DEAD MAN RUNNING

How an Underfunded, Grassroots,
Conservative Congressional Candidate Took on the
Popular Liberal Democrat Incumbent and the Republican
Party Establishment, and Forced a Change in Congress

Rob Curnock

ISBN 978-1-64515-318-4 (paperback)
ISBN 978-1-64515-319-1 (digital)

Christian Faith Publishing, Inc.
832 Park Avenue
Meadville, PA 16335
www.christianfaithpublishing.com

Many names have been changed in Dead Man Running to protect the privacy of non-public individuals appearing in this book. These changes in no way alter the veracity or description of the actual events herein.

Although there are many conversations described in this book, most are not retold to the reader verbatim. However, these conversations *are* based on the author's (and others') recollections and are written with the intent to convey the truest and most accurate reflection of those verbal interactions and incidents.

Printed in the United States of America

ACKNOWLEDGMENTS

I want to express my unceasing gratitude to my good friend Steve Toon and my wonderful wife Karen for their incredible help in editing and organizing this literary political true-life adventure.

* * * * *

I also want to thank everyone who played a part in helping make this specific political change described in *Dead Man Running*. Electoral conflict is not for the faint of heart, but it is the very core of a Representative Republic. Even those who find themselves on opposite sides in the conflict don't necessarily have to lose their humanity in the process...or the aftermath.

I pray that's the case in this political saga.

CONTENTS

INTRODUCTION

As the train drew closer to my destination of the seat of American political power, the clean, sleek subway car I had settled into grew crowded. More commuters gathered, many government workers making their way to their jobs manning the ranks of the federal bureaucracy. Others were probably tourists, lobbyists, and other assorted citizens. As each station approached, I was struck by the faux familiarity I was experiencing, names of places and areas that I recognized from my history books and news reports: Arlington National Cemetery, Foggy Bottom, The Pentagon. Each stop brought me closer to my eventual goal on so many levels—Capitol Hill.

I had dressed in what has become a quasi-uniform for most congressmen, a dark blue suit, white shirt, and red tie. I figured I could at least look the part for my day on Capitol Hill. My apparel appeal evidently worked.

Periodically, the light disappeared outside of the car as the subway passed into tunnels or underground sections. The windows suddenly became mirrors, and I was acutely aware that most of the people reflected around me were looking intently at me. On several occasions, while facing inward, I inadvertently met the eyes of one. Maybe it was my imagination, but it appeared to me they were trying to discern if I was indeed a denizen of Congress and, if so, did they perhaps recognize me? I assume it's not uncommon for regular commuters to spot the occasional elected official heading for their jobs in the Capitol Building. It's amazing what the right suit can do for you.

I had spent the night in my hotel in suburban Washington, D.C., anticipating the gravity of the next day's events. This was the first real political action committee that was even willing to hear me out. My candidacy was dismissed out of hand by virtually every other entity involved in donating to congressional campaigns. As an incumbent, Democrat Congressman Chet Edwards' financial reports were wall-to-wall with business and organizational donations. Although I had no desire to fund my campaign entirely with "professional" donors, and I would press on no matter what, this meeting presented an opportunity to establish some sort of credibility with the political donor class.

The train arrived at the Capitol Hill station and I joined hundreds of other commuters converging on the impressive four-story escalators heading to the surface. I emerged into the bright sunlight of a beautiful Washington morning. Still several hours away from my appointed time at the national Republican headquarters, I decided to explore my surroundings and take in the sights at the center of the American political universe.

The Capitol building sits atop a wide hill with federal and political buildings ringing three sides of the property. On the sidewalk in front of the congressional and senatorial offices, I encountered a small group of protesters holding signs for and against various assorted causes and issues. I watched bemusedly as these people desperately looked for some sort of recognition and attention from both the foot and vehicular traffic surrounding the halls of Congress. I found that I actually agreed with more than a few signs.

I walked up the street at one side of the Capitol and quickly recognized the Supreme Court. Pausing for a few moments, I soaked it in and pondered the enormity of what I was seeing. As a history buff, it was sobering to be standing on the ground where so much history had been created over the centuries.

The National Republican Congressional Committee building is adjacent to the Capitol. After passing security and establishing my business for being there, I was buzzed into the interior of the building and directed to where I would have my meeting with my potential supporters.

I sat down and drank in all the sights of the waiting area. This was definitely another world. With plush decor and ornate furnishings surrounding me, I pondered that I wasn't in Waco, Texas, anymore. Suddenly I understood why so many otherwise well-grounded individuals succumb to the mindset of Washington and all its seductive power and prestige. It reinforced in me the thought that if you aren't well grounded in your purpose and mission for being in Washington, you could easily lose sight of the real world that sent you there.

Unexpectedly, feelings of doubt soon overwhelmed me. *Who am I to be sitting here? I'm just little Rob Curnock from Waco. This is the big leagues. These people are important. What am I thinking? I have no business here.*

It was a slight and momentary questioning of my entire purpose and what I had been striving to accomplish for the last eight months and, in reality, the past six years.

I determined then and there that no matter what might lie ahead, I must stay focused on my reason for seeking Congress. I had a mission, ideology, and a goal. If I lost sight of any of those, I would betray everything I believed in as a person, a political office holder, and as a Christian, who quietly heeds a higher calling.

Nervously, I went over my thoughts. I wanted to make sure I made the most of this one-time chance to make some allies in our battle to secure a seat for like-minded conservatives. As the stress level rose, I realized this was no good. If I rehearsed, I would come off as contrived—an actor. My passion for redirecting our nation's priorities is no act for personal gain.

While I struggled with the human civilized version of the old instinctual biological quandary of fight or flight, a middle-aged woman came toward me from out of the double doors at the end of the hall. She had a smile on her face. "Are you Rob?" Although we had never met in person, it gave me comfort when I immediately recognized her voice from our phone calls.

Shortly thereafter she ushered me into a large meeting hall, with tables ringing the entire room. Thirty or so men and women sat around the tables. Some ate; others glanced at papers. A few made eye contact and nodded. My hostess warmly introduced me and turned me loose to tell my story.

Once again, as had happened before on the campaign, my flight turned to fight. As I gazed around the room and glanced out the sunny windows toward the Capitol across the way, I quickly focused on the true reason for my far-reaching, Davidian quest. Yes, as trite as it sounds, the country that I grew up in is quickly disappearing, and if I'm not willing to fight for this incredible gift from our Founding Fathers, then who would?

If I have integrity, I have no choice but to fight on. If not, I'm nothing more than a scared bystander who's watching a mob about to lynch someone and is unwilling to speak up and stop what is about to occur. It definitely takes courage, maybe even a bit of craziness, but if it's right, it has to be done. I have to stand up for traditional values and express those values for the average, like-minded Americans who may not have that ability to communicate.

I launched.

"The left-wing Democrats keep inching closer and closer to a mild, secular socialism, and are dragging this country down a path that will eventually be calamitous. The moderate Republican establishment leadership is either unwilling or unable to forestall the proactive Democrats in their relentless and aggressive pursuit of transforming America into something unrecognizable from the constitutional foundation of a great nation established on the unique concept of personal freedoms. We're in a battle for the very life of America as we've known it. The country is divided, and business-as-usual incumbents have a virtual choke hold on political races—especially for Congress."

As I spoke, all doubt on my part departed.

"This very interesting congressional race in Texas is one that's completely under the radar. The national Republican Party won't touch it. They say this seat is unwinnable, and they won't risk any more time, energy, or money on trying to get it. The state Republican Party is focused on other seats, and the local party is totally demoralized by past defeats to this guy.

"But the Republican leadership is dead wrong and missing an incredible opportunity by ignoring my candidacy. If they aren't going to help me, then at least get out of the way and stop telling people *not* to give to this race that they perceive as hopeless. And yes, I'm aware enough to understand the lay of the land, and I know that what I'm trying to do is difficult, but it absolutely can be done. And here's why."

Those eating had stopped; those shuffling papers looked up. I had their attention.

"I'm currently a small business owner in Waco. I've also been involved in local politics for a lot of years. But more importantly, I'm a former TV political reporter who knows and understands what I'm talking about. This is a seat we can flip over to the Republican column in the tight battle for the House.

"Here's the key: This district is currently sixty-five percent Republican based on statewide and national election results. The only reason the long-time current Democrat has been winning is because of the power of his incumbency and his ability to fool enough Republican voters into thinking he's actually a conservative Democrat. He's not and never was.

"You may have heard of him. His name is Chet Edwards. He was actually on Barack Obama's short list for vice president, at the suggestion of none other than Nancy Pelosi."

A number raised their eyebrows and glanced around the room at one another.

"But that prestigious honor—and I use that term loosely—is what has turned this completely around. I can tell you for a fact, Obama has absolutely no chance in Texas, and my opponent has now been outed as the Liberal he is, even though he's always passed himself off as a conservative in a district that is one of the most conservative in the country.

"Most candidates in those proverbial 'unwinnable' races have to overcome heavy Democrat numbers to win. I don't! In this case, all I have to do is convince enough Republican voters to stay Republican—and we're only talking about six percent of that group. I'm telling you, this seat is there for the taking.

"As I said, the party has washed their hands of this one. We've got a great dedicated grassroots organization on the ground, but we can't get any institutional financing or strategic support.

"I'm here asking for your help.

"Give me a chance to stand up to Pelosi and the Left and become one more voice for the preservation of the greatest nation on the face of the earth. I was told I was crazy for taking on this impossible battle, and in the experts' eyes, maybe I am. However, when you're doing what's right and the life of your country is at stake, you fight whatever battles you need to, no matter how hopeless they appear.

"I'm also dangerous—dangerous to the status quo and the business-as-usual crowd now running Washington, because I'm an idealist. Not some crazy, wild-eyed nut-job tilting at windmills, but a reasonable, clear-visioned fighter with a steely resolve to join other conservative idealists who understand the gravity of the danger this country is now in. I don't need a new job, career, or adventure. I'm in this race because I'm an idealist, and idealists aren't easily compromised or corrupted in a place like Washington.

"It may seem impossible, but with just a little help we'll win it. We may win it *without* any help, but I hope you'll join me in this fight.

"This is your chance to make a real difference. This is *our* chance to steal a seat from the unsuspecting Democrats and the incumbent Chet Edwards. This is really a fight to win back traditional American values."

PART I

Born to Be Conservative

CHAPTER 1

Political Awakenings

I, like most Americans, always viewed politics, particularly at the federal level, as some unreachable, unattainable world, populated only by the super rich or super connected. Washington, D.C., is a special place, reserved for special people. In other words, the average citizen need not apply. As much as we Americans revile and complain about Congress, when it comes to individual Representatives or Senators, most people are impressed and, yes, often in awe of that officeholder. It comes with the territory. The cult of personality in today's media society for wielders of power are strong factors in creating that aura of specialness in the minds of the average voter.

Ironically, this mindset is the antithesis of the stated ideals of the Founding Fathers. The incredible theory behind the political miracle called the United States is clearly and precisely laid out in all our founding documents, and specifically the Constitution. Yes, we know, in reality, that the first citizen statesmen were mostly the upper crust white males of society, but they were the ones who codified the notion that the government should be open to all free men. And more critically, in spite of all their flaws that the Left thrills at pointing out today, these Founding Fathers were also the ones who created a constitutional mechanism to eventually modify the political system, which allowed for the inclusion of political equality for all citizens. This was a never-before-tried system that truly set this nation apart from all other nations or city states that had ever come before.

The notion of—*gasp!* — holding an elected office myself, first came into my head one day while working my job as a television news reporter. Although I, unlike most people in their early twenties, had strong opinions on most issues in the political realm, I still never saw myself as anything but a spectator in the world of politics.

My first personal and practical experience in the democratic process came, naturally enough, after my first registration as a high school senior in 1976. My independent streak caused me to register as a Democrat, a last teenage rebellious gasp of "I'll be my own man" to my parents, who were die-hard, working-class conservative Republicans. It seemed like a good idea at the time, but that giddy feeling of satisfaction didn't last long. Although the two parties were at odds on many key issues, at this point, they still seemed to be in general agreement on the mission and basic makeup of the American nation. In some respects, it seemed like nothing more than a matter of a preference for something as innocuous as, "Do I prefer vanilla ice cream or chocolate?" What does it matter? It's all ice cream.

However, I knew deep down that, in spite of my rebellious declaration, I had serious internal conflicts with the values of the changing Democrat Party. After all, I had grown up in the truly tumultuous time and place of suburban Chicago in the late Sixties. As a child, seeing the news coverage of the riots in downtown Chicago during the Democrat National Convention was truly disturbing. I spent much of my youth complacent and happy in the "Leave It to Beaver" era, in a well-ordered, safe and secure world. But the nightly visions in the network news was rending the comfortable fabric of my well-being and pushing me down the political road that I eventually came to travel.

Life intervened and I never carried out the contrarian vote which would've affirmed my rebellious declaration of parental independence. My father retired from his long career at the Veterans Administration Hospital, and my parents chose to relocate from Chicago to a small town in Arkansas. Reluctantly leaving my childhood world in the shadow of the second largest city in America to a small town of less than six thousand was the epitome of culture shock. I had just graduated high school and was planning on going to college. I didn't know where, but I knew that it was critical to my future.

Unfortunately, my ability to pay for college was in serious jeopardy. My parents had exhausted their finances putting my older sisters through college. That meant that if I was going to attend, I would have to fund it myself. As a nervous eighteen-year-old, with great reluctance and limited options, I moved with my parents to Berryville, Arkansas.

I spent the next several months trying to map out some sort of a future. I had to find a path forward to get to college. Jobs at that time were scarce, leaving me with the dilemma of either securing adequate funding or looking into part-time education at perhaps the University of Arkansas. It was in the midst of this incredibly difficult life choice scramble that I remembered a conversation with one of my rarely seen uncles.

On one of his sporadic visits to my childhood home, during a brief conversation, he had asked me if I wanted to work during a summer at one of "his" factories in Buffalo, New York. If so, he would see what he could do. It was one of those conversations that seemed irrelevant at the time, and was generally forgotten in the head of a young teenager with much more pressing matters at hand, like what would my friends and I be doing that evening?

Still, when the mind is scraping for any solution to a difficult problem, it's amazing what will trigger a memory of a long-forgotten event or conversation. So, years later, while soul searching in the backwoods of Arkansas, that conversation arose out of the murky past. I didn't know my uncle well from just a few exposures over my childhood, so I asked my mom if this was an option we could explore. She agreed and called my uncle. He agreed, made arrangements to find me employment in a General Motors factory, and graciously opened their home to me for as long as needed. Soon, I was on my way to Buffalo in October of 1976, to who knows what.

Just out of high school, I might as well have been Christopher Columbus searching for a new world. I loaded my banged-up 1973 Chevy and headed to Buffalo by way of Chicago. The stop in Chicago allowed me to briefly see friends and gather myself for the final push into the unknown. I studied maps and drove east. It's funny how traumatic that event was, and it seared memories into my brain never forgotten. To this day, the playing of certain songs such as "Devil Woman" bring me right back to that fateful trip.

Following two nerve-racking hours through Cleveland rush hour, I reached the eastern edge of town, exhausted and frustrated. I'd been on the road for ten hours and was feeling the effects of stress. Northeast of Cleveland toward Erie, Pennsylvania, as darkness began to fall, I pulled over to rest and quickly fell asleep.

I woke with a start in darkness broken only by the glare of a far-off rest area parking lot light. For a brief, panic-filled moment, I didn't know where I was or where I was going. As I recovered my bearings, the overwhelming question gripped me, *What the heck am I doing?! I don't even remember what my aunt and uncle look like, and I'm going to live in their house, in a place I've never even been near?! This is crazy!*

However, this was a continuation of the lesson I was learning since my childhood. Life usually doesn't go as planned, so you've just got to go with the flow and take the road laid out in front of you. So, with fear and trepidation, I pushed on.

Several hours later I pulled into the driveway of the house that was to become my home for the next few years, although I had no idea at the time. I was met at the door by a couple of wonderful strangers who opened their home and a whole new world to me. My aunt and uncle were good people who were willing to lend a hand to a relative in need, and for their generosity, I will be forever grateful. The experience changed my life in ways that I never comprehended until years later.

In fact, my mindset was that I would work in a Chevrolet factory, making incredibly good money for that day and my age, and then quickly move on once I had enough for a semester or two at some college, somewhere.

In my mind, even though my new Buffalo family was gracious and welcoming, I felt like an intruder. That was the reason why, after several months, I was literally still living out of my suitcase laid open on the second twin bed in my room. It took my uncle coming into my room and adamantly telling me to put my clothes in the dresser and closet and make myself at home because I wasn't going anywhere anytime soon, for me to finally unpack my suitcase.

Life with my relatives in Buffalo was a radical change for me on many different levels, but it was the political coming of age that set the stage for my chance to take advantage of an incredible opportunity years later to run for the U.S. Congress.

As luck would have it, my aunt was on the other end of the political spectrum from me and virtually everyone I had ever known in my sheltered life. My oldest female cousin, who wasn't living with her parents at the time, cast some light on how that may have happened. Her theory was that, after having had her children, my aunt chose to go to college and become a teacher—in the late Sixties. Yes, those 1960s, which became renowned for radical leftist political thought and life. The housewife who had come of age in the 1950s attending garden parties and teas, was influenced to trade in that lifestyle for the burgeoning liberalism of the anti-Vietnam War Left. It was soon evident to me that she and I were in opposing corners of some great political boxing ring.

This would turn out to be my political proving ground. Two female cousins still lived at home. One was a year older than I and off at college most of the time, the other was younger and still in high school. However, as with most children, they were both heavily influenced by their mother, and adopted her liberal dogma with gleeful enthusiasm. My uncle was a product of his time and, although a Republican, he was busy running a major factory and didn't really focus his precious family time on politics.

But he did enjoy the brand-new entertainment at home: Rob baiting. Rob, the conservative evangelical Christian from the Midwest, was suddenly the center of every political argument one could imagine. The jousting would get heated at times, but generally it was just like any other verbal contact sport: no blood, no foul. Besides, I learned another valuable skill that most married men already know: sometimes, even if you can, you just don't want to win the argument. I was living in their house, and you don't push too far. You may wind up gaining the satisfaction of "winning" an argument, while losing a nice place to eat and sleep. I didn't want to find out.

It didn't matter what the issue, my two cousins and aunt relished every attempt to pound their conservative cousin into ideological submission--from gun control to abortion, to taxes to the death penalty, sex, and religion. It was all on the table and ripe for the picking. Fortunately, at the end of the day, we still stayed civil and remained 'family.' However, it was at this point that I began to learn something about myself.

Although I'd always been an independent and rebellious sort, for the first time in my life, I realized that I did care about those issues and what I believed in. And the more I was pushed, the more I pushed back. But it wasn't enough to just have opinions; I had to be able to defend and justify my beliefs. Of course, even that wasn't always enough because, after all, I was arguing with liberal Democrats. If there's one thing I've learned over the years since, fact and logic have no influence with most true-believer Democrats. At any rate, this was an incredible training ground for future political discourse and the rough and tumble of "professional" politics.

CHAPTER 2

Union Man

True to his word, my uncle was able to get me a slot on the payroll of the General Motors system in Western New York. These were mainly factories in and around Buffalo that made parts for cars that were then shipped over to Detroit for the assembly lines. At the time, these were considered plum manufacturing jobs, and I got my first exposure to the relatively new concept of affirmative action.

GM was predominantly hiring only minorities, women or Vietnam vets back from the war zones in Southeast Asia. My uncle was able to slip his white, male nephew into this select workforce of the small Chevrolet forge facility just upriver from Niagara Falls, in a blue-collar suburb called Tonawanda.

The work was mind-numbingly repetitive. The forge had two sides: A hot side, where all the blast furnaces created red-hot steel to be formed into car parts like idler levers, yokes and links; and a cold side where brake pedals were assembled. I had no idea what most of these things were used for and didn't much care. The work was hot, dirty, physically demanding, and painfully boring. I dreaded going into work every day for the start of the second shift at 4:00 P.M., lasting until 12:30 A.M. It was the least desirable of the three shifts in operation and, as such, all the new hires with the least seniority wound up in second shift.

Talk about a culture shock. At eighteen, I was definitely the youngest autoworker out of several hundred employed at the Tonawanda

Forge. In fact, my first foreman was a black woman who delighted in telling everyone around that I was the baby in her crew. Much to the amusement of my coworkers, from that point on, she just referred to me as "Baby," and most everybody else followed suit. I was a little embarrassed, but it didn't bother me, because I knew she wasn't trying to be derogatory or mean.

After several months on the cold side, I moved to the hot side when a slot came open. It was difficult work, but it paid more per hour. There, I worked side by side with guys who were not too far removed from the horrors and surrealism of the war zone of 'Nam. They had seen and done things that I could only wonder at. When a few did open up with me about their experiences, I could only shake my head. These guys may have been a few years older than I in age, but they were light years ahead of me in real-world life experience.

Like all the GM factories in the system, the forge was a closed shop. That meant that if I wanted to work, I had to join the United Auto Workers union. When going through the initial hiring paper-work, I was a little perplexed as to why I had to join the UAW, but no one asked me if I wanted to or not. I was just told to sign the papers. I did as directed and, *voila*, I was suddenly a conscript in the ranks of Big Labor.

Growing up, I always heard about the activities of unions in the news, and it was universally bad for the rest of us not in the union. I understood the original need for many unions to combat abuses of big greedy industrialists, but it just seemed like the unions were in a constant state of trying to shut down entire segments of society merely to achieve their own desires by any means possible. And they didn't care who else got hurt.

So, now I was in the uncomfortable position of belonging to an organization I had heard about, but always feared. More impor-tantly, I also wasn't thrilled about seeing a portion of every paycheck I received for my hard labor automatically deducted for union dues.

I got a quick introduction to the mindset of the hardcore union guys after several days on the job.

As a new guy, I was assigned to make brake pedals on the cold side. It was about the most menial job you could hold in the forge. You placed a flat, curved piece of steel and a specially-shaped steel bar in a welding machine in front of you. You pressed the buttons and watched as a small wisp of smoke curled up from the plate and bar as the two pieces were forever welded together. Within a few seconds, you had made a brake pedal. You pulled it out of the machine and tossed it into a rotating bin for other components to be added at other stations. Someone else in some other factory would put the rubber over the foot plate. Try doing that for an entire eight-hour shift. For someone like me, boredom set in after about—oh—the second brake pedal of the shift.

On this particular night, I'd only been on the job a few days. I was daydreaming about anything else and worked at a solid, steady pace, tossing out completed brake pedals in a near-robotic trance.

Suddenly, I was aware of a couple of burly guys in their hard hats, blue overalls, and heavy work boots standing behind me. I hadn't even noticed them until they were in my personal space on either side of me. The factory was loud and we all wore earplugs and hardhats. After watching me intently for a few moments, they began raising my level of discomfort exponentially.

Then, one shouted over the din, "Hey, what are you doing?!"

Naively thinking they were genuinely curious about my present job, I turned around and said innocently enough, "I'm making brake pedals."

"No, I asked you what you're *doing!*" he shot back with a sneer, making it clear that he was not happy with my answer, or my activity.

Not knowing what they meant or wanted me to say, and not wanting any trouble with a couple of guys who were bigger and older than I, I just shrugged my shoulders and turned up my hands in a questioning motion. With obvious resignation and confusion, I replied, "I don't know. I thought I was making brake pedals."

He said angrily, "What you're doing is putting us out of work. Slow down!" Seeing my surprised confusion, he added a terse explanation.

"You're new, so you don't understand. The faster you work, the sooner the contract gets filled—and we don't have jobs. Get it?"

I nodded in affirmation, mainly because I mostly just wanted them to go away and leave me alone.

"All right then, slow it down!" he shouted back at me as they moved away to the end of the long aisle. I stood watching them until they went around a corner and out of view. I then went back to work—at twice my previous speed and with an angry determination that arose from my newfound education of the union way of working.

I'm sure my foreman was pleased at the end of the shift, wondering how she got so much productivity out of her "baby." It just took the right motivation. And for me, motivation is to tell me not to do something, because then I will generally do the opposite—if I don't see the sense in what I'm being told to do.

What we at the factory called lunch, the rest of the world would call dinner, as it came at 7:15 every night. Most of the workers hung out in the cafeteria playing cards, socializing, and eating their dinners. Others would go to the parking lot and drink copious amounts of alcohol or smoke dope before returning to the line for the second half of the shift. They would be in trouble if caught, but nobody ever seemed to get caught. Besides, most of the guys using mind-altering

26

substances did it on such a regular basis, they had gotten good about concealing their condition.

I regularly took my lunch break at my usual sanctuary. I always packed my lunch and liked to read, so I found that if I went upstairs to the immense men's locker room, which consisted of row after row of benches and lockers, I could eat in relative peace with virtually no distractions, as few were up there during the shift. I positioned myself in front of my opened locker and would sit, or even carefully balance myself, to recline on the anchored, long wooden benches. There I could rest, read or eat my lunch in welcomed quiet solitude.

One night, I had finished my sandwich and was thoroughly engrossed in the doings of Frodo in the *Lord of the Rings*, when my solitude was abruptly interrupted by three guys whom I didn't know, that had suddenly appeared at the end of my long, empty aisle. They made their way toward me, and one stopped at what was evidently his locker on the other side of the aisle just behind where I was sitting.

They hadn't said a whole lot until they got right behind me.

I was about to get another lesson in Big Labor politics.

At the time, the UAW's labor contract with General Motors was under intense negotiations in Detroit, and from what we had been hearing, things were not going well. The leader of the three broke the quiet by loudly proclaiming that he was awaiting the decision of whether or not we, the union, would soon be taking a strike vote.

"And when we do vote to strike, everybody's going out," he continued loudly, though standing right behind me.

"That's right!"

"Damn straight!" first one, then the other two, loudly affirmed.

By now, I had left poor Frodo on the outskirts of Mordor and was fully aware that I was facing a threat of my own, right there at my locker in Buffalo. I didn't move, but just kept my face buried in my book. I was trying to make it look like I was oblivious to their conversation.

"Everybody will go out!" he paused for effect. "And that means…everybody!"

I was now barely breathing, but still acting like I didn't even know they were there. However, they were now standing around me, making me the focus of their comments.

I now had no idea what the poor Hobbit Frodo was doing, as I was only pretending that I was still intently reading. I may have even mindlessly turned a page. My heart was racing, along with my mind, wondering how far these guys were willing to go to make their point with me. All three were big. I didn't like my odds in the nearly deserted locker room. *Why is it always the bigger guys?* I asked myself.

He continued with a threatening tone. "And anyone who doesn't walk out will be (*expletive*) carried out. Feet first!"

With that, he slammed his locker closed emphatically, causing me to startle. I finally glanced up at them. They were all glaring down at me. I immediately turned back to my book.

"That's right!" the other two chimed in, while laughing menacingly as they moved away.

I kept pretending to read. I eventually let out a deep breath after I could see out of the corner of my eye that the last guy had gone around the end of the locker row.

Yet another lesson learned.

Intimidation is the preferred tool of choice for hard-core union members. And it works. I quickly came to understand why big labor unions are so critical to the success of the Democrat Party. But they also created a life-long, right-to-work conservative, who would stand up to them whenever possible in the world of politics.

I did not want to be anything like them.

I soon realized the absurdity of the union mentality when I had been on the job for several months. At the time, the United Coalminers had been striking the coal industry. Because our giant blast furnaces at the forge ran on coal, we definitely had an interest in what was happening with that strike. Piled outside the facility, mountains of coal were delivered by train. Our coal reserve mountains were slowly dwindling to tiny mounds.

No one, including the coal miner's union, had expected the strike to last very long, but it dragged on. I didn't know the particulars of why they were striking, but I did know that our jobs were now threatened if they didn't settle soon and get coal moving. Without coal, our furnaces would soon go dark.

While on strike, the coalminers had been living off their strike fund. That's money unions collect from their members and designate for distribution for their members to live on, in case of a strike. It's supposed to help take the place of a paycheck when they shut down their employers.

The only problem was their strike fund was about to run out and they were getting pressure from their own members to settle. The coal strike was in jeopardy. For us at Tonawanda Forge, that was good news.

However, that's when I realized that I, and most workers, are just useless pawns in the world of Big Labor. Word filtered down to us that the UAW leadership had decided that they did not want our union "brothers" in the coal strike to fail. So, in a show of solidarity, they decided to take money from our strike fund and donate it to the coal miners. This would keep their strike going.

This was not up for a vote among UAW members. The grand poobahs didn't care what the rank-and-file thought. They made an executive decision to hand our money over, to accomplish their own ends.

For many of us lowly autoworkers toiling in the forge, there was quiet frustration and anger. All we knew was that our own UAW leadership was taking our dues, without our permission, and giving it away to a group whose actions would soon be putting us out of work! In the bigger picture, the entire auto industry would soon go down, like a bunch of dominoes falling. When we shut down, that meant other factories would not be getting their parts, and eventually the auto assembly plants in Detroit would grind to a halt.

But at the forge, that frustration and anger generally stayed quiet and was only whispered among trusted friends. Intimidation works.

The absurdity of this situation was not lost on me as I learned yet another political lesson—this one like a slap across the face. These were the same leaders who have prominent seats at the table of power in the Democrat Party. These same tactics are used overwhelmingly to fund Democrat political campaigns at all levels. There's just something wrong about that.

Another conservative is born.

In spite of the conditions and convoluted mindset of the union world, I went to work thrilled at the amount of money I would be making. Besides, there was nothing I could do about it anyway, so I just went to work thinking that I would bank as much money as possible, get enough to go to college somewhere, and be on my way.

My uncle did not want me to be seduced by the relatively big money I would be making as nothing more than a high school graduate. He was adamant that I should attend college and not be satisfied with just having a good job. In fact, he had purposely placed me in what he thought was the worst factory in the area to make sure I would hate it and never succumb to the youthful fancy of big, easy money, making parts for cars.

My uncle was brilliant and had succeeded in his plan, with spectacular results.

Four o'clock became a daily time of execution—of my joy of life. The thought of going in to the factory filled me with a benign sense of dread. It was incredibly depressing to face that drive in to work every day, but I was not a quitter. In fact, the thought never even crossed my mind.

Well, okay, it did cross my mind almost every day with every piece of red-hot steel I tossed around on the line, but I focused on why I was there and what I was trying to achieve. I would even grab up any voluntary overtime that came my way. It just brought me that much closer to achieving my eventual goal of college.

There was a brief moment of doubt a long year-and-a-half later in my time at the forge. Somebody in management evidently liked my work habits and recommended me for a foreman's job. At barely twenty years old, I was offered a spot in GM's foreman training school. It was an incredible honor, but it also created a dilemma for me.

This was management!

This was getting off the line!

This was even more money!

And this was a way to move up in a General Motors career track!

Heady stuff.

I wavered briefly and went to my uncle for advice. As a high-level GM man, he seemed genuinely proud and pleased that I was offered such an honor. But there was no hesitation on his part as to what my answer should be to the company.

"No!" he said with absolute certitude. "It's an honor and impressive, but you go to college and get an education."

He was right. I knew deep down inside that there was no way I was willing to do this the rest of my working life, no matter what form it took in the manufacturing sector.

The goal of a college degree stayed right smack in front of my nose.

While working in the General Motors factory, I also attended the University of Buffalo to get basic courses out of the way. UB, as it was known in the Northeast was, alas, a holdover from the radical Sixties. Although generally a large commuter school, it had a sizable element of students and faculty from the New York City area, who were as left-wing as most good New York City residents.

Like any college student who is relying on a passing grade to get a degree and create a life after college, I kept my mouth shut and my opinions to myself. Plus, for the first time in my life, I was exposed to Communism and communist thinking. That was in my Sociology 101 class. The professor had coke-bottle-bottom glasses, clothes that would appear to be rejected by even the Salvation Army, a heavy speech impediment, and a "done-it-himself" haircut, which proved that, evidently, you can cut hair with a butter knife. I never understood why he kept ranting about the "means to production," "bourgeois indifference," "oppression of the worker," and the "inequities of capitalism." All I knew was that I needed to pass his course, so I just kept quiet, took notes, and quietly wondered how this nut ever became a tenured college professor holding my future in his hands.

After almost three years at the factory, I finally had the funds to make a transfer to Baylor University in Texas. A private Baptist school in the Southwest, this was as far from UB and the forge as you could get culturally and intellectually. And I was extremely happy about that.

In my heart, I knew I was home.

CHAPTER 3

Back from the U.S.S.R.

As part of my foreign language requirements at Baylor, I enrolled in a difficult Russian class. Due to my lax attitude and lack of class-room preparation, my grade averaged a C-plus. But, evidently, my professor saw something in me and, by the end of my second year, she presented me with a scholarship to join a group to tour the Soviet Union for a month. Not only would I get a chance to see the focus of the Cold War I grew up fearing, but I would get a crash course in speaking this difficult language. And, as an added bonus, I would earn four badly needed credits toward my degree work, which was now coming to a close in Waco.

I truly found Russians to be like people everywhere. Some were nice, some were jerks, some were polite, some were rude. It was like any place, including America, except for the political sys-tem. However, there was an extraordinary sense of oppression. I can't explain it easily, but it was truly real. In that police state, you could walk down any street, in any city, at 2:00 in the morning (which we did a few times) and feel perfectly safe. But at what price? Some in our group were seriously concerned about being observed, mon-itored, and bugged. That's not something that had me all that wor-ried because I had nothing to hide, but it did make you think. And besides, if the Soviet leadership was concerned about the doings of a nondescript American college student and wanted to waste valuable time, energy, and manpower listening to my meaningless and often inane conversations, then, hey, have at it. If that's what they were focused on, America had the Cold War in the bag.

In fact, I was probably naively cavalier about the whole thing and was determined to make the most of my experience. We were assigned a guide to stay with us throughout the trip, and, of course, she was approved by the KGB. "Who knows if she was reporting on us every day? Who cares?" was my attitude. I was determined to push the boundaries whenever and wherever possible. Our poor handler probably felt she was dealing with a rambunctious preschooler who was forever breaking small rules.

Like when we were on a plane and I pulled out my camera to take pictures of what I thought was a cool cloud bank. I took the shot and heard that familiar "No photograph" coming from the front of the plane. Of course, it was my scolding guide admonishing me in her heavy Russian accent. Fortunately, by this time, we had developed a relationship, and it was becoming common practice for her to scold me.

"I was just taking a picture of clouds," I shouted back across the plane, pointing out the window. The entire cabin was now paying attention.

"No! You cannot do this—is forbidden," she said.

"You guys have pink clouds over here in the Soviet Union?" I asked sarcastically, but good naturedly.

When most of the group laughed, she broke into a smile herself but, trying to regain some control, blurted out her usual, frustrated, yet good-natured accusation of, "You are CIA spy!"

"And you are KGB agent!" I quickly shot back, using a mock Russian accent.

As everyone was now laughing, she started laughing as well, wagged her finger at me, shook her exasperated head and sat back down.

I got my picture. It wasn't until I got back to America and had my film developed that I saw that it wasn't that good of a picture after all.

Everything was controlled. The people were limited to options in life that we, here in America, take for granted. We visited stores everywhere in the Soviet Union that had few selections, brands, or quality goods from which to choose by American standards. In the Soviet Union, these were the best stores they had. And in a perfect example of this flawed system, their own people were not allowed to shop in them. They were reserved for the elites and tourists, as were their "fancy" hotels, most of which made our Motel 6 look like a five-star Hilton.

The problem was, their system didn't work. There was no free market, and no ordinary citizen had the opportunity to get ahead. In principle, no one was allowed to have more than anyone else. This is basically the forerunner of Barack Obama's effort to eliminate "income inequality" in America. Of course, in the Soviet Union, anyone in the Communist Party working for the State could get ahead and did. But for the general, miserable population, there was no reason to work harder than the next guy. As a result, the quality of workmanship, manufactured goods, and services were absolutely dismal by our free market standards.

That was the "official" situation. Of course, human nature being what it is, a very real black market thrived there. This was how many enterprising average people got a little ahead, or just plain survived.

Going into the Soviet Union, we heard the stories of the infamous black market, so I decided to experience it myself. This wasn't some sinister method of obtaining illegal goods. In reality, this was the only way Russians could get many basic goods that we in the capitalist West take for granted. Because we were the first Americans to be allowed in the country since the outbreak of the Soviet invasion of Afghanistan, we were an oddity and attracted attention wherever we went. Add to that my willingness to bravely try out my Russian language skills by acting as interpreter for those in our group who spoke no Russian; it wasn't long before opportunities began to present themselves.

"You are Americans, no?"

"Yes."

"You like Soviet Union?"

"Oh yes, very nice."

"I like to speak English with you."

"Sure."

"That is nice shirt."

"You mean my University of Buffalo sweatshirt?"

"Yes, very nice. You sell?"

"Hmmm, I don't know; how much do you want to pay?"

"Seventy rubles."

Really?" I thought, trying to quickly do the currency conversion in my head. *Wow, that comes out to about $35 for this old sweatshirt that cost me $6 brand new.*

"Well, sure, why not?!"

This scenario repeated several times throughout the trip as I did my best to single-handedly conquer the Soviet Union with capitalism. I sold a used pair of jeans for a large number of rubles and bartered for other impossible-to-buy items using my emergency supply of Milky Way bars, among other things. I wound up with more money coming out of the Soviet Union than I had going in. Unfortunately, as a communist totalitarianist state, it was a closed system. You had to declare all dollars converted to rubles upon entry, so you better have *fewer* rubles to convert back to dollars when you come out! Fortunately, several members of our group were well under their allotted monetary amounts, and they graciously agreed to take some of my rubles through at Customs.

The trip opened up a new world to me. To this day, when people find out I spent a month in the Soviet Union, their first question is usually, "Was it fun?" I respond, "No, not really. I had a good time with most of the people in our group, but the Soviet Union was not 'fun.' It was extremely interesting, especially for the history buff in me, but it was not fun. That being said, it's an experience I wouldn't trade for the world."

The number one lesson I came back with was that communism/socialism is not "fun," and I've lived by the mantra that I will do everything in my power to make sure we don't get that type of political system here in America. Communism is truly not viable, and it definitely isn't fair when moved beyond theory. More importantly, it allowed me to see the end result of the world's first real socialist/statist philosophy at work. It was an effective real-world lesson, in what comes of a government controlling every aspect of an economy. It's not pretty for the average citizen. It's demeaning, oppressive, and crushes the human spirit.

After a month under the yoke of that "other" system, I was never in my life so glad to see America. It's also the reason I will fight, to the bitter end, those who, by design or by accident, would turn us into some sort of kinder, gentler version of the old Soviet Union. That foundational philosophy is with me to this day and serves as fuel for the fire-in-the-belly it takes to put myself in the harm's way of a major political campaign.

CHAPTER 4

Belly of the Beast

The last of my conservative affirmations from my higher educational experience came a couple of months later. After completing most of my course work at Baylor University, I was left three upper level credits short of graduating. As I was paying for my own education, I returned to Buffalo to save my quickly diminishing funds. I petitioned the dean at Baylor to get those last three credits at the University of Buffalo so that I could save on the living costs of going back to Texas for a semester for a single class. However, I was left with few choices during the summer sessions that would meet the requirements for my degree in Communications. Out of desperation, I settled on a women's study course titled, "Racism and Sexism in the Media." Although skeptical, I assumed it at least had something to do with the media, my area of study.

Panic quickly overtook this young white male conservative Christian's mind when I sat down on the first day of class. The teacher was the epitome of a radical feminist. With unshaven underarms and legs, no bra, makeup or hair care, she informed us that our grade would be determined by class participation in discussions and assigned readings and papers. And as there were only about twelve of us, we would sit in a circle to be more intimate. In other words, my degree was hanging in the balance by the subjective whims of a radical feminist, and there would be no hiding. I was a dead man.

I determined right then and there that I *had* to keep my mouth shut and do whatever it took to get a passing grade. After all, how bad could it be?

Oh, it could be bad.

She closed the first class by handing out pamphlets announcing activities for those interested in gay and lesbian issues. From that point on, my educational purgatory grew deeper and darker than I ever could have imagined.

We were forced to read essays on topics such as why women make better lovers for women. The answer, of course, is because they know what pleasures their own bodies. Or, how all the major networks were actually radical, right-wing patriarchal organizations actively working for the subjugation of minorities and women. It's amazing how "perspective" can affect someone's thinking. If you took the totality of political thought and placed it on a horizontal line going from left to right, to this crazy lady and her ilk on the extreme far-Left, it would only be natural to see the mainstream national media and traditional culture as something off to the far right. To those of us to the right of center, we look at that same exact media and see it off to the far left.

I tried—I truly tried—to keep to myself, but it became more difficult with each bizarre session. I continually closed my eyes to find inner calm. The class was comprised of about nine women and three men, including me. Looking around for a potential ally proved hopeless. The women were mostly feminist adherents. One of the two guys was from New York City and he practically volunteered to castrate himself if that would help the feminist cause. The other guy was obviously in the class at the direction of his girlfriend, whom he literally clung to like she was the last life preserver on a sinking ship.

I was on my own, and no help was coming. Of course, they knew I was on my own as well when, increasingly, in a reflexive reaction, I would close my eyes in a valiant attempt at self-preservation of sanity, as outrageous discussion points were made. I would open them, only to see eleven sets of eyes now staring straight at me from around that dreaded circle of desks. In case you're questioning my math skills, the twelfth pair of eyes belonged to that other male, who never took them off his girlfriend, the life preserver. But I still kept my mouth closed. I thought I was being discreet in my reactions, but evidently there is no such thing as discreet when you're sitting in a small circle of zealots.

There finally came a day when closing my eyes no longer sufficed. The feminist professor actually discussed, with all seriousness, the theory that white males invented homicide in an effort to keep minorities and women in subjugation. As my head landed on my desk with a loud thud, I knew the proverbial jig was up.

"Mr. Curnock, do you have a thought on this?" asked the she-beast teacher, with dripping sarcasm.

"Well, I was just wondering, if that's the case, why do minorities commit murders?" I asked, knowing that my entire college degree was now hanging by a slender feminist thread, but I couldn't stop myself.

"Because, obviously, white males put societal pressure on them. This inevitably forces many minorities to commit murder just to deal with the inequities created by the oppressive white patriarchal society they're forced to exist within. America is, at its very core, a racist and sexist society. It's clearly a method white males have always used to control minorities and women who resist," she answered with a smug condescension belying her wonderment at how I could be so ignorant as to not understand that obvious truth.

I closed my eyes again. I was now truly a dead man, no pun intended.

From that point on, every discussion statement ended with every head turning to me with that look of, "Okay, what possible objection could this crazy white Neanderthal come up with this time?" The lone exception was that mute, pathetic boyfriend. I could've used his help. I assumed he was on my side as, after all, at least he appeared to be blatantly heterosexual.

In the end, I managed to keep my comments minimal, tried to guess what she wanted on the dreaded papers, gave it to her, and escaped with a C-plus. I got my degree, but I also got another valuable lesson on politics and dealing with being stuck in an incredibly hostile environment: You don't have to compromise your core beliefs to accomplish a task that needs completing.

Just accept the fact that, you won't get an "A" if the other side is calling the shots, but you can get things done.

Welcome to politics in the big wide world.

CHAPTER 5

Media Biases and Darn Liberals

After sending out resume video tapes to stations all over the country, incredibly, I got an offer to be a general assignments television reporter for KWTX in the city I had just moved away from—Waco. I felt lucky to get in the business. I realized how lucky years later.

One thing about television news, for all its apparent glamour and influence, it is nonetheless completely shackled by the manacles of extreme political correctness. As a result, the inertia of its politics, whether unintentional or by design, overtly or cloaked, tend to slant leftward. This lesson was pounded home to me when, after several years on the job, a reporter position came open. I thought I would be helpful and recommend someone I knew to the news director.

Imagine my surprise when he informed me that, although he was not allowed to formally state the situation, he was under strict instructions and pressure to hire either a minority male, or a female of any kind. And, of course, this mindset was rife at the Federal Communications Commission, which grants TV station licenses and sets the agenda on a Washington-based political standard. I was stunned.

"You mean, we're not going to just get somebody good that can do the job?" I argued. "That's ridiculous!"

"That's just the way it is," was his response.

Yet another lesson in politics, and another brick in the solid foundation of my common-sense conservative philosophy.

As fate would have it, by way of my eagerly volunteering for every political story I could get my hands on, I soon evolved into the station's political reporter. I covered everything--from night meetings of small-town councils where I was literally the only person in the room not on the council, to state capital proceedings, to even a one-on-one interview with the vice president of the United States, and everything in between.

The reaction to me arriving with TV camera in hand was usually a story in itself, when covering a small-town council. The first question the startled council members often asked *me* was, "What are you doing here?" I had enough tact to not admit that it just happened to be a slow news night and the news director was looking for anything to fill the newscast. At the other end of the spectrum, there was the realization on their part that, if we were there covering their proceedings, they knew why we were there, especially when we joined an angry throng of constituents venting loud, vocal, and often angry frustration with some local problem. That wasn't something that beleaguered council members wanted to see on the evening newscast. This was a real education for me on the actual workings of small government.

My first press conference of a statewide political figure exposed my ignorance in a humbling and embarrassing manner. The Democrat lieutenant governor was holding forth on some pertinent issues in front of numerous reporters and cameras from major media outlets from across the state. After all, Bill Hobby was a powerful state figure, who had the ability to attract media no matter where he went. Assuming that my news director sent me to the news conference for a reason, I decided to earn my pay by speaking up and asking what I knew would be an important question. Sensing my opening, after the "major" reporters paused, I asked him a gem that I knew would elicit a newscast leading response.

He showed no expression whatsoever as I gave it everything I had. He listened, then paused and completely ignored my question as he matter-of-factly stated, "You understand, I'm the *lieutenant* governor, not the governor. That's not my role," as he looked around for the next question. Ouch! This young TV reporter was never again going to worry about developing a massive ego.

My reporting resume grew by leaps and bounds after that, and I made it a point to never be humiliated again. As geographical luck would have it, although Waco was a medium-sized media market, we seemed to be a required stop for all manner of politicians and candidates. I soon had the opportunity to personally meet or question everyone from presidents and presidential candidates, to statewide figures, down to local office holders from all over Central Texas. I learned a lot and experienced even more.

One of the first lessons I learned was that the most controversial of "trade" secrets was absolutely true. As an experienced political reporter, I could attest beyond a shadow of a doubt—the press is biased.

As a reporter, you have the power to frame a story however you see fit, as long as you do the job you're sent to do, which is to cover an event. Most reporters won't be overtly slanted, but make no mistake, they will slant their stories because they are viewing events through a filter of their own values and beliefs. Unfortunately for America, the vast majority of national reporters and producers working for the major networks are solidly on the Left politically, and to someone who knows what to look for, it can be infuriatingly obvious.

For example, let's say a network covers political rallies by opposing presidential candidates. This is something I actually saw years later in the Bush-Clinton race. I remember one telling day of network coverage in that race. At the Bush rally, there were no wide establishing shots, just close ups and small groups of some pretty goofy-looking white people listening intently. A quick sound bite was played from the speech and immediately followed by the reporter talking. Then a mention, along with video, of protesters at the event. The entire report ran one minute and fifteen seconds.

The newscast then followed with the Clinton rally. It started with a wide establishing shot of the event, which showed a huge crowd of enthusiastic and loud supporters. A quick sound bite is played from the speech and the roar of the crowd in response. Young, attractive, and diverse attendees were shown clapping and emotionally responding. The reporter followed with a comment on the excitement generated by the rally. The entire report ran one minute and fifteen seconds.

Network executive producers/editors/reporters will proudly and cynically proclaim their lack of bias by pointing out that they gave both rallies exactly the same amount of coverage. But the subtle emotional responses of the average viewer are polar opposites. To someone who understands what's going on, this isn't coverage; it's extremely biased cheerleading propaganda being passed off as "news." As humans with differing sets of values, this is almost impossible to avoid.

I speak from experience. I covered a campaign stop in Waco by presidential candidate Jesse Jackson. In my mind, this man was as extreme a presidential candidate as has ever run for president—prior to Barack Obama. I despised his politics and truly felt he was a danger to America. Yet, I was told to cover him and, in essence, give him a lot of publicity as the lead story in our nightly newscast.

Because I was a professional and not willing to lose my job by making a personal statement, I knew I had to cover him straight up. But I would be darned if would do anything to help him look good. We rolled tape on his entire stump speech. But while the sympathetic national media and many others who were there kept their pack mentality viewpoints of his groundbreaking, first-black-man-to-run-for-president storyline, I decided to take the story in another direction. I wanted my viewers to go beyond the fact that he was the first "whatever." Instead, I wanted to focus on what this guy actually believed and was espousing.

I went through the speech and easily found the most outrageous statements he made and used those sound bites in my report. I didn't put any words in his mouth and let his ideas stand on their own, unedited, as he spoke them. I wanted the average viewer in Central Texas to really hear Jackson's radical philosophy, and to be as turned off as I was. I covered the story completely, accurately, and professionally, but this was my way of letting people know, "Hey, this is what this guy is really all about."

While I can accurately claim that I never editorialized in my report, the mere choice of input slanted the story the way I wanted it. *Somebody's* point of view was going to be put out there, and I was not going to follow the template of the rest of the Leftist media pack.

It was an interview opportunity with the area's congressman that actually awakened my first desire to even contemplate getting personally involved in that special world of elective federal office. We conducted the interview in Congressman Marvin Leath's back yard, who lived in a small town south of Waco. After the interview ended, the camera operator and I had some extra time to just sit and visit with the congressman "off the record." There was nothing earth shattering about this extracurricular conversation, but it struck me that the most remarkable thing about getting to know this politician was that there was nothing remarkable about him. That proverbial Wizard of Oz curtain had opened up, and, for the first time, I realized that he was just like me, except, of course, that he was financially comfortable, working in Congress, and had the ability to have a hand in changing the course of events in America.

Although a Democrat, Leath was extremely conservative. In fact, he was one of the last of the conservative Democrats elected at a time in Texas when only Democrats could win. Ronald Reagan would soon change that. Still, as I sat and listened to him talk with both humor and a raw coarseness about the personal tales of the congressional life, I knew right then and there that if ever the opportunity presented itself, that's where I wanted to make a difference.

Among other things, he talked of the absurdities of the "damn Liberals" in Washington who were screwing up the country, and why they had to be stopped. At that point, in spite of his harsh descriptive license, he won me over and awakened my passion to get into the fight.

About this same time, I was assigned to help cover a special congressional election being held in the neighboring district, some of which was in our television viewing area. This was in the mid-1980s, and the Democratic congressman in that office at the time had decided to switch parties. Thanks to the popularity of Ronald Reagan in Texas and the increasing liberal tilt of the Democrat Party at the national level, the state of Texas was trending more and more Republican. This young congressman not only saw the writing on the wall, but he also found himself in philosophical harmony with the Republican Party. He made the switch but had the rare integrity to resign his seat and re-run in a special election as a Republican. It was a class act in my mind.

I covered him several times during campaign stops in our television viewing area. It was my first practical exposure to multi-event, same-day campaigning for a federal office. I was slightly surprised when I heard him give the same speech several times in the same day to different audiences in different towns. I'd never really thought about the logistics of long-term, multi-area campaigning. I was naive enough at the time that I thought it was crazy to give basically the same speech to everybody.

Of course, I quickly realized it was only the same speech to me, as I was following him around from event to event. I also quickly realized how effective his message was, and yes, he got the same positive audience response from that repetitive message wherever he went. It was simplistic, but persuasive and memorable. It generally went the same way, with slight variations and embellishments tailored to each particular venue:

"Hello, everybody, it's great to be here in (town) with my good friend (host's or other popular local person's name). Y'all got to be mighty proud of (high school football team, etc.)."

"I'm Phil Gramm and I want to be your congressman. Y'all have known me since I was first elected to serve you as a Democrat. But the longer I spent time in Washington, the more I realized how much the Democratic leadership is out of touch with America and the values of the people of the great state of Texas. I could no longer work in the party of Tip O'Neal and still represent y'all here at home. But since I was forced to make that choice, I think it's only right for you to decide if y'all still want me. I'm still the same man I was when you first chose me to represent you in Washington."

Expound on accomplishments and values on key issues, then bring the crowd to their feet.

"I'm ready to get back to work for y'all. And you can count on me to keep doing the Lord's work in the 'Devil's city.' I'm Phil Gramm, and I need you to help me get back to work."

It was very simple and yet powerful. He handily won the special election and eventually went on to become a Texas U.S. Senator and serious presidential candidate. While he got his return ticket to Congress, I got a valuable real-world education on what it took to be an effective campaigner and candidate. I didn't think that it would ever come in handy for me personally, but I learned that there was nothing mystical about the congressional election process. I saw what worked and it wasn't rocket science!

Phil Gramm taught me a lot about politics and integrity. Although he wouldn't remember me from Adam, I went on to become a real supporter of him and his agenda. Neither one of us knew it at the time, but our paths would eventually cross again, many years later. And we would not be on the same team.

CHAPTER 6

An Opening Door

It's said that the greatest danger of anyone serving in Washington is that the world of power changes them. Ironically, that proved all too true in the case of our aforementioned conservative congressional Democrat. I'll never know why for sure, but by the time he decided to retire in 1990, he was no longer the conservative Democrat berating Liberals in his back yard in small town Texas. Over the next several years, you could see the changes in his voting record and even personal life as he evidently tried to gain power and influence in the D.C. Democratic caucus. He spent less time in the district and, over the next six years, began siding more and more with those "damned" Liberals. As a conservative idealist watching from the "real" world, it was painful to see him actually helping those Liberals foul up the country.

Congress had changed the law concerning campaign funds. After 1990, a congressman no longer "owned" whatever funds were raised in the course of a campaign or tenure in office. My formerly conservative Democrat hero evidently decided to keep his sizable war chest and get out. That would leave a vacuum and an open congressional seat. I saw this as my chance to get into the fight and seriously considered filing for the seat. I discretely talked to friends in the political world, of which I had many from my political reporting days.

One of my first mentors was the new McLennan County Republican chairman. I had covered him when he first became involved in politics himself and got elected to the state legislature as the state representative from Waco. In my mind, he was a prime example of how elective public service should be done. He came directly out of the private sector, served for several years, fought the good consistent conservative fight in Austin, came back to live in the world he helped create while in the legislature, and then turned the seat over to the next citizen statesman. I strongly believe that's what the Founding Fathers had intended for this incredible gift they called America.

After leaving the legislature, he became the McLennan County Republican chairman. I gladly agreed to take on any task he requested of me and soon became more involved in local politics by serving in various capacities that he needed. I was also getting a chance to learn how things worked behind the scenes at the grassroots level. Since we were on good terms and the chairman had run his own local campaigns as a State Rep, he was a great sounding board and source of information for what I was thinking about doing.

I was relieved that when I first mentioned it to him, he didn't laugh me out of his office. I remember thinking, *Okay, I'll take this as a sign that I'm not totally crazy. More importantly, he's not thinking that I'm totally crazy!* In fact, I was mildly surprised that he took me seriously and actually gave me advice and encouragement.

As we went back and forth discussing the pros and cons of such a potential move, we both came to the conclusion that my name recognition and visibility in the community as a result of my television job was actually a unique bonus that could work strongly in my favor.

After several constructive conversations, he urged me to take the next step and call an up-and-coming political consultant he had gotten to know in Austin while serving in the legislature. He felt that for a race of this magnitude, I would need all the professional help I could get. He believed this young Republican strategist was extremely sharp and knowledgeable. Even though we both knew I had not committed to run, he thought that I could get insight as to what it would take to get the job done.

I wasn't comfortable calling a consultant this early in the decision-making process but decided that, since the chairman was sincerely wanting to help me, I'd do as he said. I nervously sat down and dialed the direct number I was given, not knowing what to expect or to say. Besides, I thought brashly, what can this young, supposed hotshot tell me that I didn't already know from all my years as a political reporter and activist? The phone rang.

"Hello?" he answered.

"Hi, is this Karl Rove?" I asked.

"Yes, it is. What can I do for you?"

"Karl, I'm a friend of M.A. Taylor, the former rep out of Waco, and he told me I needed to talk to you about a race we're talking about me getting into."

"Sure, how's M.A. doing? He's a good man."

"He's doing great. He's now the McLennan County Republican chairman." I was relieved somewhat. At least he knew who I was talking about, so we had some common ground to begin a conversation.

"Yes, I'd heard that. So, what's going on?"

"As you probably know, Marvin Leath is quitting his congressional seat. It's the 11th congressional district which takes in Waco, Temple, and Fort Hood. With him quitting, it leaves the seat wide open."

"That's true, and who are you?" he said cutting right to the point.

"My name is Rob Curnock. I've been involved in politics in this area for a long time. I work for a local television station. I was our political reporter for a number of years, but now I just do sports on the weekends." I'd always been uncomfortable talking about my TV job with strangers because it always made me feel like I was tooting my own horn.

"Are you on the air?" he asked, now slightly more curious.

"Yes, I just do sports on the weekend, or fill in for the other sports anchors during the week. The rest of the time, I'm running my own small video production and duplication business."

"Um hum, And have you ever held any political office before?"

"No, not really, although I was a precinct chairman in McLennan County, if that counts. I've never had an opponent."

"No, that's nice, but I'm talking about a contested race."

"No, I haven't," I responded, realizing that he was not very impressed.

"OK, why do you want to run for Congress?"

"This seat should be in Republican hands. It's a conservative district and went solidly for Reagan. It's been Democrat since Reconstruction. Leath started out conservative, before changing toward the end. I've had an interest in national issues and want to find a way to work for the conservative cause. I think we can win this."

"You understand it'll take a lot of money to win a congressional race? That's a big first step you're talking about doing. Most people hold other elective offices first."

"Yes, I understand. But I believe I can bring unique things to the table. M.A. and I have talked about the fact that I've got good name recognition and high visibility in this area. So, I probably won't need as much money as the average candidate," I said, beginning to feel slightly on the defensive, even though I knew he was right.

"It'll still take a big effort to make it work, and we don't even know who else might jump in. You're going to have to have professionals to run a major congressional race."

"That's why M.A. suggested I call you," I said.

"I appreciate that, but just so you know, it takes a serious commitment for me to get involved. You'll have to be willing to spend at least several thousand dollars right up front."

"I understand, and what's that for exactly?" I asked while thinking, *This guy's crazy!*

"That's basically a consultation fee. That will get us started as we determine what it will take for you to move forward in this."

Started? We just ended, I thought.

"I understand. At this point I'm still thinking about it, but I'll certainly get back to you if I do decide to run. I appreciate your time and insight. Hopefully, we'll get to work together on this," I said, politely lying through my teeth.

"You bet, glad I could help," he said as he hung up.

I hung up, disappointed. *What an arrogant jerk. If that's what this is all about, forget it. I don't need someone like that telling me what to do. Good luck with that political consulting career. You need to at least learn some serious people skills.* I had no intention of ever calling him back. I reported to M.A. that Rove had good insights, "but I'm not at a point to make a commitment. He seems to really know his stuff, and if I ever get that far, who knows?"

Looking back with hindsight, I realize now I was mainly disappointed because, while he wasn't overtly trying to *discourage* me from running, he was the first person that I had talked to about this possible endeavor who wasn't strongly *encouraging* me. Add to that, I figure he was getting his start in the big leagues down in Austin. He was swimming in deep waters and looking at it strictly from a business perspective. All in all, he was probably right, but it's also the sad financial lesson of politics that I had yet to learn.

Frankly, the idealist in me wishes it was a lesson that I never *had* to learn.

CHAPTER 7

First Steps

Although by this time I was no longer reporting on politics, I was still on-air exclusively as a weekend sportscaster with strong ratings. I was by no means wealthy and needed my job, as the small business that I had started on the side in 1985 was not yet at a point where it could financially support me. Yet, to make any kind of political run, I would have to quit my television job. And that was a problem.

As Rove and I had discussed, the key element in virtually any high-profile political race is a little thing called name ID. It's what every candidate is trying to amass and buy with commercials, public appearances, and campaigning. That's what takes money, and lots of it. It's the focal point of most fundraising. And when fundraising is difficult, which is usually the case in contested primaries, it takes personal wealth. This, of course, is the number one reason most successful politicians are personally wealthy. It's also the reason that, generally, only wealthy individuals can make a run in a contested high-profile race. And this sadly explains why the current system is slanted for the wealthy, in either party.

The obvious catch-22 that plagued me was the fact that I would be a formidable and serious candidate because of my name ID. But if I left my TV job to run for office, my name ID would diminish quickly. Would I have enough name recognition to get elected? That was the one-hundred-and-fifty-thousand-dollar question, which also happened to be the amount of money that one political pro estimated my television position had created in name ID value.

I'd heard of the proverbial fire-in-the-belly. I now understood what it meant, because I had it, and I had it bad. Ironically, another one of my confidants at the time was the former *Democrat* county chairman of McLennan County.

I knew him through my years as a political reporter, and, although he was leading the local "enemy" camp, we truly liked each other and became friends. Yes, we would spar on political issues, but I always accused him of secretly being as conservative as I was on most issues. He would feign horror and claim, "No way," but there was always a wry smile on his face at the end of the protestation. I liked to interpret that as, "OK, so you got me, but no one else will ever know."

The main thing about this man was that he'd been involved in politics a long time in Central Texas. He knew everyone and everything political in the area. Yes, he was a Democrat, but when he started working politics, everyone in Texas was a Democrat, or they had no voice. There were certainly few elected Republicans, if any.

In fact, he later told me he was the first politico to back a young former congressional aide who was planning to run for state senator and take on the chosen establishment candidate in the Democrat primary years before. Because there was no Republican in the general election, the primary winner would be senator. His man won, and they became good friends. Shortly thereafter, my friend quit as Democrat county chairman and focused on his real estate business and as a district rep for that newly elected state senator.

That newly elected state senator was Chet Edwards.

While forming my plans, I knew I needed the help of someone who knew the district, politics, and campaigns, and it had to be someone I trusted. I turned to my Democrat friend with a crazy idea.

"Gene, I think I want to run for the open congressional seat."

"As a Republican?" he asked with a smile, knowing the answer already.

"Of course, but am I crazy to think that I could win the nomination and win the seat?"

"No," he said with all seriousness. "You're not crazy; you could win. You're well known in the district, which just happens to overlap nicely with KWTX's broadcast signal. You'd have a huge advantage over anybody else."

"But what about the money?"

"I'd guess your name ID is worth about one-hundred fifty thousand. Are you seriously thinking about this?"

"Yes, I am, but here's something even crazier. You know more people in this district than anybody, Democrat or Republican. You know more about the district, the people, and the small-town power structures than anybody. Would you ever consider helping me, even though I'm a conservative Republican?"

"You're nuts! But I do have to admit, you're one of the 'good' Republicans and would be a man of your word even if you are wrong on the issues." He paused and then burst out laughing.

"What?" I asked somewhat deflated yet honored at the same time.

"We would sure turn some heads in both camps if we teamed up together. That could actually be some fun." He laughed even more.

"I think so, but with your knowledge and experience, and me as the candidate, could we win? Realistically, that's all I want to know."

After a slight pause, he pronounced, "Hell, yes, we could win! I'm confident of that. Man, that would be fun. Are you really serious?"

"Yes, I am, but I need your help to run things."

"Let me think about this. Damn, it would be wild! Let's keep talking."

Our conversations continued for weeks, and it was clear that we were both getting more fired up about the idea of collaborating on this race. I was truly getting ready to go for it. In fact, I even set up a meeting with my bosses at the TV station to affirm that if I decided to run, I knew I would have to quit. But I didn't want them to be caught off guard.

I've always been a night owl, and one evening, a week later, as I was about to head to bed, everything came to a crashing halt. It was after one in the morning and the phone rang. It was an obviously disappointed Gene on the other end.

"Rob, did you know Chet's decided he's going after the congressional seat?" he asked.

"Yes, I'd heard the rumors, but he's a Democrat, so that really shouldn't matter, right?"

"No, that's a problem. Rob, you know he's a very close family friend. Since he's the state senator, no one will challenge him in the Democrat primary. He *will* be the nominee, and then we'd have to face him in the general, and I could never work against him."

"No, I get that, but why don't we at least get the Republican nomination and worry about the rest later."

"Rob, I know we could get that nomination, but then I'd have to quit your campaign and leave you hanging. You're a good friend, too, and I just can't do that to you. Besides, if I'm involved in this, I'd want to see it to the end and win that seat, but I can't work against Chet any more than I could work against you."

"Sure, I get that," I sighed reluctantly, knowing that he was right, but bitterly disappointed that I wouldn't have a skilled guide and partner in this major endeavor.

"Rob, I've been agonizing over this for weeks now, ever since Chet told me his plans. I'm in such turmoil I'm not eating and I'm not sleeping, which is why I'm calling this late. I really wanted to do this. I was already formulating a game plan. I know we could win. But I just will not bail out on you midway through the campaign."

"I understand, and I appreciate and am honored by the fact that you were even seriously considering it. I was confident about our chances. It means a lot to me."

"I'm sorry, Rob. I know we'd win it, but I'll still help you quietly, behind the scenes, in any way that I can."

I hung up the phone with a hollow feeling inside. I knew deep down it was over. After several agonizing months of exploration, soul searching, talking with close friends, and a vigorous mental debate, I decided to stick with my job. Ironically, I was devastated and relieved at the same time.

Texas had essentially transformed to a Republican state by this time and was definitely conservative. Three Republicans ended up fighting hard for the nomination.

Meanwhile, Chet Edwards, the likable Democrat state senator who had a portion of his district in Waco, moved to Waco and jumped in, uncontested, on the Democrat ticket. He campaigned as a conservative and won a close race in the general election over the bruised and bloodied Republican nominee.

The only problem was that, for those of us who knew him, he was not a conservative. As a political reporter who used to cover him as a state senator, I was one of those who actually understood him and his political record. His first terms reinforced what I already knew. He was the master of the somewhat common technique of voting one way in Washington but coming back to the district and talking the complete opposite. It was a breathtakingly brazen practice, but with benign television reporting and supportive, almost sycophantic newspapers throughout the district, he easily carried it off with little trouble.

As a career politician, he also knew how to play the strings of power and incumbency in a way that would put any self-respecting virtuoso to shame. One of the truly problematic practices in American politics is the pork that an incumbent can shower upon any organization or people that matter in the home district. Democrats have raised this policy to an art form and Edwards was no exception. Before long he had correctly, for this part of the country, become a stalwart supporter of veterans and the Fort Hood military base, situated in the district. As a congressman in this increasingly Republican district, Edwards was constantly able to announce this funding or that grant with consistent regularity in all the local media outlets throughout the district.

It was a standard operating procedure and quite effective. And for those of us who saw clearly through the smoke and mirrors, it was frustrating. He would vote with the increasingly liberal Democratic majority in Washington on every key issue that defined us as a nation and who we are as a people. Then, when back in the district, he carefully portrayed himself as a conservative family man with Central Texas values, even though he was actually voting with the liberal Left—alongside rising Democrat power player Nancy Pelosi, the ultra-liberal California congresswoman—to destroy those same values.

It would make any sane, up-to-speed conservative crazy, as conversations with many good-hearted and otherwise intelligent conservative voters would go along the same vein:

"Oh, I vote Republican, except for Chet Edwards. He's done so much for the vets."

"The only Democrat I ever vote for is Chet Edwards. He's been good for the district."

"Chet Edwards would never vote with Nancy Pelosi; he's a conservative."

"Edwards really works hard for the district and he's helped our company get a lot of business."

"He would never vote for abortion—he's a good family man."

"He would never vote to raise taxes; that's just Republicans saying ugly things about him."

"I've met him and he's such a nice man, and besides, he's really handsome."

No matter how much persuasion and recitation of facts, voting records, and policy statements, to more and more voters in Central Texas, Edwards was a special "conservative" Democrat, and nothing could change their minds. Of course, this was an image that the incumbent carefully constructed with continuous franking mailings and campaign ads. And as for most Democrats in today's political world, this was perfect, because it fits into their mantra: "An uninformed voter is a good, reliable voter. They win elections." And in Central Texas, which was nearly 59 percent Republican, based on consistent statewide and national election numbers, these were the Republicans who kept Edwards in office.

To myself, and other conservatives who got it, we were left sputtering, "This is ridiculous!"

About a year later, I left the television station and focused solely on my business.

However, I watched politics closely with a smoldering passion. Thanks to the liberal Democrats, the America that I grew up in was disappearing. Something had to be done. Although I genuinely liked Chet Edwards and even got to know him on a personal level, Pelosi's Central Texas ally had to be removed from office.

The stage was set, and my political course was clear.

CHAPTER 8

Getting My Mind Right

Like a political nightmare, I and other conservatives watched in stunned amazement and utter frustration as the increasingly liberal voting congressman tightened his grip on this conservative Central Texas district. Of course, the situation was exacerbated by the primary newspaper in Waco, the largest population center in the district.

The editors of the Waco *Tribune-Herald* were unabashed liberal Democrats. Their editorial page read like a Democrat Party press release daily. And since Edwards was the top Democrat in Central Texas, he had all the favorable coverage that an incumbent office holder could possibly hope for. For me, as a former television news reporter, it was almost embarrassing to witness the sycophantic coverage the congressman received in both the editorial and "news" sections of the paper.

Everything, from any amount of federal funding to the naming of a post office, was trumpeted prominently in the paper, complete with pictures and glowing testimonials from grateful constituents as well as experts' assessments of the beneficial good the congressman was bestowing on the community.

Of course, even more telling was what was not covered. Knowing this was a very conservative district, the paper was pretty good about *not* reporting the congressman's votes in Washington that might cause him problems back in the district.

For example, if something was mentioned about a particularly high-profile vote on, say, a tax hike, they would selectively report his "no" vote on an alternative procedural bill which would then make it look like he opposed the tax hike, when in reality, he would vote "yes" on the final version, which would mean Americans would indeed face higher taxes. But then, if ever confronted on it by an opponent, he could cite the alternative procedural bill vote and with some semblance of cynical truth, "accurately" claim he voted against a tax hike, all the while knowing that the vast majority of voters would never be able to figure it all out. It was an incredibly deceptive situation, but one that was carried out with the efficiency of a Swiss watch.

Basically, the paper became a staunch defender of the congressman. Thus, it became glaringly obvious to anyone who understood the lay of the land, if anyone dared take on the sitting Democrat Congressman Edwards, they would also be taking on the main newspaper. It was a daunting and intimidating challenge. I personally found out just how tough and challenging it could be later.

By this time, while I had left KWTX and was focused solely on my video business, I also accelerated my active participation in the local Republican Party.

Because I was no longer an on-air personality for a TV station, I was no longer restricted from being actively involved at any level in the political world. I served in various positions in McLennan County's Republican Party, beginning as the public relations director, a precinct chairman, a delegate to county and state conventions, and eventually adding election judge to my growing political activist resume.

Being an election judge was an eye opener into the world of politics. It educated me on the realities of the election process. These things made an indelible impression on me as to what the Republican Party was up against in the two-party system. In essence, today's elections are not a fair fight.

Early in my television career, I became casual friends with a former Division 1 football player who also worked at the station. One day he took me by complete surprise by telling me that he needed a place to live and asked if he could move in with me. I wasn't particularly interested in having a roommate. I had shed my college mindset and was enjoying the privacy of my own apartment, even though it was just off the Baylor University campus.

I searched for a polite way to turn him down, when he stunned me by adding, "That is, if you don't mind living with a black person."

Now I was in a quandary. Although it truly hadn't even been part of my mental equation and reason for not wanting a roommate, I suddenly realized that by saying no, there might be some seriously wrong messages sent, which I did not want to deal with. So, because he was a good guy and I liked him, I now had a roommate.

It was an interesting chapter in my life and gave me a new, yet frustrating, understanding of a large segment of American society. He was truly a sharp guy with a great personality who could easily move back and forth between white and black cultures. It was amazing to see the personality and dialogue transformation, depending on which group was hanging out at the apartment. He could easily talk "white" as the mood hit, or if he had black friends or family over, the "black" with all its mannerisms, slang, and intonations would appear without missing a beat.

As we were both Christians who generally adhered to the same moral values, beliefs, and lifestyles, it was an easy living situation. We never had any arguments or even suffered the basic frictions of living life with another person. Even though I was never shy about sharing my political point of view, we never even came close to having an argument or verbal confrontation. In fact, it was clear to me that our political values were in almost total agreement. But one day I got my first eye-opening lesson of how politics influenced different cultures.

President Reagan was running for his second term when a story about the campaign came on the national TV news. At the end of the report I casually threw out an innocuous question affirming in my mind what I thought I had always known.

"Are you going to be voting for Reagan?" I innocently inquired, thinking I already knew the answer and would just be getting an affirmation of that knowledge.

Without any defense or animosity, he matter-of-factly replied, "No."

"What?" I responded. "I thought you liked Reagan?"

"I do."

"So why aren't you going to vote for him? Surely, you're not going to vote for Mondale?!" I shot back with an indignant confusion.

"No, I told you I like Reagan."

So, then you're going to vote for Reagan, right?

"No, I'm not."

Seeing my total, sincere confusion, he then laid me out with what I believe has become the greatest disconnect and tragedy in American politics.

"Rob, you don't understand. Black folk don't vote Republican. I like Reagan, so I'm not going to vote for Mondale. That's how I'll give my vote to Reagan."

"But that's crazy!" I shot back vehemently.

"Sorry, you don't get it, but that's just the way it is," he said, ending the discussion, and we never talked about voting again. The pragmatic side of me thought his logic was insane, but at the end of the day, Mondale wouldn't be getting his vote. I guess that's the best to be hoped for.

Unfortunately for America, my friend was not alone, and he accurately described the general mindset of the Black culture in America.

I saw his revelation affirmed years later in my role as an election judge in a racially mixed precinct. As the judge, you have many roles to play during a full day of voting. First and foremost, you have to help people correctly make their votes count. In my particular precinct, we had tables around a big room where people would mark their ballots. In many ways it was like a classroom setting with students sitting around working on assignments. And like a classroom, if they got stuck or confused, most would raise their hands and request that I come by to help them, just like the teacher. In my experience, every single time that a black voter would ask me for help, I would get some variation of the exact same question. "How do I vote for just Democrats?" or, and more remarkably, "I was told to come in and vote straight Democrat. Where do I mark it?"

Because I'm an honest person who took election judging seriously, it took every bit of acting skill I had to cheerfully show them how to cancel out my vote. And, on top of that, it broke my heart to witness their complete ignorance of whom they were voting for— good, bad, or ugly. It's a sad state of affairs which has become even more entrenched today.

As I watched the two parties drift farther apart and traditional America begin to slowly and tragically disappear because of federal policies, my desire to help grew stronger. Our congressman was getting no real challenges in each election cycle and, with each cycle, he locked his grip on power ever tighter.

I even helped a well-meaning, but totally outclassed, novice run those first two re-election cycles, giving him advice and media help wherever possible, but it was truly like standing in front of a loco-motive with your hands up, demanding it stop. There's just no way.

In his third re-election, some "real" candidates on the Republican side finally jumped in. Again, we had another combative and bruising primary to get a nominee. The eventual winner was the son of one of the first Republican primary candidates in that very first race six years before. There were large amounts of money raised and it looked like a real challenge could emerge this time in the fall. Sadly, in the end, the young Republican challenger was primarily focused on the abortion issue and was never able to convince enough Republican voters that he was a real substantive alternative to the Democrat incumbent.

CHAPTER 9

An Unexpected Catalyst

By Edwards' fourth re-election, the Republicans were so demoralized and defeated that they officially gave up and didn't even field a candidate. Such was the power of incumbency, embellished by this photogenic and personable office holder. Yet while this was going on in a conservative Central Texas district, aside from the few districts purposely concocted by the Justice Department to create safe minority seats, the rest of Texas was rapidly moving to the right.

As a small business owner and connected conservative, I vowed this would not stand. Somebody with an ability to articulate the conservative point of view, while understanding and handling the pressure of the "big stage" of a media campaign, had to challenge this congressman. If I had anything to say about it, he would never again have a free ride on Election Day.

The next election cycle brought a new first-time challenger into the mix. A retired oil executive had decided to challenge Edwards. I knew nothing about Ramsey Farley, but as a Republican voter, I was thrilled that we had someone willing to challenge him. It was still early in the process and, although we knew we at least had a candidate, word began filtering around the district in Republican circles that, perhaps, this challenger might not be a winning candidate.

As someone connected to the process, I began to hear that this particular candidate was a decent and well-meaning man, but he was new to this type of politics and didn't have the people skills or charisma to get the job done. As time progressed and the deadline for filing approached, I heard from elected officials and political types who had met the challenger. Virtually everyone quietly whispered that they were getting more and more convinced that he didn't stand a chance for any number of reasons.

I felt those old stirrings and seriously considered offering myself up as an alternative. After all, in my mind, the state of the nation was rapidly deteriorating with the continued dominance of an increasingly liberal Congress. We were a conservative district, yet we kept sending back to Washington someone who was helping the Democrats "destroy" the country. I conferred with close friends and political allies and formulated a game plan. I had talked about running for Congress before, but it never got beyond talk. However, this time, the dedicated ideological conservative in me said it was time to "belly up to the bar," as my old Democrat county chairman friend had put it. He told me the number one political fact of life, "Lots of people talk about running for office, but very few have the courage to actually do it, because win or lose, it truly changes your life." Was he ever right.

I soon came to the conclusion that I had to do this. I calculated that, with my media background, I had the ability to easily handle the pressures of dealing with reporters and cameras. With my production company, I had the ability to generate my own advertising and commercials. And finally, with my political experience, I could intelligently understand and discuss the issues. With the addition of my still fairly strong name recognition from my TV days, I thought I could mount a pretty good campaign with a lot less money than would be needed for any other normal candidate.

But I also didn't want to be "that guy" who, because of ego, bad judgment, or whatever, would jump into something he had no business jumping into, mucking it up for everyone else. So, I decided that I would mind my business and quietly watch to see if someone who could actually win would get into the race. I planned to wait until late on the very last day and, if no else was in, I would jump. Along the way, I continued to discreetly talk with close friends and confidants about my plan. I was truly amazed and gratified to get overwhelming encouragement, enthusiasm, and vows of support from everyone.

However, as the deadline drew closer, I wavered daily. One moment I was fired up and ready to go, thinking, *It has to be done!* The next moment I was looking at the monumental challenge and asking, *Who am I to do this? I'm just a small business owner.* If I won the primary, I would be taking on a professional career politician who appears on TV newscasts or the front page of all the newspapers. I would be taking on the same guy who hobnobs with the likes of President Clinton and House Speaker Nancy Pelosi. *This is crazy, I can't do this!* It was an agonizing, ongoing mental battle that seesawed back and forth for months.

With a couple of weeks to go before the filing deadline, a bizarre event occurred that forced my hand on my decision. As mentioned before, Chet Edwards was genuinely a likable guy whom I'd known loosely in social settings for years, going back to my days as a young reporter when I used to cover him. But he was more than that: He was a regular customer at my video production business. He or his wife regularly brought in family videos to be duplicated and edited.

One day I was standing in the parking lot of my business, talking with a conservative friend about my possible political intentions. The conversation became intense, with him affirming that I needed to do it because we had to get that "two-faced liberal Chet Edwards out of there." During the course of the conversation, my friend suddenly stopped in mid-sentence and stared over my shoulder. His faced turned white like he had just seen a ghost.

"Rob, it's him!"

"Who?"

"Chet! He's driving up!"

I turned around to see the congressman pull into the parking lot. My stomach knotted up like I'd just started down the top of a rollercoaster. I'd been talking about him and his policies, but I hadn't seen him personally in probably over a year.

"What are you going to do?" my friend asked with absolute panic.

I mustered all the calm I could and said, "I guess I'll tell him."

"Do you want me to stick around?"

"No, I've got to do it alone. He's basically a good guy, I owe him that much."

With complete relief, my friend beat a hasty retreat to his car and sped off.

In the meantime, Chet had gotten out of his car and said hello. He said he was coming by to pick up an order his wife had left earlier.

"Great, the girls will take care of you," I said as I followed him in and went into my office nearby.

I sat down and agonized about what to do next as I listened to him getting his order. After all, I hadn't officially done anything, so did I really have to talk to him? I asked myself, *But, if you actually do jump in and don't say anything to him, you're gutless with no character.* My answer was clear.

As I heard him finishing up I knew I had no choice. I yelled out, "Hey, Chet, you got a minute? I need to talk to you," as I headed out of my office with my heart pounding through my chest.

"Sure, Rob. What's up?" he said, as we both walked out to his car.

"Well, this is kind of awkward," I stammered, noticeably uncomfortable.

"What's the matter?"

"You know I've been involved in Republican politics around here for a long time, right?"

"Sure," he said with confusion and slight concern coming across his face.

"And you know we go way back, right?" I hesitated before continuing. "Oh man, this is awkward."

"Sure…oh," he said with what he thought was sudden understanding. "They've asked you to support someone running against me?" He thought he had it figured out.

"No, it's a little more awkward than that," I responded. And before he could say anything else, I blurted out, "Chet, I've got to run against you. Your Democrat policies are killing small businesses," I said, pointing back at my building. "I've known you a long time and you're a good guy, but you're supporting people in Washington who are destroying this country."

"Oh, wow," he said with surprised resignation. "That is something. I knew Ramsey was going to run, but I thought he was it."

That's the trouble," I said. "You'll kill him. We've got to take this seat, and everyone I've talked to thinks I have a better shot. I've got to run."

"Is anyone else in the race?" he asked.

"No. That's why I feel like I've got do it."

After a slight pause, he said, "Well, Rob, if somehow I were to lose the seat to any Republican in this district, I'd prefer it was you, because I know you've got integrity and are a decent guy."

"Thanks, Chet, that's extremely gracious of you. The feeling is mutual."

"I'd just like to ask you one thing."

"Sure. What?"

He surprised me with his request.

"If you win the primary, and I think you will, let's agree to not let it get nasty. You'll have Republican consultants from Washington coming in here to work your campaign, and I'll have the pros on my side, and it could get extremely nasty. That's how they do things. Let's just keep it civil between you and me."

"Absolutely. You know this isn't personal; it's purely ideological." I felt relieved.

"Have you filed yet?" he asked.

"No, not yet. What about you?" I asked, hoping against hope that maybe he wouldn't. After all, he was the powerful incumbent and, with two weeks to go, he still hadn't filed. Maybe he changed his mind and would quit.

I hid my disappointment when he said, "No, but I'm heading down next week."

Having by now regained my overall composure, I loosened things up by asking with a smile, "Hey, if you want, we could drive down to Austin together and save money on gas."

He laughed, but declined, and we shook hands and parted on much better terms than could have been hoped for. Surprisingly, I felt like the world had been lifted off my shoulders. But, although I knew I had done the right thing by telling him, I also knew I had lost a decent customer. All in all, I suppose it was a fair trade-off.

At the same time, I realized the magnitude of what I had just done. I was now essentially committed to the race. The internal arguing was over. In my mind it was official. I'm a man of my word and that meant I had to run if nothing else changed. And so far, there was absolutely no hint of anything changing. As it turned out, bizarrely, the man I was trying to remove from office is the one who had serendipitously forced my hand and made my decision.

A few weeks later, the status of the race remained unchanged, and I was relegated to keeping my word to myself and, ironically, the congressman. I waited until the last possible day, then committed to drive to Austin with a friend.

The hour and a half drive was about as tense as could be, with me internalizing what I was about to do. As the stress began to increase exponentially, the emotions did likewise. Once again, I was wrestling with all the fears and doubts that had plagued me for months. Who was I to challenge the man who was friends with the president of the United States, and had the ear of the Speaker of the House? Despicable as both individuals were to me, that was still heady stuff.

And beyond that, I asked myself, *Was I being a jerk to the man who had already announced on the Republican side? How would I feel if someone did that to me?*

This was a real and frustrating back and forth. Aside from the political calculations, I thought, *I'm not even married yet.* Would that mean anything? It would be awesome to have someone to team up with in this incredible endeavor. But there were more important things hanging in the balance than my personal life. Then again, what would people think?

And then there was the intimidation factor. The congressman had all the power. He had all the media. He was a professional politician who'd been involved in this sort of thing his entire adult life.

I turned over every mental rock trying to convince myself that this was the right thing to do.

Who was I? I was nobody! But that's the problem. He's a life-long politician and that's not the way this country should work. The professional political class are the ones screwing things up, I told myself with complete sincerity.

What right do I have to do this? We like to believe the system is supposed to be completely open, and anyone can become anything. But we all know, in reality, that's not how it works.

But we have to win. I can do it. After all, things are too important in America to just let a political novice become cannon fodder for a powerful incumbent and kill any hope we have to take this seat, I argued back defiantly with myself. *America's in a death spiral and Edwards is helping take us there. This is too important for my petty fears and desires. Much bigger issues are at stake.*

Meanwhile, as the stripes in the road whizzed by on the one hundred miles separating Austin from Waco, we rapidly approached my destiny. My considerate friend could sense I was struggling, so conversation, though encouraging, was kept to a minimum. Even as I internally debated, with my emotions swinging wildly back and forth, each moment drew us ever closer to what was clearly becoming the boldest thing I had ever done in my life.

CHAPTER 10

Moment of Truth

When we arrived at the Republican Party headquarters in Austin late that afternoon in August 2000, it was uneventful—even anti-climactic. The first question I asked the clerk handling the paperwork and significant filing fee was, "Has anyone else gotten into the race for District 11?"

"Just the man who filed weeks earlier."

As it was now after three o'clock in the afternoon, with the deadline of six o'clock in the evening quickly approaching, it looked like the last potential stop sign had been removed from my uphill road to removing an incumbent Liberal from the ranks of Congress. Although scared to death of taking on this task, I was more or less committed to taking the plunge.

The last hurdle was to write the check for the filing fee. As I hadn't firmly made an official public decision and had asked no one else for financial help, I knew that this filing fee of well over $3,000 was on me. The internal argument finally came to an end as I took a deep breath, signed the forms, and handed over the check. It was done. I was now officially in the primary.

As my friend and I silently headed back to the car, I just looked at him, rolled my eyes, shook my head, and said nothing. Then we both burst out laughing. It was as if the stress dam had burst. All those months of agonizing, losing sleep, and searching my own soul had come to an end. All those years of dancing around it, talking about it, dreaming about it, investigating the process, and toying with the desire to get into the fight had just culminated with a quiet submission of paperwork.

Never mind that I had no clue of my next step. I was in the battle. And for the first time in my life, instead of wringing my hands and complaining about how liberal Democrats were destroying the country, I could now actually do something! I had the opportunity to take out one of Nancy Pelosi's lieutenants. It was an incredibly satisfying feeling, and, in fact, money well spent. Oh, sure, I'd have to get past some other guy in the primary, but that was probably no big deal. I mean, I was going to get a chance to take on the congressman, and the Left, later on in the general election.

"After all these years I finally bellied up to the bar instead of just talking about it," I told my friend. "I'm actually doing it!"

We stopped at a restaurant in Austin before making the long drive back. The euphoria of finally making that big decision began to fade as we got back into the real world. I fell into deep thought as we left the car and approached the door of the restaurant. It suddenly hit me like a bucket of cold water. "What have I done?!" I blurted out with a tinge of anguish and remorse.

"What? You're running for Congress," my friend said matter-of-factly, as if telling me something I didn't know.

"I just can't believe I did it." I shook my head.

During our meal, my friend talked on about who knows what. I wasn't listening.

"What have I done?!" I blurted out for a second time, rhetorically. Then I just shook my head and we both started laughing once again. That turned out to be the running conversation all the way back to Waco--normal conversation, then me suddenly expressing my astonishment of my own audacity.

"We're talking about taking on a powerful sitting congressman. This is a former state senator who's been working in the corridors of power in Austin and Washington for the last decade. Who am I to challenge this guy? I'm just a small business owner and former sportscaster. I have no business in this race," I professed candidly.

"Yes, but somebody needs to beat him, and you wanted to do it, so it's too late now. You're in it and you can't quit," he responded straightforwardly.

"I know," I told him. "I'm okay. I just can't believe I've done it."

But now I had to figure out a game plan, I thought, realizing that, after all these months, I was like the proverbial dog who chases a car. *Okay, now that I've caught it, what do I do with it?*

PART II

Primaries

CHAPTER 11

On the Stump

I would soon learn another dictum of politics that holds true: "Expect the unexpected." I had begun to think about proceeding with the race and how I would deal with my primary opponent when I got word that caught me off guard.

The son of a successful business owner from a small city south of Waco, decided to run at the last minute. Unbelievably, Darryl had evidently shown up shortly after me and filed for the seat. That one thing that I had not expected nor wanted had happened. Here we were, going up against a strong incumbent, with three of us fighting for the nomination. This was not good, but I could either quit or go on. Because the other two were from the same small city in the southern part of the district, I had at least one advantage in that they would probably scavenge from each other's support base, while Waco was clear for me. Besides, there was nothing else for me to do, because I'm not a quitter.

With the primary election less than three months away and no organization or donated funds, I was scrambling. Bethany, a family friend, volunteered to run the campaign on short notice. She was unemployed at the time but experienced in working for several organizations. Of course, it was with the understanding that we could only pay her once we succeeded raising money.

The problem was, this was a primary. Raising money for a primary is generally difficult. Of course, it makes it even harder when the candidate just simply wasn't willing to ask for money. Yes, I knew that was what a candidate was supposed to do, but I never realized before how hard it was. I was a small business owner who had worked for everything I had, and I had always done things myself. It became apparent to me and my campaign manager that I was going to have a problem with "begging," as I put it. We started operating under the assumption that the only donations we were going to get were from those who would approach us to give. I would personally pay for the rest of what we needed, to the extent I could.

My two opponents were well-financed, however, and seemed to have no problem buying whatever they needed. We decided to wage a bare-bones campaign and hope for the best, using personal appearances and free news media as much as possible. Other than that, we would buy yard signs, bumper stickers, limited printed material, and, at the end, TV and radio commercials, which I would produce at my own company. I would buy the time at the stations and donate the production work from my company. A friend graciously offered to donate an unused portion of his business as a campaign headquarters as an in-kind contribution.

It doesn't seem like much from a professional point of view, but this turned out to be fairly effective. We did have the ability to compete with my opponents.

We were encouraged by how the race was shaping up. I learned quickly that I'm a pretty good stump speaker. I had been on television and always knew that when the camera light came on, I was talking to a couple hundred thousand people at any given time. However, now I had to be able to talk in front of crowds. It could be ten people, it could be two hundred. For the first time in my life, I was forced to face an audience in person and make sense with a clear, concise message.

It turns out, I had an aptitude for public speaking. I also quickly formulated a speaking style that was conversational and, more importantly, from the heart. I developed the technique of talking to a large crowd the same way I would talk to any single individual. In that way, I was, in essence, holding a conversation with the audience. Granted, it was a one-way conversation (unless people asked questions), but it was effective at putting everyone at ease.

It served me well early on. It was obvious from the start that my two opponents were extremely uncomfortable when it came to giving speeches. In our first joint appearances, the distinctions in style, personality, and communication skills were striking. I spoke off the top of my head and straight from my heart directly to the audience; my conservative beliefs by now were ingrained and needed no rehearsal. My opponents, though, would nervously stumble through written statements, making everyone in the room feel uncomfortable—including myself. It was like the feeling you get when listening to the singer of the national anthem forget the words midway through the song.

Because of the developing performance chasm widening between us in meetings, it became clear to everyone involved that the other two primary candidates had to change their tactics. Over time, first one, then the other began to eventually stop reading and instead tried memorizing their speeches. It was an improvement, but still painful. The human side of me began to feel sorry for them. I had to keep reminding myself that they were the enemy and needed to be defeated, if I were to get the chance to take on the real target of this race.

The key for me was to constantly focus on why I was in the race. I never lost sight of the end goal, which was to win that seat for a conservative and help save traditional conservative America. It may sound grandiose and even corny, but it was real. Evidently, a lot of people were as corny as I. The positive response after meetings was encouraging as people would sidle up, pledge their support, and take our materials.

A turning point for my campaign speaking confidence came at a meeting in the southern region of the district. My two primary opponents were from that city, and I was apprehensive about this forum being on their home turf. It was held at a local restaurant with community and business leaders in attendance. This was my first big event in "enemy" territory. Frankly, I expected the worst.

The crowd was large, and every seat was taken. We sat on a dais at the front of the hall with the meeting's leadership, and a nice lunch and organizational business preceded our comments. In deference to my nerves, I followed what became a standard routine of eating very little or nothing before speaking. I certainly did not want to be a victim of an accidental belch or intestinal issues while in front of any crowd. Of course, this was politics, after all, and you had to walk a fine line of being rude by turning down a gracious meal. I learned to size up each situation and act accordingly. In this case, as we were in front of everyone, I chose the pick and nibble routine, looking like I was eating, but not really.

We were each given five minutes to talk, the order chosen randomly. I drew second, which was not as bad as going first, but not as good as going last, to my way of thinking.

My first opponent was still not weaned from his written speeches and stumbled as usual through his prepared text. He introduced himself with his usual resume, and then went over the standard issues that one would expect for a group of business leaders. He covered several infrastructure and economic policies that he would support and enact if elected to Congress. From my seat at the front, I watched the audience intently, as subtly as I could, while still listening to my opponent.

As I observed the audience, it was clear to me that they were as bored as I was. Yes, these were good things that a congressman could do, but this was the primary. Yes, people need to know what you stand for and what you want to accomplish, but I looked at it from the average Republican voter's point of view. The only thing I want to know is, "How are you going to accomplish knocking off the powerful Democrat incumbent?" People listened, but you could actually see their lack of interest from their blank, emotionless faces. People were looking at their watches or just sitting motionless with no reaction whatsoever to what was being said. At the end of the speech, there were no perceptible changes of emotion, just polite, perfunctory, and brief applause.

These were "his" people, and this is their response? I thought. It's probably understandable, though, because that's not what I would want to hear if I were out there listening to a candidate!

I grew bolder inside as I listened to the host introduce me as the next candidate. I knew that there were undoubtedly Republicans in the audience who feared the incumbent, and some who even possibly liked him and were among those who kept him in office by splitting their tickets. I also understood that the room was virtually stacked with friends and business acquaintances of my two primary opponents. This was not good for me, but in a way, it was almost liberating.

As I stepped over to the podium, my nervousness and apprehension began to disappear. In fact, it was replaced by the white-hot anger of what we were up against in this campaign, and what we had to do to overcome it. *I have absolutely nothing to lose here, so forget the political niceties and tell them exactly what you're thinking*, I told myself as I began to speak.

I introduced myself. Even though most people likely knew me from my television days, I always proceeded on the assumption that nobody did. I did not want to come off as arrogant by thinking I was a legend in my own mind. I briefly covered our common ground by mentioning my small business ownership in Waco. I then quickly went over the past Republican political activities and positions I'd held, as I was the only one of the three who had been actively involved in local politics for most of my adult life.

As I spoke of my accomplishments and resume, the response in the room looked identical to the first speaker's: blank, emotionless stares of polite attention. A few looked at their laps or their empty lunch plates. A bored sip of iced tea here and there. Occasional glancing at watches with the quiet resignation that they had two more speeches to sit through before they could escape to the rest of their day.

I wrapped up my background quickly and shifted into what I really wanted to talk about.

"Look," I said smoothly, changing my tone, pace, and emotion. "I'm not running because of my resume or past political involvement. I'm not running because I'm looking for a new job, a new career, or an adventure. I'm running because our country is in trouble and it starts right here in Central Texas, with a congressman who votes wrong on all the major issues and values facing America.

"And let's get something straight before I go any further. I'm a conservative before I'm a Republican," I said emphatically. "We've got a congressman who goes to Washington and votes with the liberal Democrats on every major issue, and then comes back here and tells everybody how conservative he is, because he knows the average voter doesn't pay attention. Well, I do pay attention, and we don't need a congressman who stands for the Washington values of Bill Clinton and Teddy Kennedy. We want a congressman who'll stand for the common-sense values of Central Texas, not the liberal policies of Massachusetts!" I said with even more fire as I felt the passion rising inside me.

And then something amazing happened. The heads that had been looking down all raised up almost as one. I could see that "Aha." I may not have their votes, but I sure had their attention.

"I'm sure we're all conservatives up here on the stage, or we wouldn't be taking on Edwards. I'll bet there's probably not a dime's worth of difference between us on the major issues, so what we've got to look at is, who can beat Chet?" A few heads bobbed up and down in agreement. I was emboldened.

"This is a 58 percent Republican district. There's no way he should be winning here, but he has been, and we've got to stop him. We've got to put someone against him who has the knowledge and experience to intellectually challenge him on the issues. Someone who knows the media and can negate any advantage he has in that area. Someone who can effectively communicate our values and what we stand for."

Most of the room now looked like a sea of Bobblehead dolls. I was fired up because I was getting through to them. They understood what we were up against and they were affirming my every pronouncement.

"Sure, he takes care of Fort Hood, but so what? That's his job! Any congressman is going to take care of his district, and he should, as long as it doesn't hurt the rest of the country." Most heads were now emphatically bobbing in silent approval.

"You've got a choice to make if we're going to take our seat," I said, pounding the lectern. Autopilot took over as I let my true feelings surface. "We've got to put up someone who can walk like a congressman, talk like a congressman, and look like a congressman," I said, trying to draw a subtle distinction between myself and my opponents without directly referring to either of them.

"We *can* beat this guy! He's out of touch with this district and wrong on all the major issues that define who we are as a people and where we're going as a nation. "We can win, but we've got to nominate the right person, or it won't happen. I hope you'll give me a chance to take back our seat with a win in November."

Solid enthusiastic applause immediately followed my ending. People around the room looked at each other with silent nods and raised eyebrows. My campaign manager and traveling supporter were beaming as they applauded from their seats near the back.

Who knew if it meant anything? But at least I shared my heart and gave it all I had.

My heart was still pounding as I wondered what the last speaker would do. But I really didn't care. I had made my point.

Fortunately, he had memorized his speech and was not going to deviate in the slightest. It was exactly the type of speech a consultant would tell his client to give. It basically covered the same ground as the first gentleman and the audience's response returned to normal, followed by brief, polite applause.

The meeting soon closed, and supporters made their way to their chosen candidate. It was obvious my opponents were well connected as they did have their followers. Being an outsider, I didn't know what to expect. I assumed if no one approached me, I'd slip out and quickly retreat back to Waco.

I was wrong. As I stepped down from the dais, one person after another stopped me to tell me how much they appreciated what I had to say. And almost to a person, they grabbed my arm and leaned over to whisper, while furtively looking around at the others still mingling in the room, what to me were incredibly encouraging bombshells:

"I had been supporting Darryl, because we've done business with his father forever, but it's obvious you're the one that can beat Chet."

"We've known Ramsey for years and were behind him, but we've got to have someone that can win this race, and it's clear that's you. You've got our support."

"We thought we were behind Darryl, but you're the only one with the passion that can take this seat. We can't do anything publicly because they're our friends, but you've got our votes."

"We believe it's going to take someone who's willing to fight and, from what you showed us today, it's clear you're the guy that can get the message out and beat Chet."

"Didn't know anything about you other than you used to do the sports, but you're so fired up, and that's what we need. We're behind you."

It was amazing. It took me quite a bit of time to make it back to my team members. It was like running a gauntlet of well-wishers and new supporters. I was absolutely stunned and elated. I finally made it back to my team. They were still beaming.

"Rob, it's awesome!" gushed a truly relieved Bethany. "People have been coming by since the end of the meeting and telling us you're the one. A few gave me their cards and want to be contacted. This is unbelievable!"

As we drove back to Waco, it was satisfying to know I had passed what I thought was our first major test. But it was more exciting to realize that I could effectively communicate to a large crowd and elicit a positive response. It was clear to me that, although I may not have been a learned scholar or skilled orator, I knew how to communicate. I was not interested in giving a speech. What I wanted to do was talk to a group the same way I would with a single individual. I assumed that as conservative voters, we all shared a mission and a core set of values. I was doing nothing more than speaking what we all were thinking.

This was the beginning of my metamorphosis into a campaigner. I enjoyed seeing the response of people as they bought into our message. I also realized that not everybody was coming on board, and that fact was enough to keep me humble.

For the most part, primaries are made up of meetings that showcase candidates from one party. Yet, occasionally, a veteran's group, business organization, or service club might hold candidate forums with all candidates from every party invited to speak. In these cases, Chet rarely showed. After all, he was the sitting congressman. To appear in person would lend credibility to future opponents. If deemed important enough, he would always send a surrogate to make sure he had a presence.

At these meetings, both Democrats and Republicans were in the audience. In such situations, I toned down my normal message to appear a little less partisan. I focused on issues or values I felt we all might have in common, even though I knew there was little or no chance of winning these Democrats over. I also didn't change my habit of working the room before or after the program by talking with and meeting as many people as possible, even though I knew I might face hostility. Surprisingly, I enjoyed it.

I learned to identify whether a person was a Republican or a Democrat within five seconds with almost absolute certainty. Aside from the obvious Democrat who refuses to shake your hand, many attendees of these political events will engage in conversation either because they aren't completely sure for whom they are voting, they are being polite, or they want to interact with any "live" candidate. As in any police investigation, motive is key, and Democrats almost always have different motives when it comes to casting their vote. Their first comment would invariably tell me which side they were on. Even if they didn't mean to, they always started with some variation of the same question or statement.

"Hi, I'm Rob Curnock," I'd say in introduction. "I'm running for Congress and would sure appreciate it if you'd give me some consideration when you vote for Congress." Their next response was always a variation of the same theme if they were on the 'other' side:

"Okay, all I want to know is, what will you do for me if I give you my vote?"

"Why should I vote for you? How will you help me?"

"Convince me on how you'll improve my life."

Although caught off guard the first time I was asked this, thereafter I always responded with a variation of the same answer:

"I'll do everything I can to make sure you get to keep as much of your paycheck as possible by cutting government spending and lowering your taxes. I'll keep the government out of your way as much as possible, so you can exercise your constitutional right to pursue happiness. I'll fight to protect your right to own guns. I'll do whatever possible to support our troops wherever and whenever they are protecting this country."

And I invariably got the same response from them showing that they were clearly not impressed with my answer: "Hmmm...," "Oh, okay," or just silence. It was automatic.

It was at this moment they declared they were Democrats for Chet. It's sad but true, and it explains why the country is so divided today. It sounds harsh and overly simplified, but in my experience campaigning, it was absolutely gospel. Democrats tend to base their vote on how they can improve their personal lot in life and what they can get from the rich, the government, or their politicians.

On the other hand, Republicans generally vote on bigger themes or issues, like keeping a more intrusive government at bay, protecting individual rights under the Constitution, or keeping America exceptional.

That's exactly why I had to win this seat in Congress.

CHAPTER 12

Didn't See It Coming

Not too long after that lunch meeting, I got a call from the husband of the Republican county chairman for that particular county. This chairman was respected with strong connections in her part of the district. I also knew that, officially, a chairman wasn't supposed to take sides in any contested primary. Yet, from my own experiences working closely with the chairman in my own county, I knew what is supposed to be and what actually is, are sometimes two different things. After all, they are voters and political players themselves, and as such, they will generally get behind someone and quietly tell people who they are voting for. It's a wink-and-nod scenario, but it can also mean a lot of votes since, in a contested primary, many voters will call a county chairman to get advice for whom to vote.

We at Curnock for Congress headquarters were elated when he called and asked me to join him for a private breakfast meeting. I drove down thinking that, *Alright, my speech the other day worked! We're most likely going to get him to come on board, which means, indirectly, we've probably got the support of his wife, the county chairman, as well.*

This could be a major coup.

At the restaurant we sat down to break bread and talk politics. It was a thoroughly enjoyable breakfast as we covered all sorts of topics and realized we were in agreement on virtually every issue.

We had talked effortlessly for almost an hour when he broached the topic of me and the importance of taking out the incumbent. I liked where we were going with this conversation. This felt like the political equivalent of that feeling a woman gets when expecting a boyfriend to pop the question. Enough of the small talk. Tell me you're on board with us!

"Rob, you know it takes a real patriot to do what you're doing. Not many people are willing to take on someone like Chet. It certainly won't be easy," he began in earnest.

"Yes, I know, but we've got the numbers in this district, and if we get the right candidate, I'm confident we can win," I said trying to close the deal. "But we've got to get the right person out of this primary, or it'll be more of the same," I restated for emphasis.

"You're absolutely right, and that's why I wanted to talk to you. This is extremely critical."

"You've got that right," I jumped in.

"We've got to stop chewing ourselves up in these primaries. We've done it every time. Our eventual winner comes out wounded and diminished, while Chet is sitting there fresh, rested, and ready with money he didn't have to spend in a primary. He's just waiting to pounce. It's been a disaster for us every time."

"That's my point exactly," I affirmed, thinking we were beginning to get stuck in some endless loop of affirming each other's take on the race. "I certainly didn't see this three-way primary coming. Look, we both know why I chose to go after the nomination. We all know Ramsey doesn't have what it takes to win this thing. I felt that I had a much better chance."

"I agree, we both know Ramsey can't beat Chet," he emphasized.

"We got messed up with Darryl entering the race," I continued. "I had no idea he was getting into the race. I went down on the last day and specifically asked if anyone else had filed. If I had known he was in it, I would never have run."

"Yes, he filed at the last hour, which is why you missed him."

"Frankly, I'm not all that impressed with Darryl, either. He seems like a really nice guy, but I kinda get the idea his father is trying to make him a congressman to give him something to do with his life."

"No, there's more there than you realize," the chairman's husband said thoughtfully. And suddenly, slowly, it began to dawn on me--there was more than I realized to our conversation.

He continued. "Rob, I know you're in this for the right reasons, and that's why I know you're a patriot."

That phrase again. Where were we going with this?

"And a real patriot sometimes has to do something for the good of the cause, even if it's not what they want to do."

I didn't like where this was going. "Okay?..."

"For the good of our chances to get rid of Chet, we need to cut down this primary." He finally lowered the boom. "Rob, Darryl can win this."

He might as well have punched me across the table. "He's got serious money behind him, he's well liked in this community, and he'll be able to win in November. I know you don't like hearing this, but that's just the way things are," he said matter-of-factly.

With my own controlled matter-of-fact voice, I countered, "I don't agree at all," even though inside I was crushed. I would never let him know that. "So, what are you proposing I do?"

"I certainly can't tell you what to do, but for the good of our effort, you need to get out," he said, plainly telling me what to do.

"You're telling me to quit?!"

"That's what I'm saying. I know it's not easy, but you know it's the right thing to do. And a lot of people will show their gratitude for you taking one for the team on this. I know you'll be in future races and you'll have a lot of support from folks who'll know what you did here. Darryl will easily beat Ramsey once you're out, and after Darryl's the congressman, you *will* benefit from doing this, if you know what I mean."

"Did Darryl put you up to this?" I asked accusingly.

"No, he doesn't know anything about this."

"Well, I'll tell you what," I said, controlling my anger and disappointment. "I don't agree, and I'm certainly not going to quit. But I absolutely do agree with you that we need to change the congressman in this area. I'll do whatever I can, but not that."

That ended the visit. We both made a concerted effort to end on as good of terms as possible, which we did. I understood he was just doing what he could for his preferred candidate, but, boy, that was brazen on his part.

I also learned another valuable lesson in the world of campaigning: Anything can happen, good or bad. Here, I thought I was going to get a real boost to my campaign, but instead, I realized someone else would get that support. Worse yet, it dawned on me that there were, in fact, people actually wanting me to quit and get out of the way. Wow.

While disappointing, I believe it made me a better candidate. I now knew to expect the unexpected, and you should never get too emotionally high or too emotionally low. This was a lesson that would serve me well in years to come.

CHAPTER 13

Election Night

As the primary progressed, I learned valuable lessons of how a major campaign works and, more importantly, how I personally worked in the pressure cooker. Of course, in my case, campaigning was not my only job. Because I was not financially independent, I still had to spend time working. My business was my only source of income, so I became a part-time candidate running a full-time race. It made for long, hectic days and nights in that two-month primary period. But because I believed in what I was doing, even though it was tiring and at times crazy, I did it with all the energy and excitement I could muster.

In our race, the two candidates from the same city began to go after each other with escalating vigor. Their initial congeniality gave way to downright dislike for each other on a visceral level.

Even though I spent some portion of most every day with my two opponents, I began to feel strangely isolated and on my own, which was fine with me. I focused on my own game plan and did what I felt I needed to do to win. As they seemed to be fighting over the same voting turf, I went about my own business of trying to get the votes necessary to win the primary. My team and I felt good about the response we were seeing at the live events. We felt that my campaign skills were improving with each forum, press conference, or debate. Our confidence grew as people truly seemed to respond to both our message and my speaking style.

The stakes for the other two rose each day, and the pressure for them to win grew in direct correlation to the amount of money each was now spending. Darryl, seemingly funded by his father's connections, quickly moved toward a quarter of a million dollars in campaign expenditures. Farley chose to go the borrowing route, and his debt began to exceed the $200,000 level, as well.

Their sniping and vitriol went back and forth, generally behind the scenes. Evidently, there was absolutely no love lost between these two. Surprisingly, they or their campaign staff shared their feelings about the other camp with me when the other, or his surrogates, were not around. No doubt, it was because neither camp saw me as a threat. I was out of their line of fire and glad to be.

The end of this first campaign was strangely uneventful. As Election Day drew nearer, my opponents were going at it. The Curnock for Congress campaign had no money to do polling, so we had no idea where we stood. We received positive feedback and pledges of support from all our live events, and more and more people responded positively to our limited running of TV ads. We felt guardedly positive about our odds on Election Day. Besides, we assumed—hoped—that the other two candidates would split their support in their southern part of the district and I'd take the lion's share in Waco, the bigger population center. It was sound political reasoning, but sheer conjecture since we had no polling on which to rely.

In hindsight, I should have been more cognizant of that old adage of politics: "You're only attacked if you're a threat." And the bigger the threat, the more frequent, uglier, and vicious the attacks. As I was being left alone, evidently, I was perceived by the others as the political equivalent of a predator bunny rabbit.

On Election Day, aside from taking time out to vote, I spent the whole of the day at work. A strange sensation came over me in the voting booth. It was surreal seeing my name on a ballot. After staring at the ballot and soaking it in for a few seconds, I think I made the right choice—and voted for myself. And no, I didn't feel the least bit self-serving for doing so.

My campaign staff argued whether or not I should do last-minute campaigning outside of some polling places. I was adamant that this was the voters' day, and I did not want to infringe on their walk into the polling stations. Besides, rightly or wrongly, when I go to vote, I get annoyed having to walk through a gauntlet of people trying to influence my vote. My philosophy is that if I hadn't gotten the persuasion job done earlier, there was no hope.

My first ever election night was about as low key as possible. I've never felt comfortable about the concept of holding a big victory or watch party when there is even a remote possibility you might not win. And besides, in this case, we had run a low-key campaign, financially. However, we did want to thank our friends, supporters, and volunteers for their efforts and help. Our voluntary staff gathered at our donated headquarters to watch the results and invited folks to stop by anytime during the evening for light refreshments. The media also needed to have a place to come for the standard campaign interviews.

Although *low key* is the perfect descriptive term for our campaign and victory party, my emotions were anything but low key. After several months of stepping out of my comfort zone on so many levels and working so hard to accomplish such a high-profile goal, knowing that it all came down to the vote count that evening was incredibly stressful. It was a combination of intense anticipation and excitement, mixed with an extreme fear of losing, and a dread of seeing it all come to an end.

But we believed we had reason for optimism.

Although I'd been to dozens of watch parties over the years as a reporter, volunteer, or friend, this was the first time I would be the focal point of it all. I was the one who would be declared the winner—or the loser. I really didn't know how I would react.

A few television reporters stopped by, early after the polls closed, to do some interviews for playback during the evening as the results came in. And supporters started drifting in and out to wish us luck, as many of them made the rounds to all the different local watch parties for all the candidates in local races. Our little core group of supporters waited nervously for the first results to come in on the TVs we had strategically placed around the headquarters showing all three local news channels.

Finally, the first early voting ballots came in. And then, just like that, it was essentially over. We all watched in stunned silence as the initial results came in, with me dead last.

Oh, it wasn't horrible, but I knew it wasn't good. We all kept trying to cheer ourselves up by telling ourselves that there were still a lot of votes out there to be counted and we could make up the ground. But it never did happen. Every update on every station showed basic numbers all through the night. That blasted percentage just would not budge, and, one by one, they called the race and declared the other two would be in a runoff. I was eliminated with about 20 percent of the vote.

I felt gut shot. All we could do was console ourselves with the fact that we did the best we could with the resources we had, but in the end, the voters evidently felt that the other two would have a better chance of taking on the incumbent. I was surprised at my own emotions. Yes, I was disappointed and sad about losing, but it's not like I was ready to jump off the nearest bridge. I was more disappointed for my supporters, volunteers, and few financial donors. I felt like I had let them down and needed to make it right for them somehow. And as a clear indication of just how much I was, in fact, *not* a politician, my only thought was, *I need to pay these donors back, because they gave to me, and I failed to deliver.* That was the competitive businessman in me talking. I thought in terms of a "money-back" guarantee.

But the overwhelming emotion crashing over me was embarrassment. After we all said our goodbyes and thank-you's for the last three months, I was left alone with my thoughts as I got into my car to drive to my dark and quiet home. I was just plain embarrassed. I don't like to lose. I knew politics. I knew this district. People knew me. Yet, I came in last, in a three-way race against two complete raw political novices. I was just plain embarrassed.

I knew I couldn't sleep and I was too wired to go home, so I did the only thing I could think of that might help ease the shame. I decided to erase any evidence that I was even in this race. Although we had volunteers lined up to remove yard signs from polling places, I did it myself. There I was, driving around to all the long-darkened polling places with their forest of yard signs clustered about their entrances. Come light of day, my name would not be among those candidates still advertising their prospects long after all choices were already made. As irrational as it seems, as far as I was concerned, I didn't want people to even know I had run.

By 1:30 in the morning, I finally began to feel the need for sleep as the sting of the results faded. It also felt good to think I had wiped my "loser" name clear from the majority of polling places around Waco. I headed home, said hello to my cat, who was truly glad to see me and ambivalent of the day's election results. In her tiny cat world, I would always be number one. I fell into my bed exhausted, both physically and mentally, and slept like a rock. I slept more soundly than I had since I first began formulating this political adventure some six months before.

I awoke around 10:00 the next morning and simply headed into my business. It was a new day and the stress and busyness of the two-month campaign was at last over. I was not a wealthy man. I had to get back to work. I had to get back to my normal life.

Friends and supporters were wonderful over the next week or so as they thanked me for running and kept pointing out all the positive things we had accomplished—not the least of which was, if you looked at the final hard numbers of vote tallies and money spent, I had actually done very well. Maybe, just maybe, there wasn't anything to be ashamed about.

At the end of the day, I was not in debt, had paid all of my bills, and wound up spending a little over $12,000. For that, I received about 20 percent of the vote. On the other hand, my opponents each got around 40 percent of the vote. One had spent about $220,000, so far, and the other had put himself in debt for about the same amount. And they now had to continue to spend in the runoff. In that respect, I could take some pride in what we had accomplished, as well as the fact that I didn't betray my own conservative fiscal principles. I didn't spend money I didn't have and didn't rely on someone else to pay for my campaign debts. It may not have been good politics, but it allowed me to hold my head up post-election.

In fact, one could argue that I certainly got my money's worth. My $12,000 held up pretty well against their combined half a million plus.

CHAPTER 14

Living for Another Day

Still, I wasn't ready to brag about what I had accomplished any time soon, and just went about my business and personal life. But, evidently, I still had a small role to play in this primary drama.

Within weeks, both opponents reached out to me to ask for my endorsement. As I had gotten along fine with both candidates, I had no problem entertaining the idea for either. For me, it came down to who wanted it more. Darryl had an intermediary call me and set it up for me to talk to him and let him make his case. Ramsey, smartly, called me himself and made his own case right from the start.

I was torn and felt both had positives and both had negatives going into the general election. So, there didn't seem to be a clear choice in the "who can best beat Chet" department. I leaned to staying out of it because the last thing I wanted was political enemies in my own party. However, after talking with a number of supporters, political and elected officials in whom I trusted, almost all of them urged me to support Ramsey.

I talked with each candidate again and Ramsey made it clear that if he won the seat, he'd only be in Washington for two to three terms at most, and that I would be *his* endorsed successor. It was obvious to me that Darryl would make a career of it.

Ramsey offered to keep alive my dreams of somehow getting into the fight. So between that and almost everybody I knew wanting me to endorse Ramsey, I threw my support to him. Then came the hard part. I owed it to Darryl to let him know. I called him, apologized, and let him then his wife vent. Understandably, they were not happy. I felt absolutely horrible because they were truly decent people, and I knew I was hurting them badly. It was not my finest hour, and I vowed to never get myself in a position like that again.

An ecstatic Ramsey campaign quickly assembled press conferences in the two key cities in the district, and we made it official. It turned out to have a major impact on the race. I went back to work on my business and stayed directly out of the runoff, in deference to Darryl, while my campaign manager Bethany, independently and of her own volition, agreed to join Ramsey's staff.

I was told later by Ramsey himself that, after my endorsement, he heard that Darryl's father decided to pull the money plug on his son's campaign. For all intents and purposes, the primary race was over. Sadly, in hindsight, so was the general election. I didn't know it then, but this would turn out to be a bad matchup for the Republicans.

Because of the unique cleverness of my own TV commercials, Ramsey did ask me to have my company do his television and radio commercials for the general election. I agreed and did all of them for a cover-my-cost, bare bones, minimal price, while donating most of the cost to his campaign. Of course, I had to carefully stay within federal election limits.

I hoped for the best, but one incident late in the general election made me feel like my original assessment of Ramsey's chances was correct. Other than the commercials, I went back to my business and watched the race unfold as a civilian. One night, I got a call from my former campaign manager, now a key player in Ramsey's campaign.

"Rob, it's Bethany, you're not going to believe this." She was extremely distraught.

"What's up?"

"I'm at the debate between Ramsey and Chet, and it's a disaster!"

"You're there now? What happened?"

"It just finished up and I'm standing off to the side of the stage. You wouldn't believe it; it's just been a total disaster. I am so embarrassed. Before the debate, Ramsey demanded to have the questions in advance, so he could be prepared beforehand."

"That's not good, that makes him look like he can't think on his feet. And that's really not good if he's on the stage trying to debate Chet."

"Oh, it's a whole lot worse than that. He wrote his responses on note cards, so he could read them when it was his turn."

"Are you kidding me? That's terrible."

"Oh, Rob, it's worse. He mixed up his cards and read the wrong answer to one of the questions. It was totally humiliating. I can't believe it." She was truly upset, and I didn't blame her.

"Oh, man, I knew he wasn't very smooth, but I didn't think it could get that bad. Well, hopefully, not many people saw the debate. Unless it gets reported, the only ones that will know about it are the people in the audience."

"What a disaster. I just thought you would want to know, and I had to talk to somebody. I'm so upset, but I've got to get back out there."

I hung up, thinking, *That's exactly why I felt the need to run against him for the nomination in the first place, but it's too late now. We've just got to hope that he can appeal to enough Republicans to pull off the upset. He may not be able to communicate it very well, but at least he's right on the issues.* But, man, I wish it was me taking on Chet. My fire in the belly rekindled brighter than ever.

Later I was invited to his home for the election victory party. He had a large group of people who all turned up hoping to see Chet finally get bounced. As the results began appearing on the televisions, it was clear it wasn't going to happen. By the time the race was called, Ramsey had finished with a respectable 44 percent of the vote to Chet Edwards' 56 percent. But, from what I understood of the district and of his candidacy, I had the sense that it was probably going to be Ramsey's high-water mark.

I was one of the last to leave his home that night. Before going, I got a chance to have a little one-on-one time with Ramsey in his kitchen. Surprisingly, he was in good spirits. I was disappointed on several levels but was thinking ahead to the next cycle. I mustered the courage to ask him point-blank if he would go again. He quickly and definitively answered "No, I'm done."

I showed no real response, but deep inside I was thrilled. I knew if he were to run again, there would be a lot of Republican voters who might think it was only fair to give him another chance. Yet I was convinced that if he got the nomination again, the numbers would be even worse. This just wasn't a good matchup for us on so many levels.

I left thinking that I would keep an eye on the situation over the coming year and see what developed. We still had a job to do in this district. Once again, the Republican's political public enemy number one was on the loose. We had to get him out of there. He and the liberal Washington Democrats were starting to pull the country hard to the left. We had to remove Pelosi's ally. We just had to put up a good candidate to topple Chet.

Personally, I was emotionally recovered from my loss, and, in spite of my third-place finish, I still believed I had a huge upside. I had only spent a little over $12,000 while both my opponents had spent or borrowed between them more than half a million. I had little organization and no professionals in my camp, yet at the end of the day, I got that respectable 20 percent of the vote.

Lots of great people in and out of politics had also thanked me for running and urged me to not give up. Some were likely just being polite, but most sincerely pledged their support if I would run again. Many expressed amazement that I was able to get a respectable amount of the vote when I was so heavily outspent.

That was music to my ears and a comfort to my soul. So, I told myself, *Let's see how things play out in the coming year.*

Then I returned to my life and business.

CHAPTER 15

Unfinished Business

In the following year, I went back to being an election judge and running my business, which was busier than ever, but I kept abreast of the political situation. Soon, it was time again for someone to make their intentions known regarding challenging for the congressional seat in District 11. I still had a mild interest in giving it another shot, believing that I now had experience and knowledge under my belt. The wounds from the first go-around had mostly faded, and I anxiously watched to see who would surface to take on the "unbeatable" incumbent. I intended to do absolutely nothing if the primary was contested; I wasn't interested in going through that again. I, like everybody, waited to see if any elected Republican office holders from the area would take up the cause, take advantage of the favorable Republican numbers, and take on the giant.

McLennan County Republican Chairman M.A. Taylor kept me apprised of the situation. Several county chairmen from around the district were organizing an effort to avoid another contested primary and rally around one candidate. That was exactly what we needed, but who would be the one candidate that everyone would agree to rally behind?

M.A. laughed and said, "Ah, yes, that's the problem. That's always the problem."

"Who've they got?"

"A few chairmen from the southern part of the district are trying to talk one of their state representatives into running. I don't think it'll happen. Nobody wants to risk their own seat to gamble on the long shot of taking on that phony, liberal SOB Edwards. Otherwise, nothing's certain, although several folks have expressed interest."

"That so?"

"Yes, but most of them have no business running, and hopefully someone will talk some sense to them. I always try, but you know how it is. Nobody really listens."

Then he turned to me and asked, "What about you? You still want some more pain and aggravation?" he laughed. "They're planning on holding a meeting down in Temple for all those who have expressed any interest. They want me to be a part of it, but hell, it ain't gonna do any good. If somebody wants to run, they're gonna run. I've always said, it only takes one person to talk somebody *into* running, but a hundred can't talk them *out* of it."

"I agree, we don't need a contested primary, but if Ramsey goes again, I promise you he won't win—and he won't do better."

"I believe you're right about that. What the hell, maybe you should go down there and see what happens. Then you can let me know how they're wasting their time."

"I can check it out, but those are the people that tried to get me to quit last cycle," I reminded him. "On top of that, I hurt their chosen candidate when I endorsed Ramsey. I don't think they're going to be real happy to see me."

"Piss on 'em. You got every right to run. Besides, I think it's gonna take someone from Waco to beat Chet."

The number of people at the meeting surprised me. Twenty people sat at tables assembled in a giant square in a large room. I found the last empty chair and sat down. One of the county chairmen from the congressional district explained the need to have only one candidate in the upcoming primary as the only way to beat Chet. She declared that we couldn't afford any more divisive primaries in which the eventual winner limped out battered and bruised to take on a strong and politically healthy incumbent.

Most, but not all, nodded in agreement. I recognized some from my past political dealings and from the last primary, but I was startled to see Ramsey across the room. Obviously, his promise on election night to not run again wasn't written in stone.

Many of the potential candidates I'd never met before. After going around the room and introducing ourselves, at least eight declared that they were "thinking about" jumping into the race. Another county chairman proclaimed they were persuading a local state rep to jump into the race. If she did it, he said, then the rest of us should just get behind her. That was *his* plan, of course.

Just then, the man from that area who had lost the very first race to Chet in 1990, strolled into the room. He asked to speak and was given the floor. He said that, in reality, *he* was the only one who could beat Chet, but he was making too much money in his business to even think about getting back into politics. And as he wasn't running, the one in the room that had the best shot to beat Edwards was Ramsey. Ramsey smiled broadly in agreement with this seemingly spontaneous declaration of unsolicited political wisdom. That first nominee then turned around and left.

Months later I learned he supported Ramsey the whole time, that Ramsey was indeed going to run again, and this was most likely a surreptitious theatrical attempt to scare away everyone else.

The meeting wrapped up with the chairman in charge asking us to think carefully about what we were going to do, and to keep in mind that we needed to get behind one candidate.

If Ramsey goes again, we lose again, I thought. If that particular state rep agrees to jump in, then she'd probably put up a good battle and maybe we'd have a chance. Over the next couple of weeks, word got around that the state rep would not challenge Chet, and Ramsey would indeed run again. And, apparently, he was the only one. It felt like déjà vu. This is where I came in two years ago, only this time I knew with absolute certainty that Ramsey could not win. With encouragement from my own county chairman and past supporters, I once again seriously explored my options.

I conjectured, from my past experience, that I needed at least $100,000 to make a credible run. And that would be only enough to run a bare bones campaign, with me once again supplying radio and TV ads. But that would give us enough to buy the time and at least do yard signs, bumper stickers, and a limited mailing. Things like office space and phones would again have to be donated by supporters and volunteers.

Almost to a person, everyone I talked with agreed that Ramsey would be a sure loss again and they encouraged me to run. I even secured a couple of serious financial commitments from people I knew had access to sources of money. They were solid guys that had a proven track record of success. For me, this was the turning point. Between the two, they promised me they'd raise upward of $70,000 if I would go again. I took this as a sign that—this time—it would be different.

As the filing deadline approached, I again waited until the last week to see if someone else surfaced. All was quiet, so with those significant financial commitments in my back pocket, I confidently went back down to Austin a week in advance of the deadline and filed. Once again, things didn't go as planned. Near the last day, a third candidate jumped in from a small town in the very southern-most part of the district. "Carl" was a political consultant and was at the meeting that night but hadn't spoken to anyone about his plans. He quietly slipped in and surprised everyone.

My only thought: *Unbelievable. Here we go again.*

CHAPTER 16

Defection

I assumed this race would be similar to the first go-around, except that I would have more money to work with. Once again, my assumptions proved to be woefully off base, right from the start. Instead, I got my first real experience with the turmoil and nastiness that I had mostly escaped the first time.

Now that I was in the race again, I needed to establish a campaign staff. Coincidentally, several days after filing, Rick, a new supporter, questioned me on my plans and offered to lead the fundraising effort. Importantly, he was a financial planner with connections to big money clients, and a great salesman as well. I considered it a blessing and eagerly agreed. He then recommended and volunteered his wife to run the campaign. Although she hadn't run a political campaign previously, she had similar skills from her professional career. And it just so happened that she was between jobs.

Upon meeting Donna, I knew immediately she would be excellent for the position, and opportunistically offered her the job of campaign manager. I considered it another blessing. She agreed to join the campaign in a voluntary capacity, until her husband was able to raise funds. Once those funds materialized, we could pay her a modest amount. I was getting excited. It looked like the pieces were falling into place.

The last critical piece, I thought, would be to contact my first campaign manager about rejoining the team. I assumed Bethany would surely come back to the campaign if I did run, but because of my late decision, had not spoken to her about the possibility. She hadn't reached out to me either. I wanted her involved in the campaign in any way she wanted; she was my friend, she had led my first campaign, and I'm a loyal person. But more importantly, Bethany now had the political knowledge and experience. She could teach our new, inexperienced campaign manager the ropes and the district.

It was only at this point that I realized it could be awkward asking her to take on a role other than as my campaign manager. Would it be a problem? Either way, I had to find out as soon as possible. I anticipated she could work with the new campaign manager in an administrative advisory capacity. When I approached her, however, she was noncommittal. Unfortunately, I discovered too late, when she had jumped to the Ramsey campaign following the first primary, she had become a key player in his campaign and, most importantly, was a paid staffer.

"Ramsey wants me to work for his campaign again—and for a good salary," she said dropping an unexpected bomb on me.

Although we were long-time family friends, the idea of volunteering to do for me what she had gotten paid to do in the Farley campaign didn't appeal to her anymore, which I could totally understand. She pressed me about paying her to work the campaign. I was somewhat taken aback at the loss of that original idealism that we had shared in the first go-around. I explained that I had good financial commitments this time, but I couldn't promise her a salary from the as-yet nonexistent campaign fund. And more importantly, I couldn't pay her when I couldn't pay Donna yet, who was campaign manager.

"Are you thinking about going to Ramsey?" I asked, genuinely alarmed. "You told me what a disaster of a candidate he was last year. We both know he can't win."

"He's better known throughout the district now and, with the experience," she justified. "He might be able to do what he needs to win." She sounded as if she were trying to convince herself as much as me.

"You can't really believe that? Maybe he's a decent guy, but he was a mess as a candidate! He had his chance and blew it badly. You know I've got a much better chance to win this seat."

"Rob, I know you may be a better candidate, but he wants me and he's willing to pay, and right now I've got to think of my family. I need to help us out financially. If you can pay me, of course, I'd rather work with you."

Racking my brain, I quickly came up with what a possible scenario. I offered to hire her as a contractor for Dub-L Tape, my business, and she could advise me personally on campaign matters in addition to Dub-L Tape duties. I was rather pleased with my Solomon-like solution.

"I don't know; I guess that might work. Let me think about it," she said, underwhelmed with my brilliance, and promised to get back with an answer in a couple of days.

A candidate forum was scheduled at Baylor University in Waco a few days following. It would be the first of the new campaign, and I wanted Bethany on board. I became apprehensive when the days slipped by with no word from her.

Finally, she called the afternoon of the event, with several hours to go before that first meeting started.

"Rob, it's been very difficult, and I know you won't want to hear this, but I've decided to work for Ramsey," she said uneasily.

"What?! You're kidding me?!" I said, stifling a combination of anger, disbelief, and hurt all at once. "Why would you do that?"

"He needs me, and he's offered good money to oversee his campaign."

"Of course, he 'needs' you—because it's a two-fer," I argued urgently but calmly. I had already assessed the situation and gotten control of my emotions. I knew getting upset or argumentative would probably do no good and could wind up hurting me in the long run. "He knows if he gets you, he hurts me—big time! He had to get you away from me. It's his best strategic political move, and I can't believe you're letting him do it."

"I know this isn't easy, but we'll still be friends," she assured. "For the sake of my family, I just couldn't turn down the money. I'm sorry."

"What about my plan to pay you what you said you wanted through Dub-L Tape?"

"But that wouldn't come from the campaign. I think I can do this professionally, and to put it on my resume, I need to be paid from a campaign. That's very important to me from a career standpoint."

"I understand, but I'm gonna be honest with you; I think this is a really bad move on your part. First of all, how's Farley even going to pay you? I've heard his campaign is still in debt by almost a quarter of a million dollars from the last race and that he owes people money. That's not a sound financial foundation. You better make sure he can deliver what he says he can."

"I think he can," she said with a fair amount of confidence.

"More importantly, Bethany, we've been good friends for a long time. I'm sure it won't end because of this, but that's exactly why I'm begging you to think this through. If you do this, it hurts me badly, and there's just no way that our friendship will ever be the same. We've been through a lot together, and to possibly destroy things over a temporary job? This is just plain bad."

"It's strictly a financial decision; there's nothing personal in this. I won't let it hurt our friendship," she said.

Of course it was personal—very personal. This was the most important calling of my life, and on a grander scale, the traditional values of our country hung in the balance. But no amount of talking was going to change her mindset. Before hanging up, she reminded me she had all the files from our first campaign and would return those to me as soon as possible. In my distraction from the conversation, I offhandedly said, "Sure, whatever." Maybe I should have paid more attention.

The last turn of the knife in the gut came that evening, as Ramsey had already assigned her to be at this meeting with him. Ramsey, of course, was as pleased as he could possibly be when we briefly met for a perfunctory greeting. He knew he had busted me with his acquisition of Bethany, and it appeared to me that he could barely contain his glee. Rather than give him the satisfaction of his personnel victory, I poured on a devil-may-care attitude with my normal attempt at humor, with neither one of us mentioning what we both were thinking. I greeted Bethany and her husband, acting as if absolutely nothing was wrong.

From a campaign standpoint, the meeting went fine. Following the meeting, in the milling about and talking, Bethany's husband positioned himself next to me. I could tell he was uncomfortable and ill at ease, even more so than I.

"I hope you understand there's nothing personal in this," he explained of his wife's decision. "It's just like two opposing football coaches on the sideline. When it's all over, we'll just shake hands and get back to life, but we're still friends. It's nothing personal."

At that point I let my emotional guard down just a little and lowered my voice so that only he could hear me: "Yes, but this ain't no football game," I said. "If Bethany's successful and does her job, she will destroy me politically. And since *I'm* the candidate, it's *very* personal to me."

He went quiet and we parted. It was painful, but we never mentioned it again, even as our paths crossed through the coming months and years. Once again, I was left thinking, *Welcome to the pain of politics.* Unfortunately, in this particular campaign, this was only the beginning.

CHAPTER 17

First Rule of Primaries

Donna proved fantastic. She had much to learn about politics, but she was excellent at organizing and had people skills. In a short time, we had an impressive campaign office up and running, courtesy of gracious donors. While that was awesome, her husband Rick soon found that raising money for us was a bit more difficult than anticipated. The basic rule of fundraising in a primary was again proving unrelenting and ironclad.

The dampening effect on raising money in a contested primary, for just the opportunity to later take on a powerful and perceived popular incumbent, is formidable. Even if a donor is willing to publicly oppose the sitting congressman, the common practice is to stay on the sidelines and wait for the nominee to be chosen. Only then will regular donors kick in—after the primary is over. It's a hard sell to bring in money for the primary. Even in the general election, the success of fundraising is directly correlated to the strength of the incumbent: the more powerful the incumbent, the tougher the sell for a challenger.

It didn't take long for Rick to realize the difficulty of the task—there wasn't much interest in betting on such a long shot.

I was disappointed my official fund raiser wasn't making progress, but I wasn't panicking, either. After all, I had those early commitments from some friends I was sure would come in. However, as weeks passed, and the friends made no effort to get in contact with me to finalize the donations, I began to get concerned. Even though it felt unseemly to me and went against all of my personal sensibilities, I decided I had to gently push these friends to secure the funds we were soon going to need.

I reluctantly made the calls to subtly convince them to make good on their "pledges." I was surprised and alarmed when they seemed to have forgotten their commitment to my race. I didn't get the feeling that they had changed their minds or stopped supporting me, only that these were Type A individuals who had a lot going on in their own worlds. I was just one more item on their daily agenda.

I hoped my wake-up calls would spur them to action. Instead, they just hit the proverbial snooze button and said they would make some calls and get back to me. Another week passed, and certain campaign items were coming due. We needed their donations. Again, I hated it, but I had to ask them to deliver on their pledges. By this time, though, I had that feeling of "they ain't coming through." I wanted to be positive, but at the same time, I thought this should have gone smoother.

My intuition came to fruition. The two different men I most counted on for the bulk of the pledged money both informed me they had had no luck. Everybody they had assumed would chip in, declined for any number or reasons. Business was bad, times were tight, they'd wait until after the primary. A couple potentials actually liked the incumbent and wouldn't support any challenger. My friends had failed. They apologized and assured me that none of the no's were because of me personally. On the contrary, everyone remembered me from television and liked me, but they just weren't going to write those checks at this point.

My friends seemed surprised and embarrassed that they couldn't make it happen. All I could do was thank them for trying, act like it was no big deal, and move on. Yet this was tough to swallow.

The motivating factor for launching this second primary was because I believed I had a solid financial foundation. As I was still not personally wealthy, this financial support to take on primary challengers was critical to the goal of facing and displacing the liberal incumbent. This support was now nonexistent, and I had no real fundraising path forward. *Unbelievable*, I gloomily thought. I kept this sentiment to myself, as the well-known mantra in politics is that you must keep yourself and those around you upbeat and positive. But, at that point, I felt like a brave but unaware World War 1 military officer leading a charge through enemy fire, only to turn around and realize his men are still hunkered down in the trenches. *This can't be good.*

I had two choices: I could quit or cut back on expenses and fund it myself. At my core, I'm not a quitter, and I still believed in what we were doing. Now I had to put my money where my mouth was. If this was my calling, then circumstances would work out—one way or the other. And I truly believed this was what I was called to do, even if it came down to me, my campaign manager, and a relatively few faithful supporters.

It was what it was.

Money or no money, I would still do the best I could as a candidate and get out our message of conservative values and our ability to defeat the Democrat incumbent in the fall. I'd continue to meet voters and try to win them over with reason, logic, and common sense. Besides, I enjoy meeting people, interacting with my old friends in the electronic media, and being a part of the political process. It was an incredible opportunity and an honor.

It just looked like I wouldn't have a whole lot of tools with which to work. Still, the number one candidate's rule remained in effect: I had to stay upbeat and not let my staff know we were in a difficult spot.

On we charged.

CHAPTER 18

Going Personal

The goal of any campaign is to win more votes than the other candidate no matter what it takes. Of course, for the rare candidate with character, the boundaries of doing whatever it takes is set by staying with what is moral, ethical, and legal. I believe character is one of the greatest and yet rarest personality traits that a person can possess in politics—or life. I try to exhibit character in every facet of my life. It most likely stems from my quaint yet heartfelt notion that, at the end of this life, I will answer to a higher power.

Sticking within moral, ethical, and legal boundaries is extremely difficult when your opponents have *no* such qualms about campaign tactics. And, quite honestly, it isn't always your opponent that may have character shortcomings. Often it is supporters, campaign workers, or especially, the political pros. That's where things can get truly nasty and give politics its well-deserved reputation as a dirty, cutthroat business.

It is.

I remember that awkward conversation with Chet in my business parking lot and his warning of consultants from Washington. That would be one of the few things in the political world in which he proved absolutely correct.

Although most general elections get unpleasant, that's the nature of the beast and I totally understand and accept that. As long as the debate sticks to politics, I can easily deal with it. I may not like it, but I've come to expect it and don't get bent out of shape when I am on the receiving end of ridiculous political attacks. To me, *that's* politics.

What is surprising, though, is the contested intra-party primaries where politics can, and generally do, take a dark and nasty turn. The difference between a general election and a primary is that primary candidates tend to be on the same page with their political values, goals, and beliefs, in contrast to the general election debate. So, in reality, the focus of primaries often tends to move off of politics and into the personal realm. This is true of pretty much any race from local dog-catcher to President of the U.S.

We've all heard of the politics of personal destruction, in which candidates tear down the reputation of their opponents by fact or insinuation. Because political values in same-party primaries tend to be identical, it's hard to move a voter when all a candidate can say is, "Me, too," or "I agree" on debate questions. It's here in the primaries where the politics of personal destruction are raised to an art, as the common goal of winning involves getting voters to like you, or conversely, to dislike or distrust your opponent. Victory often comes back to a personal separation between candidates, and that's where it gets ugly.

Losing my first campaign manager to Ramsey was a blow, but it was nothing more than a tactical victory on his part. He had actually pulled off a savvy political maneuver. However, I got my first indication that tactics were turning personal a few weeks into the campaign.

Conservative radio talk show host Lynn Woolley, invited me to do a live radio show out of the southern part of the district. Lynn, a friend from my media days, invited all candidates from many different races to come on his show during campaigns. He had seen

through Chet Edwards early on and regularly pointed out the incon-
sistencies in his role as a liberal-voting congressman in conservative
Central Texas. In keeping with federal fairness rules for electronic
media, the incumbent always had a standing invitation to appear on
the show to answer questions or plead his case. As might be expected,
the congressman never chose to avail himself of that invitation.

Needless to say, this was a great opportunity to reach local
conservative voters in an unfiltered manner. Lynn was giving me an
opportunity to have an hour alone and unencumbered without the
usual format of sharing the stage with your primary opponents. I
looked forward to the show and looked forward to taking advantage
of the free-wheeling interview, complete with call-in questions. This
was my type of forum.

Because Lynn and I were in the same place philosophically, the
friendly format show went well. I got the rare opportunity to lay out
my political agenda and espouse conservative values. He also gave me
a soapbox to explain why I thought I would be the best man to beat
Chet. I had several chances to go after my primary opponents, but
that wasn't my style. I knew Ramsey's problems as a candidate, but
I really didn't want to publicly point them out. It just wasn't seemly.
As for the other opponent, Carl, I'd really grown to like the guy.
Besides, I didn't feel like he was a threat, and we got along fine at all
the functions. He agreed with me on the problems facing Ramsey as
a candidate, but neither one of us wanted to go there publicly. We
both just stuck to our own issues and strategy and stayed away from
the negative.

Apparently all three of us candidates weren't using the same
strategy of playing nice, it turned out.

We took a couple of calls from listeners on standard issues with
give and take. As an old media guy, I thought it was "good radio."
But then the third caller went in a slightly different direction. I didn't
think anything of it—a question on something about me person-

ally—so I just started to answer. But before I could get another word out, the host suddenly cut in.

"We're not going there," Lynn said curtly to the caller. "We've brought Rob on to answer questions about the campaign and his philosophy, and why you all might want to vote for him. We're sticking to the issues, and if you callers can't do that, then we're just not going to take any more calls. I mean it!"

I was on the other side of the table with my eyebrows pushing up to the ceiling, wondering what the heck that was about. I'd never heard Lynn go off on a caller like that. The caller, of course, hung up and we moved along. We took a few more calls, he threw some more questions at me, and the show was over.

Off the air, Lynn looked at me and said, "I could tell you were a little surprised when you saw me shut down that one guy, but I'm not going to put up with that crap. They need to keep this to politics. That really pissed me off."

I shrugged. "I thought it was a little odd, and I was certainly ready to answer. But, man, you really let him have it."

Then he stopped and looked at me and asked, "Don't you know what's going on around here?" like he thought I would have known.

"Know what?" I asked, puzzled.

He turned around and picked up a piece of paper and pushed it across the table in front of me. "Haven't you seen this? It's been going out all over the place. I've gotten three of them myself, and it's a bunch of bullsh--."

It was a printed copy of an email. The title: "Questions to Ask Rob Curnock." It listed a dozen or so questions for media and voters to confront me with in forums or meetings. I scanned it briefly, not getting much past the first couple.

"Why isn't Rob married?" with the not-so-subtle implication that I was a homosexual.

"Does Rob have a close, personal relationship with Chet Edwards?" A not-so-subtle accusation that I was purposely working with Chet to mess things up in the Republican primary. In other words, I was secretly in the race to help Chet.

Inside, I was livid. After looking at it briefly, I tossed it back to Lynn.

"What a crock. Who's putting out this nonsense?"

"I'm not sure, but I've definitely gotten some of it from Ramsey supporters. I don't know if it's from his campaign or not, but it's still bullsh--. I've known you a long time, and this is just garbage."

"No one who's ever known me has even remotely accused me of being a homosexual."

"I know," Lynn affirmed shaking his head.

"And this Chet nonsense is almost laughable. These idiots have no idea how much effort and work I've put into getting rid of Chet. I've been working in Republican politics around here when their boy Ramsey was off doing his oil thing. He's never done squat to help us get rid of Chet," I vented.

"I know," Lynn repeated.

"And I don't ever attack Chet personally because anybody with any common sense knows that people actually like Chet on a personal level. If you start calling him names and attacking him, the soft ticket splitters that we need to win will just start defending him. Whoever put this crap out is a moron."

"It's pathetic, but I thought you knew. Since you didn't, I thought you should be aware of it."

"I appreciate it. I'll consider the source and ignore it. They're the losers."

"Welcome to politics," Lynn laughed. "Looking on the bright side, you're obviously being seen as a threat."

"I guess I've arrived."

We both laughed, but I walked out of the studios with mixed emotions. I was angry because I thought, *How dare they?* I was mildly amused because, at least, now I was being taken seriously. However, I was also alarmed, wondering, *How ugly could this get?*

It was going to get a lot uglier.

CHAPTER 19

Ambush

Politics really does bring out the best and worst in people. Maybe it's the finality of a winner-take-all competition, or maybe the clash of the Type A individuals who typically get involved in high-visibility, high-stakes campaigns. Whatever the cause, as a primary moves along, stress levels rise exponentially. Mole hills do become mountains. Small, insignificant incidents become magnified and amplified to bizarre proportions, completely out of touch with any sense of reality. In other words, the campaign exists in and creates a dimension all its own.

Campaign staff, volunteers, supporters, donors and, yes, candidates begin looking for any edge they can to move on to the next round. Where and how they look for that edge depends, to a large extent, on the personality and values of the individuals involved.

Which it is depends on who they truly are in everyday real life.

In the heat of a campaign, you constantly make choices that test moral, ethical, and legal parameters. Once, a sincere, loyal, and well-meaning Hispanic supporter approached me discreetly and asked if he could volunteer for my campaign. I was honored, but a little surprised, because he was not normally political in any way, shape or form. I had known him personally for some time and, although he was a nice guy to me, let's just say he had rough edges. I'd classify him as the epitome of the low-information voter if, in fact, he even actually voted. On the other hand, I was truly encouraged that my running for office had evidently sparked his interest in the political process.

"I'd like to help any way I can. We've got to beat Chet Edwards, and you're the only guy that can do it," he said proudly.

"Thanks, I appreciate that, and I'd be happy to have you on board. What would you like to do?"

"I don't know. Do you have something like a dirty tricks squad?" he asked with absolute sincerity.

"Excuse me?!" I exclaimed, caught off guard. If I'd been drinking something, I would've done a Hollywood spit take. "What are you talking about?!" I asked as I tried to keep from bursting out laughing.

"Don't you need people to go around and steal the other guy's signs, or knock 'em over, or put up your signs and bumper stickers where they aren't supposed to be? I could also show up at their meetings and harass the other guys and give 'em grief when they try to speak."

"Are you serious?!" I asked with absolute stunned amusement.

"I've heard about it on television. Every campaign has a dirty tricks squad, and I'd be real good at it. I'd do a good job for you, and it would be a blast."

At this point, I couldn't contain my laughter any longer. That started him laughing.

"C'mon, I'm not a Democrat. I don't have a dirty tricks squad. I don't even have a clean tricks squad."

"Well, then you need to get one, and I'm your guy," he said still laughing.

"I appreciate the offer, but that's not my style. I do want you to help in other ways if you're willing. Still, I'm truly honored that you want to help."

The good news is that he still wanted to help and stayed with me through the campaign.

I had perceived in him a childlike naiveté concerning politics and dirty tricks; however, I soon came to find out that, in many respects, maybe I was the naive political child. I knew that such shenanigans go on behind the scenes, but just because I didn't want to engage in those activities, that certainly didn't mean an opponent wouldn't.

On one of those rare days when nothing beckoned on the campaign calendar, I was working at my business when a reporter from a local television affiliate called, wanting to ask a few questions. *Cool. Free publicity*, I thought.

Once we started talking, I suddenly realized who he was.

The reporter was a young fire-breather on the local ABC-TV affiliate trying to make a name for himself in the vein of Woodward and Bernstein. In our city, we didn't have investigative television reporters, as it generally took a lot of resources to do it effectively and was beyond the financial capability of most small-market television stations. Nonetheless, this station promoted his "investigative" stories, so I deduced he had a motive for the call.

"Mr. Curnock, I understand you're having trouble with the Federal Election Commission concerning reports that you haven't filed on time." He dove in like an aggressive prosecuting attorney.

The Federal Election Commission—another reason many "average" citizens have difficulty succeeding in the election process. An arcane and complicated maze of rules, regulations, and paperwork is required to participate in a federal campaign. Like anything the federal government does, there is no simple, straightforward, and easy way to understand and fully comply with all that is required.

To highlight this modern-day rule of thumb, read the Constitution. This all-important, founding document is relatively simple, concise, and understandable to the average citizen. Now read any portion of the Affordable Care Act (Obamacare). Today's legislative accomplishments are written by bureaucrats and lawyers and can only be understood by other bureaucrats and lawyers—and even that's a crap shoot.

The Federal Election Code is almost as complicated as the tax code. The average citizen has little hope of understanding either. More ominously, you can find yourself running afoul of some rule either by an error of commission or omission, without even knowing it, until your opponent—or an antagonistic investigative reporter—somehow digs it up. Of course, it is usually as a result of your opponent making that tattle-tale phone call designed to get you in trouble. It almost takes a professional to stay on top of all the reporting and paperwork, and my campaign did not have a professional. In fact, we had no professionals on our campaign, just a conscientious and competent volunteer treasurer who did a remarkable job doing it as well as he did.

My heart started racing as I held the phone. This didn't sound like positive free publicity coming my way. In fact, it looked like some very public and ugly trouble.

"Uh, no. My treasurer had a question concerning a trigger date on when a finance report from over a year ago was due, because we never officially shut down the campaign account from the last primary. He contacted the FEC and left several messages about the situation. We need to know exactly what they want and when. He's still waiting for an answer."

"But wasn't it due several weeks ago?" he pressed on aggressively.

Now I was in dangerous territory. I wasn't going to throw my treasurer under the bus, and yet I hadn't been focusing on that part of the campaign. I was locked in on campaigning and getting votes, not the mundane and confusing paperwork intricacies. That's what I had a treasurer for. But how could I say that to this reporter?

"I'll have to get back to you on that. I need to talk to my treasurer. I'm not sure where that's all at, at this point," I offered.

"I'd like to come by and talk to you on camera about this. How soon can we do it?" he pressed.

"I'll be glad to talk to you as soon as I know more. I'm not trying to dodge you. I just need to know exactly what's going on."

"You're the candidate—shouldn't you know what's happening at all times?" he shot back.

At this point, I was battling emotions. I was thinking, *Look, you little punk, you're talking to a former reporter myself. I know exactly what you're doing, and it isn't going to work.* I wanted to reach through the phone and smack him, but I also knew the nature of the beast. I had to give him answers or it would only get worse for me if he thought I was hiding something. That would feed his aggressive, suspicious nature in trying to uncover a blockbuster story.

"Look, I promise you I'll get everything together and will be glad to sit down with you," I responded. "I have absolutely nothing to hide. I'll call you back as soon as I know something."

"I'll be waiting..."

I hung up agitated, angry, and slightly nervous. I should have seen this coming. Ramsey had actually mentioned it to me once over the last couple of weeks. He even sent me a personal email saying something about him still wanting to see my financial report. I chalked it all up to Ramsey just trying to get under my skin and ignored him. Besides, I assumed my treasurer was handling things.

In fact, Ramsey had brought it up after a forum a week earlier. The other candidate heard him warn me to get that report in. Since Carl and I had begun to form a loose friendship on the campaign trail, he asked me what Ramsey was talking about.

"I don't know. I think he's just trying to harass me about an FEC report for which he thinks we may have missed a deadline," I answered.

"Yes, I know; those reports are confusing and impossible to keep up with," he laughed.

"How are you doing it? Have you had any problems?" I asked him.

"Actually, I'm lucky. I used to work in a congressional office. They're helping me out by having one of the experts on the staff handle it for me. I don't even have to think about it. They make sure everything is done properly."

"I'm jealous. We're just trying to stay on top of it as best we can."

"It's not easy unless you pretty much do it for a living," he chuckled.

When I hung up with the reporter, I immediately called my treasurer. He had heard back from the FEC. They said we "should have" had it in on the 20th of that month, but to submit the paperwork as soon as possible. It was a technicality, he was told, and as we were in contact with them and making a good faith effort to comply, if we filed as soon as possible, "all would be fine." My treasurer then hit me with a slight problem.

"I'll do it right away, but we need some data from the last primary," he said. "Do you have it?"

"Oh crap, no. That's from the last campaign, and Bethany kept all the files. She said she'd get them to me weeks ago, but never did. And now she's working for Ramsey! I've got to get those back," I said in a slight panic.

I called Bethany next. No answer. I left a friendly yet concise message. "Hey, Bethany, I *really* need to get my files back ASAP. Call me or let me know how we can make that happen. Thanks."

Hours passed. No files, no return call.

In the meantime, rumors were exploding in my campaign inner circle. All the key people smelled a rat. They wanted me to call the police and report that my files were stolen by Bethany or, at the very least, they wanted me to contact a lawyer and threaten her with legal action if we didn't get the files back immediately. To a person, they all believed she was somehow mixed up in this on behalf of Ramsey. It caused a bit of hard feelings among us all when I defended Bethany and assured them that she would never do something like that to me.

"We've been friends too long. There's just no way. I'm sure she'll give them back as soon as she gets my message," I assured them.

They all looked at each other and back at me, while shaking their heads. It was obvious that they thought I was crazy and handling it all wrong. However, as I was the candidate, it was my call. But they clearly didn't like it.

The rest of that evening, I heard nothing back from Bethany. Doubts began to creep into my mind. I wondered if I wasn't a fool after all.

The first thing next morning, I called Bethany again. No answer. Another message. Hours passed and still nothing.

Finally, by that afternoon, I knew I had to call the reporter back. I absolutely could not afford to let him think I was avoiding him. I could think of nothing else to do but tell him everything I knew, just lay it out for him, and let the chips fall where they may.

Ironically, the FEC was appeased for now and they were the ones that mattered. We just had to get the filing to them as soon as we could. It was the darned reporter, who had no actual standing in the matter, who was causing all the heartburn. My question was, how did he even get onto the story? It's not like this is the type of thing that normally makes our local TV news. I soon had an inadvertent answer when I called him back.

"Thank you for getting back to me," he said with all the politeness of a traffic cop who's just pulled you over for speeding. "Did you get the information from your treasurer? And are you ready to answer some questions on camera?"

"Sure, you bet. It's just like I told you the other day. We've kept the FEC in the loop on this thing and we just need to get it filed as soon as we can. It was just confusion over the starting date. Now we know. We'll get it in as soon as we get all the information we need."

"You don't have all the information you need? Why is that?" he asked, thinking that he was tripping me up.

"That information is in my old files from the last campaign. And my old campaign manager still has them. But there may be a problem," I acknowledged.

"I would think this is important enough that you would get them. Why is that a problem?"

"I've been trying to get them back from her, but we haven't connected."

"Who's your former campaign manager? I don't understand why you're not getting them back."

"It's Bethany. The problem is, she now works for Ramsey. She's one of his key people."

What he said next told me all I needed to know about the origins of his story.

He said absolutely nothing.

For a few seconds, there was just total silence. It appeared he was taken completely off guard by that last bit of critical information. He finally recovered slightly.

"Oh... I didn't know that," he said calmly.

"Yes, I'm telling you, there's a lot going on here that you probably aren't aware of. I'm a former reporter like you; I'm not going to hide anything from you. I know you're just trying to do your job, but you've been sicced on me by someone who's obviously trying to make political trouble for me. I think you'll see this is clearly not what you thought it was or had been told it was."

"You're right about that. I'm not sure what we'll want to do about this now, but I'd still like to talk to you on camera. I'm just not sure how we'll play this. Would you still be willing to talk?" he asked. His mood had softened considerably.

"Sure, just say when."

"How about the day after tomorrow, at 10:00 a.m. in your business office?"

"I'll be here, and we can talk about whatever you want. Who knows, I may even have my files back by then," I joked.

We hung up and I began to assess all that had happened over the last several days. My staff was on the warpath to get those files back by any means necessary. It had caused a slight rift, as they thought I was refusing to accept that I was being totally screwed around by Ramsey and my former campaign manager.

The FEC was waiting, and my treasurer was feeling like he'd let the campaign down. It's clear that the reporter had softened his intention to blow me out of the water with his investigative bombshell, but we still had an interview set up for him to do who knows what. And on top of it all, I still needed those stupid files.

I didn't want to go after my former campaign manager, but it looked like I was going to have to do something—something potentially drastic. Something I seriously did not want to do.

Another day passed. Still no word. Still no files. My political adventure was certainly losing much of its enjoyable qualities. I didn't like where this looked like it was going to have to go.

The following morning, I showed up at my business office to get ready for the interview. I still didn't know where this was going to lead, but, oh well. Amazingly, I walked up to my office and, lo and behold, sitting next to my locked office door was my missing box of files.

Stunned, I asked an employee where that box came from. "Some man brought it by yesterday before we closed and after you left. He said you needed that stuff. I told him to leave it by the door. He didn't say anything else. I figured you knew all about it."

"Unbelievable!" I said as I went in to my office. I was totally ticked off and left the box untouched. Within a few minutes, the reporter and his cameraman showed up and started setting up for the interview. We chatted for a bit before getting started.

"Did your files ever show up?' he asked.

"Funny you should ask," I said. "Come with me."

We stepped out the door and I pointed at the box they had stepped around to get into my office. "There are my files. They were sitting there when I got in this morning. I haven't even touched them. Amazing how they showed up in time for my interview with you."

He shook his head. "I think I've been used—and that really pisses me off," he said angrily. "It's pretty clear this is not what I was told it was. Let me just ask you a few questions and see where it goes."

He never did share what he was told, and I never pressed.

"Welcome to the world of politics."

On camera, I repeated everything I had told him on the phone. He gave me every opportunity to blast my former campaign manager and Ramsey. In fact, he tried to lead me down that road. I refused to follow him, thinking that no good would come of it. Besides, I thought, I had no proof of anything and it's possible, just possible, that the files being returned the night before my television interview was just a coincidence. Either way, I was going to let it go. My angry campaign staff ended up reluctantly following my lead.

The reporter left. He never ran the story.

CHAPTER 20

Procedural Error

The potential crisis was averted, but that was because this particular reporter and his news organization had no agenda or axe to grind. And, quite honestly, I was probably the beneficiary of an opponent who handled the entire incident quite clumsily when fomenting the story. It turns out I would not be so lucky the next time. And it would turn out to be my own actions in the area of detailed campaign regulatory paperwork that would cause me problems and give my political enemies just enough rope to—while maybe not hang me—certainly trip me up.

The trouble started innocently enough as an innocuous attempt to pay for some commercial time. I was on my way to a campaign event in the south of the district and would pass by the TV station on which I was placing ads. The station's prepaid policy concerning political ads was the industry standard. We were in the latter stages of the campaign, so I was anxious to get our commercials on the air as quickly as possible. As I would be driving right by the station, I was happy to save mail time by just dropping off a check for payment to get it started right then.

Due to my lack of significant fundraising, I was essentially self-funding the campaign. We had a campaign checking account into which I would deposit money on an as-needed basis. My treasurer and I were the only ones who could sign checks. In my personal world, I had a corporate bank account of which I was the sole stockholder and the only person who could sign checks. I also had my personal account for which I was the only one who could sign checks.

On this day, I called the station just before I left and got a final total for the buy, so I could write a check for the exact amount. After hearing the total, I knew there wasn't enough money in the campaign account. The last thing I wanted to do was bounce a check. I certainly didn't have time to transfer money around right then, because I was literally rushing out the office door to make my meeting. To avoid writing a hot check, I thought, *I'll just give them a company check to cover it, then repay it from my personal account. I'll get the accounting in order as soon as I have a chance.*

I never gave it another thought.

In the meantime, the primary was drawing to a close, and things were getting busier and more hectic. It was late on a Thursday afternoon before the Tuesday election when I got a call from the reporter from the Waco *Tribune-Herald* assigned to cover our race. I felt we were on pretty good terms and, being a former reporter, I had some empathy for his job. I went out of my way to work with him whenever he was writing a story or covering an event. I found him to be relatively accurate and fair in the primary coverage. From what I could tell, he didn't seem to have an agenda that was overtly obvious in his reporting.

That fact, however, did not change my opinion about newspapers or the *Trib* in particular. Early on in the campaign, I had made a conscious effort to avoid reading the newspapers in the district like the plague. As noted, the Waco *Trib* was hopelessly biased in its support of the incumbent. I saw this as a fact and knew I could do nothing to change it. Therefore, I just had to focus on my own message and work as much as possible with the less agenda-driven television and radio stations. Besides, the electronic media were "my" people. I still had many friends and supporters in the stations, whom I knew had my back. I neither expected them to help me, nor to promote my campaign, but I was confident they at least wouldn't go about trying to help Edwards at my expense. I couldn't say the same for the newspaper.

There was method to my madness. The most important, yet least obvious, thing that a candidate can bring to his own campaign is his attitude and state of mind. It affects every volunteer in the organization and can influence each voter whose support you're trying to garner. The candidate has to stay upbeat and optimistic at all costs because those attitudes will show through. For me, that meant avoiding the newspaper at all costs.

Right at the start, I told my surprised volunteer staff that I would not be following the campaign by reading the paper or watching any television coverage. I explained that, as a candidate, I had to stay positive. If every time I opened the paper and saw the usual positive Edwards articles about him getting this funding or performing some other high profile 'congressional' activity, I would become totally discouraged and begin to question why I was even in the race.

Think about it: three local "nobodies" are fighting just to get the Republican nomination. Meanwhile, the congressman sits back, does his job, and ends up with affirming and positive widespread news coverage. It sends the subconscious message to the numerous non-ideological and disengaged voters that, "Edwards is the legitimate officeholder who's doing good for the distinct. These other *schlubs* are just troublemakers who, for purely political reasons, want to block him from getting positive things done."

I knew definitely that was done by design in the paper, but I'd be darned if I'd let them discourage me by filling my mind with those powerful subtle messages. So, for my own sake and that of my campaign, I chose to ignore the paper completely.

But, understanding the importance of the media in any campaign, I cooperated with this reporter whenever possible. When I answered the phone this day, following exchanged pleasantries, he dropped the bomb on me by starting out with a simple question to establish his trap.

"You mind answering some questions for a story on campaign expenditures I'm working on?" he asked, meaning we were now going on the record. "It'll probably run this weekend."

"Sure," I said.

"Rob, when you bought commercial time at KCEN, how did you pay for it?" he asked in a suddenly serious tone.

I thought it was an odd question and wondered why he wanted to know, but didn't think anything of it when I replied, "I wrote a check."

"What kind of check?" he pressed.

"Uh…a Dub-L Tape check." I felt something much bigger coming.

"Isn't Dub-L Tape a corporation?" he continued.

"Yes, and I own 100 percent of the stock. It's my company," I said, wondering where this was going. And then he swung his haymaker.

"Don't you know it's illegal for a corporation to donate to a federal campaign?" He pounced on me like a poor man's version of Tom Cruise in the final courtroom scene in *A Few Good Men*.

My stomach went into a knot and I felt my face go flush. Although I was aware of corporate donor rules, I honestly didn't think it applied to my own personal business. I tried to keep my composure. "What are you talking about?" I asked.

"It's against the law for a corporation to donate to a campaign, even if it's your own corporation. You can't do that."

I was stunned and now, carefully yet quickly, searching for a response. My first thought was, *You're kidding me,* and *How'd you get that information?* I knew I was in a no-win situation. If I pled ignorance, which was the reality, my political opponents would say, "He wants to be a congressman making laws, and he can't even follow the rules himself!" On the other hand, if I say that, in the grand scheme of things, this can't be a big deal, it makes me look like I'm disregarding election rules. From a political and PR standpoint, this was tough. I knew I was in a bind—and so did the reporter.

I finally responded with the only explanation I could come up with at the moment, which was what basically happened.

"Look, I knew I had to reimburse my campaign for the check and that was my plan right from the start. I just didn't have any personal checks with me. I'm going to get it taken care of right away, especially now that you've pointed out to me that it's a problem. I'll get with my treasurer and make sure we get it straightened out. I just didn't realize this was a serious problem. I assure you, I'll do everything I can to make it right. I'll call you as soon as I talk to my staff."

"Okay, let me know," he responded, and we hung up.

I knew this was trouble from a political standpoint. I also knew that my only hope was to tell the truth and try to rectify the situation as quickly as possible. But it was probably too late. I had a massive knot in the pit of my stomach. I could see everything that we had been doing for the last couple of months going up in smoke. *I can't believe this. All the work of my volunteers, all the traveling, all the speeches, all the commercials, all the money, all for nothing.* One stupid little procedural error and we were possibly going to be blown out of the water. It was heartbreaking. I was absolutely crushed emotionally.

This is yet another area where incumbents or candidates with deep pockets have a real advantage. They either have someone on staff to handle the procedural paperwork and reporting timetables, or they have the money to hire a pro to do it. And they might even have a staff member whose sole task is to dig up any regulatory problems with an opponent. It's just one more thing that intimidates or discourages the average citizen from getting involved. Ironically, the paperwork is so intimately detailed and difficult to interpret, that you often hear of even well-funded, experienced candidates at the presidential level running into trouble.

I mentally regrouped as best I could. I let my staff know what happened and asked for advice. I was really just looking for someone to give me something positive to pick up my spirits. We all tried to encourage each other as much as possible, but it wasn't very effective. This was trouble, and we all knew it. I was grateful for their support and limited advice, but I already knew what I had to do.

First thing the next morning, I called the Federal Election Commission in Washington to see how much trouble we were in, and to find out if there was any way to rectify the situation. Maddeningly, I had to leave a detailed message for the official in charge of this particular congressional race. And then, like a condemned man, I watched the minutes and hours drag by, waiting and hoping for him to call me back. I prayed he would call me back that day, or I'd have nothing new to say to the reporter, and he'd write his story with what he already had. And I knew that wouldn't be good for me.

The FEC manager finally called early that afternoon. "Sorry it took a while, we've got a lot going on. What can I do for you?" he asked with genuine concern. I was pleasantly surprised and pleased in that he seemed like a truly decent guy who wanted to help.

"Evidently, I've got a major problem, and it's basically all my fault."

I told him about the commercial TV buy, using my company check, what I had intended to do about it, and finally about how a reporter was telling me I broke campaign laws.

He listened intently to the whole story, asked a few questions, then blew me out of the water with his response.

"Honestly, Rob, it's not that big of a deal."

"Seriously?" I was ready to leap out of my chair and through the ceiling.

"This reporter's making it out like I've broken the law and am in danger of going to jail." I slightly exaggerated, but he understood my point.

"No, absolutely not," he laughed. "Let me explain something to you that most people don't understand. We're not here to play 'got-cha'! Our main concern is that candidates follow the campaign rules, and to help you get in compliance if there's a problem—like this one you're dealing with."

"I had no idea," I said with newfound relief.

"It's clear from the fact that you immediately contacted us and are obviously trying to get it straightened out. Yes, what you did was incorrect, but it's easily rectified. Just make sure you reimburse your campaign with non-corporate funds. Make sure your treasurer gives us a clear paper trail of what's being done and why. And make sure all the amounts are accurate."

"He will. He's very conscientious. Boy, thanks! I feel better."

"I'd bet you probably won't make this mistake again," he chuckled, hearing that I was clearly relieved.

"You got that right! I had no clue. And I'm just amazed that the reporter was on top of this."

"This is a congressional race, right? Welcome to the big leagues. Generally, in cases like this, your *opponents* are the ones who dig it up to make trouble. Standard campaign stuff. If there's anything else, call me. And best of luck."

I was on cloud nine. A massive load was taken off my shoulders. I reached to call the reporter back to tell him the good news, but suddenly realized that I was still in a major quandary. How could I tell the reporter that the FEC official said it was "no big deal?" That was the main point and most powerful defense I had in this matter. But if I gave the reporter his name and title, which I would if asked, it wouldn't look good in print to see an FEC official claiming that a technical violation of an election law was "no big deal." If he were questioned, he likely would deny claiming it was no big deal. Then I'd look like I lied. The old reporter in me realized I had to protect my source and be very careful with this one.

I called the reporter back to make the best of the bad situation, and settled on just telling him that I was in contact with the FEC. I gave him the official's name, title, and his instructions for making it right.

"He said that would clear it up, and, as far as they're concerned, that's the end of it," I told the reporter. "There's not anything else to say, other than I made a procedural error, and I've rectified the situation. By the way, just out of curiosity, how'd you get started on this story, which I'm assuming you're still going to write?"

"Yes, we're still going to run the story, and I'll include this new information, but the final form is up to my editors, as well as when it will run."

Surprisingly, either through sympathy or obligation, he then admitted, "and we got started on this from someone calling it in for us to check out."

The FEC guy was right. Welcome to the big leagues. The only question left was, who made that call? My Republican opponents, or the incumbent congressman? I found out later who it was, from a friend who handled political advertising at one of the local TV stations. However, as I don't have any documented proof, I'll keep this one to myself. At this point, it didn't matter. Whoever made the call had accomplished their mission.

I felt better when I hung up, but still knew I was waiting for the *Trib* to detonate a bomb under my campaign. I knew it had to be sometime in the next four days, as the election was on Tuesday. I hoped it would run on Saturday as that is historically the lowest circulation day of the week. The farther out from Election Day, the better. I was just hoping for minimal damage and exposure. Still, I felt like a condemned man waiting for the hangman to pull the lever. Besides, I thought, *Surely, the paper wouldn't be so overtly partisan as to make it look like a hatchet job? That would make them look bad, as well. Surely, they wouldn't be* that *vindictive? Or stupid.*

I found out on Sunday, their highest circulation day by far.

As I didn't get the paper, I was informed of the article by a number of folks in church that morning who let me know they didn't like what the *Trib* did to me. They thought it was clear that the *Trib* was going out of its way to make me look bad. These were all friends and supporters, but I knew that there was going to be an awful lot of people who didn't know me, didn't like me, or didn't really care, and this probably did not paint a pretty picture.

After church, I reluctantly went to a convenience store and bought a paper. I had to see for myself.

It was bad.

Not only did they wait until Sunday to run the "hit" piece, it wasn't in the political section or buried somewhere else; it was on the front page, above the fold. And with the most damning headline they could muster:

"Curnock Ads Violated Campaign Law"

Complete with my picture front and center.

I rushed out feeling like a wanted criminal. I wanted to look for a hole to crawl into and hide. It felt brutal. I have always gone out of my way to avoid trouble. I've never been arrested in my life and have gotten maybe a couple tickets. As a Christian—especially a recognizable media figure—I'd always been careful to exhibit a good witness by staying out of trouble. And now I was staring at my face on the front page of the newspaper with the headline screaming "Curnock Ads Violated Campaign Law." I mean, how bad could they make it?! This headline had me indicted, convicted, and ready for execution, all in one stroke.

Never mind the fact that the headline was totally wrong and misleading. The ads did not break any campaign law; it was the method of payment that was in question. But, the paper and one of my primary opponents, or my future general election opponent, got the damage to my campaign they sought.

Even though the article itself was somewhat less defamatory than the headline, you had to dig deep into the story to read that, although I may have violated a campaign rule, it was rectified.

Still, the whole experience left me humiliated, embarrassed, and about as depressed as I'd ever felt in my entire life.

Weeks later, a friend at a television station told me of a conversation he had with the congressman at the time this was breaking.

"Was it really that big of a deal what they said Curnock did?" he asked Chet.

He told me Chet laughed and said, "No, but it sure doesn't look good in the papers, does it?"

Chet had that right.

Whether fair or unfair, accurate or inaccurate, it was done. There was nothing else to do but carry on and finish with dignity. It took some soul searching and counseling through the day with close friends to regroup emotionally and realize that I had nothing to hang my head over. This would pass.

Besides, we still had work to do. We had a whole day left to campaign.

On the positive side, none of the television stations saw it as a real story and didn't pile on. At my old station, they had a standing rule that they would never run an explosive political hit piece in the last three days of an election. They did it out of a sense of fairness, as normally candidates couldn't defend themselves in that late stage of a campaign, no matter what the veracity of the charge.

The last days were low key, but emotionally trying. I had to fight the feeling that everyone I came in contact with had seen that terrible article and was judging me. But by Tuesday morning, we were feeling as optimistic as possible. Because we had done no polling, we had no idea where we stood in the race. But we were fairly upbeat, based on all the successful live events we'd taken part in over the last two months, as well as the overwhelming positive response we'd gotten from our TV and radio commercials.

As I had done two years before, I voted and then went in to work.

CHAPTER 21

Farewell...for Now

After the polls closed, we gathered at our headquarters for a low-key "victory" party. A number of supporters dropped by and wished us well. A few television reporters came in for quick on-camera interviews, and that was pretty much it. I was anxious, uptight, and didn't know what to expect. We hoped for the best, but didn't know how much of an effect, if any, that last-minute newspaper blast would have on the results. My stomach was in knots, but, all in all, I felt stoic. If we were supposed to win, we would. If not, we gave it all we had and learned a lot, both good and bad.

In the end, it was all tragically definitive. We watched the returns on the television and, right from the get-go, Ramsey jumped out to a big lead. I bounced around the 20 percent range. Carl was below that. Those numbers held through the first few reported results, and the stations all soon called it for Ramsey. He had won convincingly. I wasn't even able to force a runoff. This was tough to swallow.

I was disappointed for both myself and those who had worked so hard on the campaign.

My emotions were a jumble from the last five days. I was hurt, tired, and mostly embarrassed. I felt like a complete failure and just wanted to hide until people forgot who I was. The combination of the newspaper attack and the fact that I had lost had taken its toll. After thanking everyone involved, we all grieved for the loss and tried to pick up our spirits as much as possible. We closed down the campaign office and prepared to go back to our civilian lives.

I was still too wired to sleep and not anxious to go home to stare at the walls, so just like after the first campaign, I did the only thing I could think of to ease the pain. I drove around picking up my own campaign signs throughout the Waco area. Once again, it was good catharsis. A little before one in the morning, I returned home exhausted and quickly went to sleep, somewhat relieved that my life could now get back to normal. I just hoped that newspaper hit piece didn't damage my business or my reputation in the community. Only time would tell.

I went back to work in the morning as if the past two months hadn't happened.

Fearing that the newspaper's article might affect my business, at one point I contacted a prominent lawyer I knew who was an expert on libel and slander. Although I knew it was a long shot, I checked with him about the *possibility* of legal action against the newspaper, because of that darned headline. After looking it over, he gave me the somewhat expected news. As a candidate for Congress, I was considered a public figure, and the normal burden of proof becomes prohibitively difficult in such a case. In other words, he agreed that, even though the headline was absolutely defamatory, because I was a public figure, I could do nothing about it.

My former campaign manager, Bethany, who had gone to work for Ramsey for the paycheck, never made it past the summer on his team. I heard through the political grapevine, and one brief conversation with her, that she quit his campaign amid accusations of, wait for it…not getting paid. I don't know how it all played out, but it ended with lawyers. Our friendship was indeed strained, if not downright uncomfortable, but neither one of us has ever discussed what happened between us again, which is fine with me.

Looking back at the primary results, I have to admit I was struck by the overwhelming sense of gratitude for those voters who had chosen to support me. That 20 percent number jumped out at me. For whatever reason, roughly 20 percent stuck with me through thick and thin. They didn't care what the newspaper or anybody else said about me. I was their guy!

I never got into the races because I was looking for anyone's approval to validate my politics or even self-worth. But this was an emotional bonus for me and helped make it all worthwhile. They didn't know it, and this may sound strange, but these faithful 20 percent were now my friends, and I would do anything to help them politically, if ever given the opportunity. They had shown me loyalty, and I would return the favor by remaining true to our shared values and political goals, whether I was officially in or out of politics.

In the coming months and years, I had a lot of well-meaning supporters encourage me to run for any number of offices from city council to state representative. For me, it wasn't something I felt motivated to do. My passion was always in federal politics and issues. I've never been interested in running just to hold *some* office.

Once again, I had escaped without serious personal financial damage, but the results were remarkably similar. In spite of the fact that I had to essentially self-finance the campaign, I was able to put on a credible effort by spending only about $15,000. According to election financial reports, Ramsey, on the other hand, went roughly another quarter million dollars into debt.

My prediction of how Ramsey would do against Chet this second time turned out to be somewhat accurate. It was fairly obvious that it just wasn't a good matchup. I briefly watched one televised debate in the fall between the two and quickly turned it off. It wasn't a fair fight on both a visual and substantive level. I'm not a political genius, but my original instincts as to why we needed a different challenger were completely validated.

In 2002, Edwards carried the 11th district once again with 52 percent.

I knew deep down that, although I had the desire and this congressional goal for all those years, for all practical purposes, I was probably done with running for office. It was hard to come to grips with it, but evidently God had other plans for me. I knew for the sake of the country, barring some unexpected or unforeseen door opening up, I would be relegated to helping someone else try to capture our congressional seat or, at the very least, maybe be fortunate enough to play a role in bringing about even some small change at the national level.

Little did I know, both would come to pass.

PART III

The Main Event

CHAPTER 22

Life Changes

After the 2002 election, I settled back into the real world, disappointed but not crushed. True, I never got the opportunity to take out the liberal congressman, but I hadn't really gone all-in either. I spent some money, but in the grand scheme of things, that was okay. I held to my own fiscal values and didn't go in any deeper than I could afford to lose. Unlike Farley, who was now half a million in debt, I was okay financially. By all accounts, I had acquitted myself admirably and had an incredible opportunity to share my conservative values with like-minded voters. More importantly, I had been supported consistently by about 20% of Republicans in the district.

But now it was time to get back to my business and the continuation of my decades-long pursuit of the love of my life. She was the real reason I was not married. It was one of those proverbial "love at first sight" situations. I was twenty years old, living in Buffalo, and joined church friends at a restaurant after a Sunday evening service.

I've forgotten everything else from that evening except that I saw the most stunningly beautiful girl I'd ever seen. Crazy as it seems, I knew from that moment she was the woman I wanted to marry. The trouble was, I later found out she had suitors stacked three deep, and I certainly didn't have the confidence or inclination to break through that phalanx of competition. So, I just observed from afar and took my shots when or if the opportunity arose. The chances came few and far between over the years. I moved away from Buffalo and made my life in Texas. Throughout a long series of bizarre events and other relationships for both of us, she and I somehow maintained an on-again, off-again, long-distance connection. But that supernatural love story is truly the content of another book which should be inaccurately found in the fiction section of any self-respecting bookstore.

While I focused on my business and personal life, I didn't completely withdraw from the political world. Although no longer a candidate, I still felt the burn to stop the onslaught of the Left any way I could. The Democrats in Washington, as always, were on the offense and continuing to chip away at the foundations of this great nation. I was determined to help fight them and stop them any way I could. I went back to serving as an election judge and stayed active to a lesser degree in local party activities.

Then something unprecedented in over a century happened. Before the 2000 census, Republicans took control of the Texas executive branch and the state legislature. By 2003, through an effort contested by the state Democrat minority, Texas congressional districts were redrawn to better represent the statewide Republican majority. Under the new map, Democrat Chet Edwards now represented the 17th District of the State of Texas which included Waco.

Because Texas was now almost completely Republican, our district was drawn up to be even more favorable to a Republican congressman. At least that was the hope on the Republican side. Voting strength numbers in presidential and statewide races showed the GOP consistently garnering about 65 percent of the vote. Surely, a good candidate could now take out our Pelosi pal and let us join the vast majority of congressional districts in the state which had almost all gone Republican.

Generally, the only exceptions were the "minority" districts. During redistricting, they were carved out to keep the Justice Department happy as Texas was still under the heel of the 1965 Voting

Rights Act. The rest of the country may wonder how certain unbelievably ignorant and radical congressmen are able to stay in office year after year. The dirty little secret is that the Justice Department, in collusion with federal judges, has carved out these special minority districts, and as long as the Republicans leave those "special" districts alone, they are free to do their constitutionally mandated job anywhere *else* in the state.

Of course, the problem is that we have now unwisely created safe seats in which the minority incumbents can never be realistically challenged. In essence, these become protected seats which will never be treated like any other congressional seat. The hypocrisy of this is evident in that it only applies to black Democrat seats. For example, when a black *Republican* gets elected, the Justice Department and federal judges are perfectly fine if that minority officeholder gets gerrymandered out of office. This situation is endemic to America, and we now have districts throughout the country that are completely immune to the competitive give-and-take of elections. As a result we have some of the most radical, corrupt, arrogant, and incompetent legislators to ever hold elected office. It is inequities like this that conservatives like me believe are destroying the country. It's the type of thing that keeps our passions burning in a desire to bring common sense and fairness back to Washington.

With a Democrat holding on to a seat in a newly created, heavily conservative, Republican district, political pros from Texas to Washington were licking their chops to flip this seat in the new District 17. Even more intriguing, this new district became the home of newly elected President George W. Bush and his Crawford ranch located just outside Waco. Any first-year political science student could see this was a seat ripe for the picking. Unfortunately, yes, *anyone* could see this was a seat ripe for the picking.

So, once again, in the 2004 election cycle, Republicans conducted another bloody three-way contested Republican primary and, thankfully, this time without me. The eventual winner was a state representative from the new northern part of the district. With the help of the National Republican Party and her extensive connections in Austin, she was able to raise well over $2 million. Vice President Dick Cheney even came down to headline a huge fundraiser. Finally, it appeared we had a chance to take on Edwards with an even footing.

By virtue of the fact that I owned a video production company, we were hired to do work for this candidate and gladly agreed to do so. I was honored that the campaign soon asked me to take on a larger volunteer role and help with other aspects of their media endeavors. I was happy to get into the fight, even if it was just in a supporting role.

Unfortunately, when the final numbers came in, our heavily backed and well-funded candidate ended up with only 47 percent of the vote. I was disappointed, but, based on my knowledge of politics and familiarity with this area, I privately understood why this would be a tough race for our candidate right from the get-go. Often, other factors determine the outcome of an election besides money and party support. In this case, those intangibles all went to the incumbent, especially when the challenger was forced to defend her own political record involving some controversial local issues.

Still, I did everything I could do to help, and one always hopes.

The 2006 cycle was more of the same. Like a bad version of the *Ground Hog Day* movie, we did it again. Anyone with a proclivity for a congressional seat would look at the numbers and surmise that this should be an easy seat to win, so candidates never seemed to be in short supply. Once again, we had a contested, nasty primary, and the winner limped out to face Edwards. In this case, it was a gentleman who looked really good on paper. He was a young, wealthy, and politically well-connected war vet with a photogenic family. He should have been good-to-go. So once again, on paper, it looked like we had a fighting chance. But once again, we were up against those darn intangibles.

One problem was, he had essentially moved into the district to run. For Republicans, this just does not help. Add to that the fact that he lacked people and communication skills, especially in comparison to the smooth and skillful incumbent. It was clear to me how this was going to go. Fortunately, I was never approached to help in this campaign, so I quietly predicted to my close friends that this would be ugly.

Although the amount of funding he had was comparable to the incumbent, the race turned out lopsided. Edwards easily won with almost 65 percent of the vote. Even though I dutifully voted for the Republican challenger, I did so while proverbially holding my nose.

It appeared that, as a result of this latest political beatdown, the leadership of the Republican Party and any potential serious congressional wannabes had finally had enough. The thinking in the political power circles was that, for now anyway, Edwards had won—this seat was his to keep.

As I was not intimately involved in this race, I was emotionally distant from the massive disappointment of losing yet again. Besides, although I loved my country, I had bigger fish to fry in my life.

My video business was doing well and keeping me occupied on a professional level. But, more importantly, my relationship with my longtime, long-term love interest was finally coming to bear. Like some long-lost lone wolf, it looked like I was coming back to the fold of traditional life. Karen and I became engaged, and she was now the focus of almost all of my attentions. The wedding was set for October of that year back in Buffalo. I merely fulfilled my responsibilities of getting my groomsmen gathered and at the church in New York. I also made the plans for the honeymoon, but other than that I just attended to my business and life.

In spring 2007, my soon-to-be best man and I were discussing upcoming wedding plans in a restaurant when, unexpectedly, a local appellate judge saw us and stopped to say hi. I had gotten to know him over my years of political involvement in local politics. He asked what I had been up to since I had withdrawn from many of my usual activities in the political world. It was good to know I was missed.

"So, Rob, where've you been? Haven't seen you in a while. What's going on?"

"I've been busy with Dub-L Tape and, believe it or not, I'm actually engaged to Karen from Buffalo."

"Congratulations, it's about time. She's a great girl," he said, having met her on one of her increasingly frequent visits to Waco over the years. "What took you so long?"

"Oh, you don't even want to go down that road, unless you've got about eight hours for me to give you an *abridged* version. It's a long, complicated, and crazy story."

"Maybe you should write a book."

"Maybe I will, but nobody'd believe it," I said. "What've you been up to?"

"Just the usual. We're trying to get candidates to run in the next cycle. We've got a great chance to pick up more seats in the courthouse."

And then he paused and asked me the innocent question which changed the direction of my life and, yes, even congressional politics in Central Texas.

"What about you? You thought about running again?"

"Not really," I said defiantly. "I had my fill of it a few years ago and, besides, I'm getting married in October. It's the first marriage for both of us, so it's a pretty big deal."

"I totally understand," he said. "I just wish we had somebody to run against Chet Edwards."

"You mean *nobody's* going to run against Chet?" I asked, mildly surprised and alarmed.

"Not so far. No one's shown any interest in taking on that battle again. You know how it is. There are folks out there who say they want to take on Chet, but it's just not realistic for them."

"Surely, somebody will jump in. What about the state reps or senator?" I named a few well-known office holders from the Waco area. "Certainly, one of them will eventually jump in. They always have in the past."

"Are you kidding? No sitting legislator is going to take a chance, based on what Chet's done to everyone else that's tried. No one wants to risk giving up their seat on a long shot. And you really can't blame them, I suppose."

"I get it, but as a voter, that sucks. I, at least, want a choice on the ballot."

"Well, what about you? People know who you are. You made a good showing in the races you were in. You can at least talk intelligently about the issues and, besides, you know the media and how to handle yourself in that type of campaign."

"I appreciate the kind words, but I don't have the money. And I'm getting married in October. I don't have the time at this point in my life."

"I understand, but it's too bad." And then he said the magic words which got my dander up.

"It's a shame—I hate to see Chet go unopposed."

He didn't know it, but them were fightin' words to me. Like a bull charging a waving red cape in front of me, I rushed in without any clearly thought-out intent.

"Shoot, if that's the case and no one else will do it, I'll at least put my name on the ballot so that, if nothing else, at least we'd have a choice."

"Really?" he asked with mild hopeful surprise.

"Sure, but *only* if no one else files. Besides, I'm getting married in October and I'm sure someone else will jump in."

"Do you mind if I share that with some folks in the party?"

"Sure," I responded with a twinge in my stomach, realizing that I was going on the record. "But again, *only* if no one else is willing to do it. And I definitely don't want my name out there publicly," I said adamantly. "In the end, we know someone else will eventually step up."

"Understood. I'll be discreet. We'll see what happens," he said as he walked away.

I turned back to my friend and asked with bemused confusion, "What just happened?!"

He shook his head in mild disbelief. "You just told the judge you'd be willing to run for Congress again. You're crazy."

Deep down, I knew he was right. Still, I had my reasons for what I may have rashly said to the judge. As a passionate, politically aware conservative living in the district of a liberal congressman, political life had been frustrating for the last eighteen years.

"I agree it would be crazy, but don't you, at least, want a choice against Chet?"

I didn't know it at the time, but that statement would become my battle cry in the coming months.

"Yeah, but you've already been down that road, and you know it wasn't a lot of fun. You've done your part, and besides—you're getting married."

"I'm sure nothing will come of it," I assured. "Someone else will get in before the deadline…they always do. So right now, it's all just meaningless talk."

To my slight surprise, over the next weeks and months, the "talk" escalated. I began receiving sporadic calls from various local party and a few elected officials saying that they'd heard I might consider getting in against Chet. I responded to each with the same statement: "Yes, I'll put my name on the ballot, *if* no one else will, just so we have a choice in the next election—but *only* if no else wants to run. If they do, I'm out. It's all theirs. I'm sure someone will come forward."

In the meantime, I let Karen know that, although highly unlikely this would move beyond talk, it was being discussed. She said she would leave it in God's hands and, if that was what we were supposed to do, she accepted that—although it wouldn't be ideal for the start of a marriage. We both focused on the wedding and the colossal life changes coming with our marriage. She would soon be relocating across the country and setting up home in my old bachelor pad for the time being—just until we could get a house built on some land I owned in another part of Waco.

After getting married in Buffalo in October, in November of 2007, we took our delayed honeymoon on a cruise from Australia to New Zealand. It was a two-week trip of a lifetime. On the other side of the planet, day-to-day issues of life back in Texas were almost completely forgotten. The little bit of political news reaching those distant shores from America was mainly surrounding Hillary Clinton and the inevitability of her becoming the first woman president of the United States. We half joked that, if she got anywhere near the White House, New Zealand would be our new home. Actually, judging by the beauty and standard-of-living of that isolated island nation, maybe it wouldn't have been such a bad trade-off.

CHAPTER 23

Into the Fight

When we returned home from our honeymoon, the calls became more frequent and even more serious. The district was comprised of eleven counties now, with Waco being the largest population center. As the congressional contest was the highest profiled local race on the ballot, it was also the highest priority for the politically active throughout the district. The thought that Chet Edwards would go unchallenged was of the utmost concern for those who saw the big picture and realized that we had to have someone who actually represented our values in Washington. Never mind the fact that Edwards was undefeated against weak and apparently strong opponents alike. Still, hope springs eternal. This was the race everyone wanted to win. However, we had *no* chance to knock off this political giant…if we didn't try.

The various county chairmen and power brokers met constantly to find someone of substance to step forward and take on the incumbent. Urging local office holders at the county or state levels proved unsuccessful. Comfortable elected officials had their own reasons for not wanting to go out and challenge the powerful and popular congressman. The standing rule of thumb was, "You'd have to be completely crazy—or naïve—to take on Edwards."

So, as the months passed, and the filing deadline rapidly approached, the "any port in a storm" approach took hold. The McLennan County leadership told the other county chairmen that, if nothing else, "We've got a small business owner in Waco who ran in the primary a few years back and made a credible showing. Even though he lost, he's a former TV guy who's well-spoken and can at least put up a good front. He's willing to do it if no one else will step forward." Undoubtedly, to my thinking, the conversations most likely continued in knowing tones, "Of course, barring some miracle or act of God, he can't possibly win, but at least we'll have a name on the ballot."

Soon, the phone calls took on an urgent tone. "Rob, are you still willing to do this? We've got folks who want to run, but they just don't understand what they're getting into and don't have the necessary skills to make a credible showing—if you know what I mean."

Yes, I knew what they meant. And I also saw that this talk of running for Congress again might actually be getting closer to reality. A nervous yet tempered excitement began to take hold of my thoughts. Karen and I discussed what this would mean if we chose to do this. It would not be easy on our new marriage. And because we had no organization, or, more importantly, no funding, with no real way to raise any (considering the long odds we would be up against), we mostly spoke of just putting my name on the ballot and doing little or no campaigning. At least, at the end of the day, voters would have a choice.

We discussed at length the upsides and the downsides, but it all boiled down to, "If this is what God wants and the doors keep opening, it's our responsibility to walk through them no matter what the cost." As it would be a team effort, it was exhilarating to know that my soul mate would be at my side, no matter what the future held. This was a new dynamic that I had never experienced before. It was liberating. Win or lose, it would be much easier with a partner at my side than it was before.

We agreed, and I passed it on to the various politicos who were acting as unofficial conduits to this anonymous possible candidate.

"Okay, I'll put my name on the ballot, but with this caveat: I'll go to Austin to file on literally the last hour of the last day, and if even a homeless bum walks up and says he's running, I'm out—the nomination is his. And more importantly, I do not want my name out in public on this."

Since the news outlets in the district kept running "Who will challenge Chet Edwards?" stories on a sporadic basis, I did not want to see my name appear in any of those. If anyone else ran, I didn't want to appear as an indecisive perennial candidate wannabe. All agreed, and we waited for the approaching deadline to see how it would unfold.

The pressure built. A few well-meaning potential candidates came forward to volunteer to beat Chet Edwards "since no one else had the guts to." Generally, they were good patriots who, like most conservatives, couldn't stomach the thought of Central Texas being represented by a congressman who worked so enthusiastically *against* our "local" President Bush and so effectively *for* Nancy Pelosi, now Speaker of the House of Representatives. But as it is with so many well-meaning folks, it's easy to *talk* about running. It's a whole other world to actually do it and realize what all is actually involved. Still, that's the great thing about America. Every citizen has the right and the freedom to get involved in the political process.

Surprisingly, the local officials kept their silence and word, saying little more than "Thanks for your willingness to step up," to other would-be suitors, "but we've got someone who's going to go. We *will* have a challenger for Chet." More surprisingly, there were no leaks to any news outlets. So far, things were falling into place, whether I really wanted them to or not.

I took my first real step of commitment in late December. My wife and I were in Buffalo with her family for our first Christmas holidays as a married couple. It was surreal, hanging out with the in-laws in total obscurity in upstate New York. Yet, if things continued as they were, I might soon be at the center of a high-profile political race.

"Heck, if this goes all the way, I would be congressman for the president of the United States. Boy, I hope the Bushes vote for me," I pondered jokingly to my in-laws. As things were still holding to form and I had given my word, I bought a plane ticket to cut my trip short to return to Texas to make the filing deadline. Karen stayed behind, both of us still not 100 percent sure I would be running. But, crazy as it seemed, it looked like this race might be on me.

Once again, I asked my best man to drive me to Austin. Eight years after the first decision, here we were making yet another emotional trek to Austin. The stress level rose significantly when my cell phone rang halfway there. It was the McLennan County Republican chairman.

"Are you going through with it, Rob?" he asked with a sense of urgency.

"We're on our way to Austin right now. I'll be there before 6:00 p.m. Anybody else pop up?" I asked almost hopefully.

"No, it looks like you're our man. I've got a room full of press outside my office who heard we had someone to run against Chet. I told them, yes, we have someone that agreed to…"

"You didn't give them my name, did you? Because if someone else shows up, I'm out," I interrupted.

"Nope, you're still incognito," he assured.

"I'll call you when it's done…then do whatever you want."

I had that old feeling of déjà vu in panic mode.

"Well, here we go again. Looks like this is it," I said to my friend, then retreated into my thoughts while again watching the road stripes zip by as we pressed toward my destiny.

We arrived at Republican headquarters in downtown Austin at about 5:30 p.m. A half hour to go. I took a deep breath and got out of the car when my cell phone rang. I wasn't going to answer but thought I'd better just in case.

It was a well-known Republican professional campaign consultant from the Waco area. Although I'd never actually worked with her, I'd known her for years from our political dealings.

"Rob, where are you?" she asked abruptly.

I thought she had somehow found out I was running and was calling to wish me well or ask for work.

"I'm in Austin."

"What are you doing?" she asked urgently.

"I'm about to file to run against Chet," I said, thinking she would be pleased.

"Do not do that!" she shot back.

"Excuse me?" I asked, truly surprised.

"You've got a bright future ahead of you in politics. If you run against Chet, you'll destroy your political future. You can't win, and it will hurt you in any future race. Think about what you're doing."

Stunned, I asked, "Are you saying you don't even want us to have a choice in November?"

"You can't win. Nobody can beat him. All you're going to do is get him upset, and he'll go into full campaign mode and get his people out...and that will hurt everyone down ballot."

I suddenly realized her motivation. "And which candidate are you working for?"

She told me. "But that's not the point! You can't beat Chet. You're throwing away a promising career. Please, just think over what you're doing. No one has been able to beat Chet. You can't win," she reiterated.

"I have twenty minutes to decide. But if I do decide to go, I want your vote," I said with a little bravado in an effort to tweak her.

"You know I'd support you, Rob."

"No, I want more than your support; I want your vote," I said, making her declare it out loud, just in case she was another closet Republican Edwards supporter.

"Sure, Rob."

I hung up with a combination of anger and disbelief. "Can you believe that?!" I rhetorically asked my friend who had been listening to the whole conversation.

Knowing the county chairman was babysitting a room full of reporters, I immediately called another of my Republican contacts back in Waco. I told him of the call I had just gotten and wanted to know if this was the predominant line of thinking back home. If so, what was I doing down here in Austin filing? After angry assurances from him that she was speaking only for herself, I hung up the phone, and my friend and I proceeded into the headquarters. I now had ten minutes to go.

While waiting to do the paperwork and pay the fee in those minutes, we ran into a mid-level state party official. He had gotten the word that I was in to file for District 17.

"Hey, Rob, I hear you're going to run against Chet Edwards. We sure would like to get him out," he said enthusiastically.

"Absolutely," I agreed. "I'm looking forward to working with you guys on this."

"Oh, no," he said without missing a beat. "We're not going down that road again. We'll be focusing on getting (former congressman) Tom Delay's old seat back and going after a couple of other congressional races we think we can win."

"Really?" I responded with all the composure I could muster. It was like being on a sports team and finding out your coach won't be coaching you during the big game. In fact, he won't even be going to the game, because he's got more important things to do. "You're not even going to try for this seat?" I asked with complete surprise.

"No," he laughed like he had just heard a cute comment from a child. "We're not going to keep beating our heads against *that* wall. We'll go after Edwards in 2012 when we've got a better shot."

"A better shot?' I asked, truly confused.

"After redistricting, when we've got better numbers."

"Better numbers?!" I shot back, barely concealing the anger building inside me. "We're already at 65 percent. How much more do you want?!"

"We've just got to focus our limited resources where we can. But—really—good luck to you, Rob. We hope you do well," he said, walking away.

I looked at my friend who was looking more uncomfortable by the moment. I shook my head in disbelief. This was getting more bizarre by the minute. We had five minutes to decide.

We were ushered back to where I had to fill out forms and write the check. With mixed emotions, I completed the paperwork and began filling out the check. My friend, who had been largely silent to this point, suddenly asked, "Rob, can I talk to you for a second?"

"Right now?" I asked, surprised and somewhat perturbed.

I looked at the clock overhead. Two minutes left.

"Yes. Right now."

It was obvious he was in emotional distress. "OK, just a second, ma'am," I said to the clerk.

"What?" I asked with a little bit of impatience.

"Don't do it!" he blurted out.

"What?!"

"I'm telling you, don't do it! You've just seen what kind of support you'll get."

"You're serious?!" I shot back. *I can't believe this*, I thought. *Now I've lost my good friend on this? What's next? I sure hope Karen forgot my phone number and doesn't call in the next ten seconds, because if she does, it's all over.*

He continued with a genuine emotional sense of urgency, "I'm your friend, and it's obvious you'll get no help. And you know Chet; it'll get nasty and he'll destroy you. You've seen what he's done to everyone else—and they had support. I don't want to see you get hurt."

"Mr. Curnock, it's time," the clerk said.

"One second," I said as I studied my friend. It was obvious that he was speaking from the heart and meant every word. In my own heart, I knew he was right. I turned back and forth, looking from him to her.

After a few seconds, without a word, I rushed over and signed the check. I thanked the clerk, turned to my friend, and said, "Let's get out of here."

6:01. It was done. As we made our way out through the maze of halls and offices, we ran into another staffer. "Thanks for running, Rob. Hope you get him."

My friend asked him for a clarification of what we had heard earlier. "You guys are saying that Chet can't be beaten. Is that true?"

"Let's just say that Chet is as close to bulletproof as you can get," he said with absolutely no idea as to the potential emotional and psychological damage his words were doing to this poor candidate who would be carrying their water in this race.

My friend was visibly crushed. I showed no response, thanked him for his time, and walked out. "Maybe we'll see you later," I said, walking out the door. It was a veiled jab dripping with sardonic irony.

I had to get out of there. I was about to explode. I was in a controlled emotional nuclear detonation, and ignition was just beyond the outer door. I said nothing to my sullen friend on the slow elevator ride down to the lobby. We walked out the front door and I could contain myself no longer. Already emotionally raw from the weight of this monumental decision, I burst with the wrath of pent-up frustrations, suddenly free from any restraints.

"This is why the Republican Party is losing everywhere!" I yelled, not necessarily to my friend. He just happened to be the only set of ears in the vicinity. And the venting detonation of a good rant was just getting started.

"We wonder why we're getting rolled up on every issue and in every race. The Democrats are constantly on the attack—and we do nothing! Our leadership won't fight. They're afraid of everything. They send in flawed loser candidates against someone like Chet and then quit when we don't win. I'm not mad because they're not helping me as the candidate—I'm mad as a voter. I get it, they think my chances are slim and none. So be it. They may be right, but at least see if there's something that could be done. At least hold my coat and give me an 'Atta boy.' The voters in District 17 have a right to expect that the party isn't going to roll over and play dead...because they're afraid Chet might get mad! Edwards has no business winning in this area, but when your leadership won't fight, who wants to follow them? I'm furious! We're losing our country and our party won't do anything about it."

I felt sorry for my friend who was driving. He got an earful. I called my county chairman and told him it was done. Then I vented all over him for several minutes as to the attitude in the state party headquarters. He commiserated with me, then I hung up to let him contact whomever he needed.

It wasn't a lack of support for me that had me riled. It was the reinforcement of my belief that the leadership of the Republican Party is just plain out of touch with its own rank and file. Those of us on the receiving end of the Democrats' seemingly endless destruction of our values and principles wonder why our leadership never adopted any of the Democrats' tactics. Those on the left never stop, never give up, and they go to any lengths to achieve their goals. We somehow never seem to learn the stupidity of bringing a knife to a gunfight.

I eventually settled down and took stock of the task ahead. It was at that point that I felt a calm come over me. It was the calm of someone who now knew the tremendous difficulty of what he had to do, but at least all the apprehension, doubt, and uncertainty of getting into the fight had been removed. Conversely, I soon felt a strange giddiness. All these years, I've wanted to do something to help the conservative cause. I wanted in the fight. I was now in it up to my neck.

No more primary 'personality' pageants. Whether I felt like it or not, whether I was alone or not, whether I had the money or not, whether I had a chance or not, I was in *the* Main Event. After all these years, I could actually do more than just complain about our congressional situation. I could do something about it. It hit me like a bolt of lightning: *What an incredible opportunity!*

I was determined right then and there to seize the moment. I was the one who had a chance to take out one of Pelosi's most reliable allies in the House. That's incredibly powerful motivation. All talk of just putting my name on the ballot to give people a choice was now completely forgotten. Although I didn't know exactly how we'd do it, I was going to give it everything I had.

The monumental irony of the moment was not lost on me. As a voter, *I* was now all that *I* had!

CHAPTER 24

Challenging Goliath

Of course, now came the hard part. The plan had always been to *just* put my name on the ballot and give our voters a choice, at the least, but now that I was thrust into the arena, my competitive nature and desire to fight for conservative values was surprisingly strong. I *had* to do something. Why *not* put up a fight? Maybe the party was right, and I couldn't win, but what did I have to lose? I'd already paid well over $3,000 just to make a point for my fellow conservatives.

If there was ever a David versus Goliath scenario, this was it. Edwards had well over $3 million in the bank. He had just pounded the last two well-financed and party-supported opponents he had faced. He had become one of Speaker of the House Nancy Pelosi's most trusted allies in Congress. He had the prestige of being a sixteen-year incumbent who could deliver the pork to his district and was experienced in the ways of Washington. He had connections and people and PACs supporting him from both sides of the aisle throughout the district and the country. Local office holders at all levels in *both* parties worked with him or for him, some overtly and some covertly, some out of fear of opposing the sitting congressman, others because they truly liked him. He had his powerful allies in the local newspaper editors, who were free agents on his team. More importantly, he knew the Republican Party had backed off of challenging him once again.

He had the aura of invincibility wrapped around him like a royal robe. All he had to do was easily dispatch a two-time failed primary candidate who had no support, no backing, and no money. This was a no-brainer. This should be a cake walk.

And he was right.

His supporters knew he was right and my supporters knew he was right. The media knew he was right and the Republican Party knew he was right. Even *I* knew he was right, but with one exception. I wasn't a starry-eyed goofball out of touch with reality, and I knew a few factors were actually in my favor.

First, for the first time in years, local Republicans would have a general election challenger that hadn't been bloodied and weakened in a difficult and nasty primary. The district had been redrawn four years earlier and it was now more Republican than ever—a solid 65 percent Republican. Second, Fort Hood, the source of much of Edwards' ability to cultivate veterans' loyalty and goodwill, was no longer in the district. Third, the current president, George W. Bush, lived in the district just outside Waco at his Crawford ranch when not in Washington. Surely, there was some benefit to that unique situation.

And on a subtler level, as the national Democrat Party moved farther to the left, Edwards was being forced to take a stand on one side or the other. It was becoming more difficult for him to camouflage his votes that offended the natural sensibilities of the traditional conservatives in Central Texas.

Keeping in the vein of David and Goliath, these were the only four stones I had to use in my sling. However, according to the Bible, David had five smooth stones when he went into battle with the giant, but God moves in mysterious ways and will provide for his servants if they have faith. Miraculously, within a couple of months,

Nancy Pelosi, of all people, would toss me a fifth stone that I hoped would wind up right between the eyes of this congressional Goliath.

At present, though, in the real world, things still looked bleak. Sure, I had a few reasons for optimism, but now what? Should I go about my business and get on with my new wife and my new life and let voters have that simple choice in November, the simple choice I myself yearned for when I entertained this crazy idea? Deep inside, the answer was, of course, *no*. I couldn't in good conscience passively let it go. That's not who I am and that's not what this race was about. It was about much bigger things than me, my wants, my needs.

My new wife Karen was as supportive and understanding as I could hope. Starting off married life on a congressional campaign trail was not the best way to ensure a lifetime of marital bliss. Newlyweds in today's society have enough stresses in the most normal of situations. Add to the mix a life in a high-stress, high-profile fish bowl. Add in an eleven-county district where every day brings long drives to get to campaign events. Toss in the unique phenomenon of being the focus of displeasure of about half of the people you meet, and in many cases, the target of downright, vitriolic hatred. It's been my personal experience that the hatred of the Left, especially regarding national issues, knows no bounds and little filtering. Putting all these factors together would not be fun.

I don't say this to whine or complain that it's too tough. I was a big boy and could deal with what came my way. That was my choice. But it would be difficult for my spouse to see her husband brutalized in an over-the-top and public fashion. As the candidate's wife, Karen had to nod and smile, but if you stood close during the nastiness, you could see wisps of white smoke coming from her ears. She did not like seeing her husband attacked, but it was the nature of the beast. She understood and accepted that, with all the dignity of an experienced political spouse and the external good nature of an academy award-winning actress.

For the first time in my adult life, though, it felt incredible to have a partner in one of my endeavors. It's amazing the difference it can make. Suddenly, you don't feel alone. For me, the synergism of having a partner you love and trust is empowering.

Shortly after word went out that I had filed, I began receiving encouraging emails from people throughout the district, with offers to help, and thanking me for standing up and challenging the incumbent when no one else would. I also began to hear from most—but not all—of the Republican county chairmen in other parts of the district, pledging their support and asking me to touch base with them as soon as possible. Everyone was positive—to my face—and looked forward to working with me in the coming year. I was actually starting to be encouraged that the unpleasant experience of the filing process was an isolated aberration and a thing of the past. I grabbed on to positive emotions and prepared for the coming battle.

My first opportunity to meet voters in the new northern part of the district came in early January. The Republican Party in this county had opened a new headquarters, and I was invited by the new county chairman to an informal housewarming. It was a two-hour drive with no program, but I could meet party activists in that area. It was the first of hundreds of road trips Karen and I would take almost daily.

I was definitely the new kid on the block. This part of the district was out of my former television station's viewing range, so no one knew me from my media days. And because they were new to the district since I had been involved in my last primary, they had no idea who I was on any level. Therefore, we were on equal footing, and it was a great chance to get the relationship off to a positive start.

The event was an informal come-and-go affair. A woman with the party sat at a registration table welcoming guests and preparing impromptu name stickers. "Hi, I'm Rob Curnock, and this is my wife Karen," I said with no further thought as we approached the sign-in table.

"Great to have you. And how do you spell the last name?" she asked, not recognizing the name. For some reason, my name has given people difficulty my entire life. She started writing on the tag.

"That's a C, not a K,…u…r…n…o…c…k."

"Oh, I'm so sorry."

"Not a problem."

"And who are you with?" she asked, wanting to know what organization I represented.

"I'm with Karen," I responded, with a lame attempt at humor, as I pointed to my wife.

"Oh…ha, ha. No, who are you with?" she politely laughed.

"I was just kidding, but I hope I'm with you!" I said, as she now looked totally confused and was probably wishing I would just move on in and mingle. "I'm the guy that's running for Congress, and I hope to be your congressman."

Her mouth dropped open as she suddenly looked more intently at me. "You're the man who's running for Congress…against Chet Edwards?!"

"That's me, and I…" But before I could say anything else, she was ignoring me and calling over to a nearby person."

"George, get Randy. This is our congressional candidate. This is Rob… I'm sorry, how did you pronounce your last name?" as she introduced me to whomever was listening around the door.

By now everyone in the immediate area was sticking out their hands to shake mine, and they all seemed genuinely glad to meet me. It was causing a bit of a stir, but it was a great relief to both Karen and me. Over and over, a variation of the same comments was repeated:

"So glad to meet you. We've got to beat that Chet."

"Thank you for stepping up and taking him on; we've got to win this seat."

"How did we ever get a Liberal like Chet as our congressman? We want a conservative congressman."

"We're with you all the way."

"Tell us how we can help you."

"You must beat that liberal Edwards!"

I learned also that I was unlike the last Republican candidate that had come through this area to take on Chet. They freely admitted they didn't much care for him and didn't want to work for him for a variety of reasons. I didn't take these conversations as simple flattery. In reality, it was a valuable lesson that people need to like you before they'll energetically work with you.

Additionally, it was heartening to see the sincere goodwill coming our way from virtually everyone. It was a new experience for me as a veteran of the nastily contested primaries, and I liked this new twist on campaigning. More importantly, it was a reversal of the maddening experience a week before at the state Republican headquarters. With the overflow of positive vibes, Karen and I began to think the unpleasantness in Austin was just a bad memory.

But the feelings were not universal after all.

I was surprised and pleased to see a woman I knew from Waco--a political pro serving as an area director for our local state senator. The senator's wide-ranging district overlapped into this northern county. He was one of the state officeholders that many in the political class hoped would take on the incumbent congressman, but he showed no interest in that fight. I hadn't seen this acquaintance in some time but had always been on good terms with her. It was good to see a friendly and familiar face.

"Hey, where the heck have you been? And what are you doing up here?" I asked with genuine curiosity.

"Hi, Rob," she smiled. "I moved up here a couple years ago to head up the senator's office in this part of the district," she said.

"Well, it's great to see you again. This is my wife Karen, whom I don't think you've ever met."

"Oh, you finally got married. Well, good for you. Nice to meet you, Karen." They shook hands.

Then her tone turned a little less friendly.

"I hear you're running against Chet."

"Yes, we'll see what we can do to get him out," I said.

"I can't believe you're going to mess with that," she said sourly and shaking her head. "Why on earth would you want to put yourself in that situation again?"

As all the good emotions of the last half hour were sucked right out of me in the blink of an eye, I responded back in serious kind.

"Well, this is the first chance I've had to actually go head-to-head with Chet. But most importantly, if I didn't do it, *nobody* was going

186

to, and Chet would've gone unchallenged. As voters, we wouldn't have even had a choice in November. The senator wasn't thinking about it, was he? Because if *he* was, I wouldn't be here right now."

Whether she meant to or not, she then gave me the proverbial sucker punch put-down.

"Oh, no. He's got a lot more sense than to take on Chet," she laughed.

"Well, somebody needed to step up, so I guess it fell to me," I said tersely but masking my building anger with a weak smile.

"Good luck; he's real strong," she replied, not meaning it in the supportive way. "You've got your work cut out for you."

"Yeah, thanks," I said, not meaning it sincerely. "Hope to see you around."

Karen and I caught each other's eye as we walked away. I rolled my eyes and whispered, "That's the kind of support we're going to get from the senator and his office." She just shook her head.

We stayed to the end and met as many people as we could. All in all, it was worth the trip, and many positives came out of it.

On the long drive home, Karen asked, "Who was that woman with the senator's office?"

"She represents most of the political class around here," I said, not hiding my contempt. "The senator has the best chance to win this seat, but like every other office holder in this district, he's not going to risk his seat by taking on Chet. That's the problem with established politicians. I get it, but as a voter, I don't like it."

"Maybe we'll get some help from him anyway?" she asked hopefully.

"I doubt it. Think about it. Locally, he's the top Republican in this area. If I were to pull this off, guess what? Suddenly, *I* become the top Republican, with all the power and prestige that it brings. While I don't care about the prestige, jealousy is a powerful emotion. If you like being the big fish in a little pond, chances are I'm not going to get a lot of support to become the bigger fish. Then there's the fear factor. I promise you, he thinks I have absolutely no chance at winning, so why would he get involved and antagonize the local congressman? I hope I'm wrong, and I've always been on good terms with him, but I'm not expecting anything."

Unfortunately, I was not wrong.

Darn it.

CHAPTER 25

Emotional Connection

This was new territory. No more candidate forums, as I had no primary opponent. I was accustomed to being one of several candidates vying for a spot, and, as such, I never expected nor received any special treatment at any event. It was a rule of thumb that no favoritism should be shown to anyone, by anyone, running the meetings. So, my first congressional candidate event came as a complete campaign culture shock.

In late January I was invited to an early candidate's forum in another one of the new northern counties in the district. Like the previous one, I knew no one in this area either, so Karen and I headed up with the anticipation of meeting new people. I would be given a bit of time to introduce myself to voters and party activists after the other contested local candidates were finished speaking.

We arrived about an hour after the start time as the last of the down-ballot constable position candidates were speaking. We came in at the back of the big room where maybe seventy people were scattered about. Immediately, someone from the party met us and asked who we were. I explained that I was the congressional candidate and we were told we could come in and say a few words to the group.

The woman was visibly surprised, and after a few pleasantries, she headed up to the front of the room where the county chairman was sitting. I felt rather bad for the candidate who was struggling through his speech at the time, because the chairman immediately popped up and headed back to us. The commotion caused most heads in the place to turn to us to see what was going on. Truly embarrassed, I tried to keep things as quiet and calm as I could, in deference to the poor candidate speaking at the podium.

Dan, their new county chairman, was a young, enthusiastic guy in his early thirties who had an outgoing personality and was visibly happy that I had accepted his invitation. He asked if I would speak last to close out the meeting, so Karen and I waited in the back of the room until my time. Before introducing the last candidates on the ballot, he announced that "our" congressional candidate had just arrived and would be speaking last. The room buzzed as everyone turned around to size us up, with many smiling and nodding their heads in approval. They even politely applauded.

This was a new experience for me. In fact, I was honestly embarrassed. I was used to being one of several candidates vying for a position, with much of the audience divided up in support of their particular candidate. In those meetings, I was just one of the crowd. Here, it appeared that most in this crowd were definitely happy to see me. While sitting in the back of the room, during the rest of the candidates' talks, a quiet, steady stream of people walked by to shake hands, nod hello, or even silently hand me notes. It was slightly unnerving yet extremely gratifying.

After the last candidate finished, Dan introduced me. As he didn't know me and had nothing specific to go by, it was a broad and impromptu introduction on the need to win this seat and get it back in conservative hands—and I should be the candidate to do it. It was exactly what I wanted. The audience warmly applauded, and I addressed my first crowd as the presumptive Republican congressional nominee.

As had been my practice in the previous primaries, I had no prepared remarks, so I thanked them for giving me a chance to spend time with them and gave them a synopsis of my business and political experience. Then I launched into a simple message of why I was in this race and why we needed to win. It was evidently what they wanted and needed to hear.

Unlike my earlier primary experience years before, where I was surprised and happy to see nodding heads throughout the audience, this was exhilarating. Not only did heads nod approvingly, but I was constantly interrupted for applause and even received one quick standing ovation! I'd gotten applause and warm responses before, but it was nowhere near the enthusiasm I was experiencing here. Everything in the primaries was tempered by the fact that the majority of the audience was usually not in your corner, whether they liked what you had to say or not. For the first time in my limited political life, I understood what it was like to connect with my audience. I understood how good politicians throughout history bonded with the crowd. It was a spontaneous, symbiotic combustion of enthusiastic, positive emotion. The more they got fired up, the more I got fired up. It was an incredible experience, which I was thrilled about and lucky to be a part of many more times in the campaign.

I don't know how long I talked, but I said everything I wanted to say, and no one showed any sign of apathy. I admitted to them that I was under no illusions of what we were up against, "but with your help, we can, and we will win this thing—no matter what all the pundits think!"

The applause was as thunderous and prolonged as could be imagined from a crowd of seventy. I made my way back to my seat waving and mouthing "thank you" to them. Before I could make it all the way back to my wife, Dan bounced up to the podium. His remarks were unsolicited, unexpected, and straight from his heart, and went straight to my heart like a shot of adrenaline and breath of fresh air.

"This is what it's all about," he said. "This is my first time to meet Rob and, frankly, I didn't know what to expect. But I'm thrilled that we've got a man like him working for us. We know this won't be easy," and he turned to me, "but for the first time, after hearing you, Rob, I have real hope. I think we can win this, and I think we will win this. You're what we've been waiting for. You're a true conservative who's not just talk; I'm convinced you're the real deal. You're the type of man we need in Washington to turn this country around. I'm pledging tonight that *I'm* going to do *everything* I can to help Rob win this, and I hope all of you will too. Rob, we're with you all the way. Thank you for standing up for us."

More enthusiastic applause.

I was glad I was not expected to say anything else. I was frantically trying to get a hold of my emotions. As I struggled to regain my composure, I just waved and mouthed more "thank- yous" to the audience and Dan. But this was truly an emotional first for me.

All my past political experiences involved me asking ambivalent voters for support and to simply give me a chance to fight for the values that we all held dear. But suddenly here was the leader of the local party spontaneously pledging to work for and with me with complete sincerity. He was assuring me that I was not alone and would not be alone in this fight. Up to now, I had heard plenty from the party officials and political naysayers who were quick to dismiss my "hopeless" campaign and belittle my efforts. And those were from my *own* political party! They should have been in my corner. After all, I was fighting for them, even if they didn't care or appreciate it.

This was an emotional turning point. I realized that "my" people were not in the power circles of Washington or Austin. My people were not the leaders of the party or the political pros. *My people* were the working-class rank and file. They were the proverbial grassroots who didn't hold all the levers of power, but who put their hearts and souls into preserving their values any way they could with whatever they had. They were the worker bees, and they would be the true life-blood and lonely allies in this Herculean task we were undertaking.

We left that evening only after meeting briefly with every person in that building that wanted to talk with me, and that was almost everyone. The county chairman asked about my conversation with a couple of people who, unbeknownst to me, were prominent and wealthy folks in the area. He expressed surprise that the two had made a point of even talking with me, as they were well-known Chet supporters and donors—even though they were strong Republicans at every other level. My newfound friends assured me there was little chance that these two benefactors could be counted on for help or even votes. However, they were pleased when I assured them those were exactly the types of voters I would go after, and I wouldn't give up on them easily. Republicans splitting their tickets for Edwards are the voters we had to win over to take the seat.

I was growing bolder, knowing that I wasn't alone, even in parts of the district where I didn't know anyone. This was one thing that made this difficult task so worthwhile. This motivated me to go on, no matter what the odds.

CHAPTER 26

Thinking on My Feet

Simple logistics dictated that campaigning in this new district would be a lot more work than before. Although the new congressional boundaries were friendlier to Republicans, the distance between major population centers was now much greater. The eleven-county district comprised four main but small cities: Waco, the largest and in the center; Bryan/College Station, home of Texas A&M University in the south; and Granbury and Burleson, in the two northernmost counties just south of Fort Worth. The rest of the district was mostly rural with small towns scattered throughout.

The good news was that the area was quite conservative in culture and politics. There was no way a liberal congressman should keep getting elected, even if he did try to paint himself as a moderate. In fact, in this part of the country, a moderate is little more than a watered-down liberal who can't make up his mind. Fortunately, Waco was right in the middle so, for me, a campaign road trip was basically two hours north or two hours south. On an almost daily basis, I was destined to spend at least four hours on the road.

Karen had ended her teaching career when we were married months before, which meant she could spend time campaigning with me. We decided to take advantage of these situations by looking at them as nice long dates. We would use the trips to get to know each other even better. As Karen explained, it would help us bond even more in our first year of marriage. In typical guy fashion, I just liked having her with me.

A few days following the first event, the president of the Republican Women's Club in another part of the northern district, having heard about my first speech, invited me to an informal meet-and-greet at a regularly scheduled business meeting. She apologized that there would be no opportunity for me to speak as the agenda had already been set. However, she promised she would make sure that I got about a minute and a half before the actual program began. It was still an opportunity to meet voters.

On the drive up, we discussed what I would say in only a minute and a half. That wasn't time to say much, so I had to make as big an impact as I could quickly. This is where my television training paid off. I thought of it as three thirty-second commercials. My first thirty seconds would feature who I was and what I did in Waco. My second thirty seconds would briefly cover why we needed to get a conservative in our congressional seat. My final thirty seconds would cover why we could win and how we needed to work together. It was up to me to keep it concise, coherent, and on time. I was only getting one chance to make a first impression. I'd have to rely on one-on-one campaigning *after* the meeting.

Sixty people filled the room. The club president wanted us to sit up front so that everyone could see us. She soon opened the meeting with the pledge of allegiance to both the United States and Texas flags. I was up shortly.

"Do you know what you're going to say?" Karen whispered.

"It's only a minute and half. I could mumble it in my sleep," I said cockily.

When another lady began going over club business matters, the president quickly made her way over to me. She leaned over and whispered to me apologetically, "Rob, I just wanted to make sure, would twenty-five minutes be enough time?"

TWENTY-FIVE MINUTES?! Are you out of your mind?! I screamed...in my head.

"Uh, that would be fine," I whispered calmly with a forced smile.

"If you need more, go as long you want. This is very important to us," she whispered. "I'll introduce you in just a few minutes."

"Okay, that's great. Thank you," I continued with that same weak, phony smile frozen on my face.

"Did she just say twenty-five minutes?!" Karen said under her breath in near panic, as we both stared forward without turning our heads. "What are you going to do?"

"I have no idea," I muttered. "I'll just talk about the congressional race."

The president was introducing me. It was go time.

As I took the podium, I went into autopilot. Taking bits and pieces from other talks I had given in the past, I said whatever I wanted and in as much detail as I wanted. But more importantly, I spoke like I was holding a normal conversation with them. It was liberating. No time constraints, a friendly audience, and a topic I was passionate about. Pretty soon I was pouring out my heart and was constantly interrupted by enthusiastic applause. I loved the fact that we were all on the same page politically. I finished what I had to say and opened it up for questions. By the time the president closed things out, I had been speaking for about fifty minutes, and the audience was still totally engaged.

I learned lessons that morning that would serve me well through the rest of my campaigning days. First, I affirmed that I could think on my feet and still make sense. That's a gift for which I'm grateful. Second, I learned that I had the ability to roll with the flow and not get rattled. That's a personality trait I'm also grateful for. You learn on the campaign trail to expect the unexpected. Third, I realized that if you absolutely believe in your core values and what you're doing, and passionately express it with conviction straight from the heart, you don't have to "think" about what to say. People of like mind will respond positively.

We left that meeting with a profound sense that good things were beginning to happen.

Many pledged their support. Our ranks were growing, and we didn't even have any organized ranks to fill! We walked away realizing that interest in our campaign and our mission was increasing, and we needed to get up and running quickly. We also suspected that, perhaps, I was a decent candidate with an ability to connect with voters. This was a great combination and, with a bit of luck, just maybe we could make good things happen.

CHAPTER 27

Getting Organized

From the onset of this crazy idea, I was of the mindset that I would just put my name on the ballot and go about my personal business. As that was quickly proving *not* to be an option, it was critical to organize this campaign, and I was starting from scratch. I needed help, and quickly. Although we had ten months until the election, panic was looming over the horizon.

If I were going to mount any type of campaign, I had to come up with a game plan. In some strange inverse variation of the theory of relativity, the days seemed to be flying by. I was being contacted for a steady stream of speaking engagements and forums. Perhaps word was spreading that I was a pretty good communicator, or perhaps I had the cachet of being the presumptive nominee for the high-profile congressional race. Even though the national and state parties had declined to, once again, challenge the incumbent, the rank-and-file on the ground were chomping at the bit to elect a conservative to this seat, and they were itching for a fight. Maybe both.

About this time, I truly began to understand that this was not "my" campaign. Unlike a primary, where support is more difficult to come by, a general election will bring out many more people who want to get involved at any level they can. In fact, folks will come out of the woodwork...both good and bad. It's not easy sometimes, but it's up to you to sort out which they are and what role they can play in the campaign. They will quickly take ownership of the challenge and offer their help no matter how long the odds. But in return, I realized that I was *their* guy, and they weren't going to let me just coast through to November. It was truly a different dynamic than the earlier primary races in which I had been involved.

Fortunately, God answers prayers. A local businessman named Porter stepped up and forcefully offered to take charge and organize the campaign. Porter was a middle-aged good old country boy. He was tough as nails with a bombastic, aggressive, and abrupt manner, but with a heart of gold if he "took a likin' to you." I'd known him for years from various local political endeavors. Unfortunately, in most of my previous primary battles, he and I were not on the same side. In sports terms, he was one of those players that nobody else in the league likes for their aggressive, hard-nosed, in-your-face style of play, but when he's on your team, you love him. That was Porter, and now he was on my team. Karen and I loved him!

Porter was the first to jump in and offer his help in any way we wanted, and to take charge, if need be, with the condition that he was still running his own busy and prosperous business first. He was also ready to go out and recruit the people needed to make things happen. That was exactly what we needed. On top of that, Porter was willing to put his money where his mouth was. He donated, what turned out to be, our seed money to the maximum federal legal limit.

About this same time, another man—Sean—whom I hadn't seen in years, suddenly surfaced to let me know that he would like to help out with my campaign in any way he could. I told him we would need a campaign headquarters, but, of course, we hadn't raised any money yet. Within days, he had a friend donate a suite of offices. Another prayer answered.

The campaign was beginning to take structure and form. Now, with some sort of campaign organization, I could focus on giving speeches and meeting voters, while others tended to the nuts and bolts of making things work.

In the meantime, the invitations to attend forums kept coming in from all over the district even though I had no primary challenger. It was a great opportunity to continue to meet people and get our name out there. However, it finally sunk in that I was on a whole new level from the old primary days. I was perplexed when my first invitation to be a keynote speaker came in for a Lincoln's Day dinner and auction in one of the northern counties.

"Why in the world would they want me to be their *keynote* speaker?!" I asked my wife with completely sincere and honest surprise. "Surely they could find a *real* speaker. I should just show up, campaign and meet people."

Karen was not amused. "You're a good speaker and you *are* a real speaker. People have been responding to all your talks. You need to start realizing that people do want to hear what you have to say. I'm not just saying this because I'm your wife—you're really good!"

I understood the point she was trying to make, but it was a whole new way of thinking for me. When running for office, a person does have to believe in himself and what he's doing. It's important to have the courage to put yourself in front of the opposition day after day, but I was now also beginning to understand why politicians can get into trouble. If you truly start believing your own campaign literature—watch out. It's the same with athletes and movie stars. The average people out there are often thrilled to meet you, and if you don't take it for what it's worth, your ego can grow by leaps and bounds. Fortunately, I had a career where I consistently received the same type of "celebrity" treatment in my community, so I had practice in not letting it go to my head.

I'm convinced that if a person isn't extremely grounded and doesn't understand their role in the grand scheme of things in life, politics or fame will mess with your thinking. That's why so many politicians develop an attitude that they are "above" everyone else. But unlike movie stars or athletes, it can be a disaster for the country with politicians. They are the ones developing laws and government, but if they are in that poisonous mindset, I believe many lose sight of the common man and what life is like in the real world. Sadly, it only gets worse as the races and offices get bigger. I've always vowed and prayed that if I was ever successful politically, I would never succumb to that mindset. So sometimes, to my wife, it appeared as if I was bending over backward the other way, to avoid displaying arrogance. It was a continuous mental balancing act.

I gratefully accepted the invitation to be their speaker and nervously prepared for my keynote debut. For the first time in all my campaigning experience, I took the time to write out notes about what I would be saying and went over mentally how the speech would be delivered. It was a good crowd of several hundred. They were attentive, enthusiastic, and welcoming. It turned out to be a great experience as, once again, I was interrupted continuously with affirming applause. For the most part, my mental muscle memory took over and I barely looked at the notes. I just talked to a bunch of like-minded voters. It was another good opportunity to hone my speaking and campaigning skills. And, yet again, afterward, we had more activists volunteering to come on board and help us win the seat.

All of this was an evolution of me as a campaigner. I always took it as a point of pride that I needed to be the best campaigner that I could be. I knew that as a serious underdog in this battle, I had to win people over, every opportunity that I got. I made it a point to critique myself and to try and improve with each event. After all, my opponent was a professional politician who'd been doing this for years. If I was going to go head-to-head with the congressman on every stage, I had to be able to communicate and campaign at his level. I took it as my responsibility to improve to the point where we would be on an equal footing, at least in presentation, if nothing else!

One thing that hadn't changed from my past primaries was that I was having to spend time at my business. I was a working class, small business owner, and because I still wasn't financially independent, I had to work to live. However, the pressure on me to campaign was starting to increase, both in my own mind and in those who were manning the campaign around me. It was frustrating to realize that I couldn't be a full-time candidate, but it was what it was. So, I just continued to attend events and talk to as many people as possible, wherever I went, and that included the many customers who came into my retail business.

As the days kept quickly passing along, we got to know the district and began to form a loose organization of enthusiastic volunteers throughout the entire district. It was obvious that we still needed a campaign manager to take things over on a day-to-day basis. I also had to develop a sense of urgency when it came to fundraising, and that was beginning to prove just as difficult as ever. Most of the resistance to donating to our race was based on the absolute ironclad belief that we stood absolutely no chance of winning. And, sadly, I understood that. I didn't like it, but I understood it.

Porter, who I named campaign chairman, was also beating the bushes and contacting all the sources he'd tapped for financial help in past political races. After several weeks, he admitted to me in total exasperation, "I ain't seen nothing like this ever! I can't get *anybody* to get involved financially at all! I don't know what's going on out there, but nobody is willing to donate anything! The best I get is 'maybe later,' and that ain't no good. I always thought I was pretty good at raising money, but, man, this is unbelievable. I could always, at least, get something, but I'm gettin' nothin'!" He said this in a combination of total frustration and simple matter of fact.

I just listened with hidden disappointment. *Here we go again,* I thought. *Lord, please don't let Porter get discouraged and quit.*

However, Porter again proved why he's somebody you want beside you on any battlefield.

"That being said, I ain't giving up. Hell no. I'll just keep on keepin' on. They ain't whupped this ol' boy yet. We'll get it done somehow, some way."

A few weeks later, while talking to another supporter about raising money—and the lack thereof—I discovered there was perhaps something more sinister at work than just the "They've got no chance at winning" syndrome. This revelation turned out to be the most disappointing and frustrating aspect of the entire 2008 campaign.

Potential donors not connected or savvy in politics will often contact the party at the local, state, or even federal level to get information about getting involved or donating money, or just to ask for information about various candidates. A supporter informed me that he knew of at least one wealthy friend that had contacted the Republican Party to inquire about giving to my specific congressional race. The Republican official told him not to waste his money, because "Curnock can't win; he has virtually no chance." He would be just throwing his money away, he was told. Instead, he should support other "winnable" races where his money *would* make a difference.

This supporter told me that his friend was convinced by the party official and ended up *not* donating to my campaign. I heard enough similar stories throughout the campaign to know that, although maybe not organized or officially sanctioned, it was definitely something being done. Maybe they were well-meaning party officials who just didn't realize or care that they were killing all hope *we* had of raising money. I'm sure it made sense from their perspective. They were convinced that they were doing the best thing for the party.

When I combined this new knowledge with my own experiences in the state headquarters the day I filed to run, it all added up. It was bad enough that the party wouldn't help me in this race, but they were, in a sense, actually working against me!

I have to admit, it was crushing to my spirit, but I kept it to myself as much as possible because I didn't want to bring down the spirits of those who had committed to the campaign. It was totally defeating to know that your own party was reportedly undercutting you in a critical race, and, in a way, working against the cause of taking back our country from the Left. My anger and disappointment centered on the fact that, while it's the party's prerogative to withhold all help and support, *for crying out loud*, don't discourage those few who might be willing to join with us.

All I could do was to focus on the things I could control, such as campaigning and meeting voters. And like my campaign chairman Porter said, "This ol' boy may be down, but I ain't whupped yet!"

CHAPTER 28

Pelosi's Gift

There are many ways to run a political race. You can attack, you can go negative, you can stick to issues, you can get personal, or you can ignore your opponent. For Edwards, it was apparent he intended to treat me as *persona non grata*. In essence, from his perspective, I didn't exist. He was the powerful and successfully entrenched incumbent. He had no reason to fear me and every reason to treat me like I was an annoying child meddling in adult affairs that I had no business being involved in. A few early meetings would have put both of us on the same stage, yet he never appeared at those meetings and, instead, sent surrogate speakers to represent him. After all, he was too busy being a congressman. I didn't begrudge him for this style of campaigning; it's just another strategy.

According to his FEC financial reports, he was also doing some high political networking. He had close to $3 million in the bank with donations coming in from wealthy donors and national PACs from all over the country and made it a point to help other Democrat candidates in other parts of the country. If you can spread your own war chest around, you're not a candidate worried about your own political life. In fact, he was evidently looking to take advantage of that time-honored tradition of creating political IOUs. Those come in especially handy if you aspire to higher political offices. It displays a mindset exuding supreme confidence that his own seat was not in jeopardy in the slightest. It's called hubris. And in this case, in his position, from his perspective, based on my status as an opponent, it was probably warranted.

Still, we were hoping that we could find something that would change the dynamics. It was not necessarily for my own personal well-being, or even the psyche of the volunteers. The main reason we needed something, anything, to change the dynamics was to get the campaign to be taken seriously by financial donors. As long as we were perceived as a hopelessly irrelevant cause, no financial heavy hitters were going to grace us with their dollars.

I'm sure that as David was walking out to meet Goliath, there probably wasn't a whole lot of wagering going David's way. The same was obviously happening here. We could get the average activists to come on board, but the party and its connected donor base was another story. My job was to figure out some way to change the way those people saw our race. And quite honestly, there really was no way I could do that. I needed a miracle.

At this time, all we could do was just soldier on and pray for some sort of divine intervention. It took a while, but eventually my prayers were answered. And, yes, God works in mysterious ways. The unforeseen miracle finally came through for me several weeks later as the national presidential primary was unfolding—on the Democratic side!

Barack Obama came out of nowhere. He was taking the Democrats and the presumptive nominee Hillary Clinton by storm. In a political party where everything is based on politically correct group-based values, in this case, race was trumping gender. Soon, the divided Democrat leadership was beginning to think that Obama was going to win, and they had to start looking beyond the primaries.

While on a national talk show, Nancy Pelosi was asked who Obama should consider for his vice-presidential running mate. Out of the blue, she answered that she would recommend *Congressman*

Chet Edwards of Texas. Yes, the same Edwards that I was now challenging for this District 17 seat.

It's always psychologically hazardous to try and follow the logic of the thinking of Pelosi, but one has to assume that, in her mind, Edwards was a good ally of hers. And from her lofty far-off point of view in Washington, D.C., Edwards was an extremely popular congressman who was continually winning in a heavily Republican district. So, of course, one would assume, her logic goes, as a southern white male from Texas, he would be the perfect geographical and sociological balance for the first black man realistically trying to win the White House.

Whatever her logic, the cat was now out of the bag. In typical Washington echo chamber fashion, the stated vice-presidential choice of the Democrat Speaker of the House took on a life of its own, and Edwards was now firmly ensconced as a highly touted potential running mate for Obama.

For *my* average supporter, this was devastating news. How could I ever hope to compete with a potential vice president? For the political pundits both in and out of the district, this was just another confirmation that the powerful Edwards was truly a force to be reckoned with, and now he had national stature. I'm sure for many casual observers, the thought was, "If it wasn't required by law, why even bother holding the election? This is basically just a waste of Chet's time. He's got more important things to deal with than spending time on a re-election campaign against an unknown, unfunded, and unsupported opponent."

As word began to get around the district, I was approached by more than a few folks who meant well but were sincerely crushed by the newfound national stature of my opponent. It was all in the same vein:

"This has to make things much more difficult for you, doesn't it?"

"Now that Chet might run as Obama's vice president, you've got to feel like he can't be beaten."

"Are you okay? Edwards now has the entire Democrat Party behind him."

"I don't see how you're going to deal with this."

"It sure gives him a lot of credibility and major stature. That can't be good for you."

I would stun them with my sincere response. "This is the best thing I could've hoped for. I'm thrilled!"

And then I explained to everyone who would listen:

"Obama is as liberal as they come. He's a dedicated Socialist with zero chance of winning Texas or, more importantly, this district. Pelosi has just outed Edwards as someone who would be politically acceptable to the philosophy of Obama. Therefore, Edwards can no longer try to pass himself off as a conservative. Edwards would never admit it, and those conservative ticket splitters who support him would give me very little credibility since I'm his opponent. But, they *will* believe Nancy Pelosi when she identifies and promotes one of her own. Edwards just got his longtime, carefully maintained "conservative" cover ripped away by Pelosi, and he's now tied to the radical leftist Obama. Finally, after eighteen years, people in this district will see that the emperor has no clothes! This is tremendous!"

The coming months would prove my theory and prognostication to be absolutely on target. Edwards may have been basking in the glow of his newfound gravitas on the national level, but on the local level, he was bleeding badly. Although not clearly evident to most pols at the time, he would eventually succumb to this grievous "honor" bestowed upon him by his friend Pelosi.

All of this charged me internally and stoked my competitive fires. There was no turning back now. There was no sticking my head in the sand and hoping for the best come Election Day.

Nancy Pelosi had handed me that fifth smooth stone.

CHAPTER 29

Trouble on Board

I needed a campaign manager but faced an incredible Catch-22. I wanted a professional to strategize and help raise money, but I had no money to pay a professional. On top of that, I was the political equivalent of an untouchable. The political professional cadre of consultants and campaign chairmen is a close-knit community, and no one of any substance was going to get involved in this "no-win" situation. The pros build their reputations on success and a winning track record. I spent many a night wide awake trying to figure out how to solve this conundrum.

Porter oversaw operations on a part-time basis while continuing to manage his own business, but even he was adamant that we had to find someone to take over. My first primary campaign manager was not an option. Unfortunately, I lost touch with my second campaign manager when she moved away. Besides, this race had a different feel to it. We needed to take it up another notch. At the end of the day, though, we could only do what we could do with the resources we had, which were little. At this late juncture, I had to find a solution.

Then, after many sleepless nights, I had an epiphany. In the coming months—even years—I would find out that it was more of a nightmare.

A long-time friend from out of state had sold his business and was recovering from surgery, essentially spending his time healing.

I'd known him for a long time and knew that, for the most part, he was in the same political camp as me. I wondered if he might not be interested in running the campaign while he recovered, if it wouldn't be too physically demanding. It would give him something to keep his mind occupied, get him involved in politics—which he loved—and it would give us somebody to oversee day-to-day operations. I thought it would be a win-win situation.

I ran the idea past Karen and my uncle. Both knew Randall, and both expressed some reservations, but agreed that if those issues were addressed, he might be a solution to our dilemma.

I called Randall and laid out my proposal for him to come to Waco and help me with this major, high-profile political campaign. I asked him if this was something he could handle physically, and if he understood what it would take to do something like this. He insisted he did, citing his experience with other political campaigns and the media. He affirmed that he could also handle non-demanding physical duties in the office. The more we talked, the more he appeared anxious to give it a go—but only if all his expenses were taken care of, including at least three trips back home before the November election to deal with personal issues. I thought this was reasonable and knew the campaign should eventually have enough money to be able to at least handle his expenses, so I agreed. He wanted to give it some final thought and would call me back as soon as possible with an answer.

I hung up thinking it appeared that we might have finally solved our campaign manager problem.

When he called back in a couple of days, I expected him to say he was on his way down. Instead, he blindsided me by his qualified answer. He said he would come to Waco, but *only* if we would pay him a significant amount of money based on a sliding scale he laid out. And this was on top of all other expenses being met. I was stunned and disappointed. In hindsight, I wish I would have said no thanks and just hung up. However, my options were limited.

"But, Randall, you know we don't have any money. That's our number one problem. We can't afford to pay *anyone* right now, at least not until we raise some significant money. And from what you're asking for, at this point, we'd have to turn everything over to you and would have nothing left for the campaign. We just can't do it," I said, completely deflated.

Out of curiosity, I asked, "And how did you even come up with those specific numbers?"

"After we talked, I called a buddy who ran *my* congressman's campaign. He told me what an experienced professional campaign manager gets paid for a congressional campaign, so that's what I want," he responded.

"But you're not an experienced campaign manager; you've never actually run a campaign—have you?"

"No, I've never officially run a campaign, but I was involved in enough others to know what needs to be done. Besides, that's why I'm asking for less than what he told me. I know I can do the job, and that's what you need, right?"

"But, Randall, we don't have any money right now. We have to raise money before we can pay you."

"That's part of the job. I'll oversee raising the money we need to win the seat."

"You'll raise the money? How? It's been very difficult raising money for this deal. It won't be easy. Have you raised money before?"

"Sure, I've been involved in numerous fundraisers. I'm actually pretty good at raising money." I could tell he was getting irritated.

"So, you're saying you can raise the money we'll need to pay you and fund the campaign?" I asked skeptically.

He was now fully annoyed. "Yes, Rob, I told you that's part of the job. I know a lot of ways to raise money. If you know what the **** you're doing—and I do—we'll get the money. The bottom line is, you need a campaign manager and you're running out of time. You need to get off your a** and make a decision to get this thing going."

"Well, if you can raise the money to pay yourself, then that's the deal. But you have to raise the money, and I want you to understand how hard it is to raise money against Edwards."

He was now totally ticked.

"I can raise the g**da**ed money. Stop acting like a little sh**, say yes, and let's get to work!"

We'd been long-distance friends for twenty-eight years, and since he was older he had always treated me like an exasperating little brother. We shared common interests like sports and politics, and we got together infrequently when I visited that area.

Yet his attitude toward me was one of the issues Karen and my uncle were concerned about.

"Alright, alright. Let me talk to Karen and Porter, my campaign chairman, and get back to you."

"Hurry up—time's wasting!"

Karen and I were taken aback that he would turn this thing into a potential money-making arrangement for him. But, in the end, we both agreed that if he could raise the money and run the campaign, things would work out the way we needed. We arranged a date for Randall to come down, found him a donated place to live, and joyfully celebrated that we had solved our campaign manager problem.

It turned out to be the worst decision I'd ever make in this campaign or any other.

Randall quickly set about getting the campaign moving forward, but, in return, he wanted complete control in every aspect--in essence, obedience from me, my wife, and all volunteers. The personal "issues" I had hoped were under control were absolutely out of control. Over the coming months, our gracious women volunteers in the office soon began to grumble and chafe about his authoritarian ways, and some stopped coming in altogether or would only come in with the stipulation that they would have nothing to do with Randall while working in the office, and things just kept getting worse.

Unbeknownst to me at the time, we even had three female volunteers complain of mild sexual harassment or improper sexual comments. I was not told by any of the women involved until well after the fact, probably to shield and protect me from the unpleasant situation. The volunteers just quietly stopped working directly in the office.

My relationship with Randall quickly deteriorated. He continued to treat me like an annoying little brother who needed to be constantly corrected and controlled. If he didn't get whatever he wanted, whenever he wanted, he would threaten to quit. This happened three times in the first month or so. My wife, in tears, and I would then do everything possible to keep him from quitting.

The situation took an emotional toll on both of us and our young marriage. Randall pitted Karen against me by emotionally manipulating her into thinking that I was not looking out for her best interests, but that only *he* truly was. When I pointed out his manipulation of her, she got mad at me. It took a couple of months, but Karen eventually realized what was happening and broke free of the hold Randall had on her. But like the other ladies in the office, she wanted no more to do with him, except when absolutely necessary.

The situation came to a breaking point when one of our first and most valuable volunteers, also our scheduler, had a conflict with Randall. He didn't like a flyer she had created for an event and felt that he needed to personally approve anything that went out from the campaign. While Randall's position did have merit, clearly his people skills were utterly lacking. This particular volunteer was no shrinking violet herself and was forceful in her own way, and she was absolutely key to what we'd been doing right from the start. She had even donated most of the furniture and desks for our office.

When I explained the delicate nature of the situation to Randall, I might as well have been talking to a wall. He was unmoved and adamant that she was out of line, and he wouldn't tolerate it. He then slammed me by saying that I was wrong for not backing him in this matter. The situation between the two of them escalated quickly and turned ugly. She went to her long-time good friend Porter, still the campaign chairman. She was ready to quit and wanted all her furniture back. Now.

Porter, who'd been with us from the start, had been privy to the dynamics between Randall and many of the volunteer staff, and had already had a few run-ins with him as well. In fact, as a result, he was now even staying clear of the campaign office for the most part, letting Randall run the show.

But now, Porter had finally had enough of Randall.

Already furious at him, Porter told this volunteer that Randall was wrong, and he would send workers from his own personal company over to move her furniture out, immediately. Porter then called me and told me that Randall had to go.

In hindsight, the correct course of action is obvious, but at the time I thought, *As bad as Randall is, how can we possibly get by without a campaign manager?*" I was like an enabling spouse in an abusive relationship; I couldn't see the totality of the situation. Yet I knew Porter was ready to walk. This was bad.

Porter and the volunteer still believed in me, the campaign, and what we were trying to accomplish, but *not* with Randall in the mix. It was him or them. Period. Porter agreed that he and I would meet with Randall the next day.

Before Porter arrived, I got there first and sat across the desk from Randall that would very likely be disappearing if this wasn't resolved immediately. I explained to him that, although the flyers were not perfect, they were for one small event.

"If it makes her and Porter happy, let it slide," I implored him.

Once again, Randall was unmoved. He then turned it around and berated me for not backing him. This was not good, and it was about to get a whole lot worse.

Porter soon arrived and came in loaded for bear. For whatever reason, he was no longer calm. He was so mad his face was blood red and his eyes were blazing. In his hand was a copy of a biting letter Randall had sent to the volunteer in question, telling her why she was wrong and needed to leave these matters to him. Porter forcefully pulled up a chair across the desk from Randall. Porter is a bear of a man and I feared that this could quickly turn violent. You would think that Randall, physically half the man that Porter was, would assess the situation and realize he was in imminent danger of getting beat up.

You would think wrong. Randall did not back down.

I was stunned and at a point of quiet panic as I mentally searched for something to say to alleviate the situation. I could think of no words that would not result in Porter quitting, or Randall quitting, and I was sure the campaign desperately needed them both. The verbal battle continued as I watched in disbelief at what I was witnessing.

I'm convinced that even Solomon would scratch his head over this one.

As the conversation grew more intense, it was obvious that Porter was getting physically wound up. I felt that it was a matter of seconds before I was going to have to somehow physically restrain him.

Suddenly, Porter stopped mid-sentence. *Here it comes*, I thought, ready to lunge and corral him. But, while glaring with a look that could kill the average human, he just furiously wadded up the letter and threw it squarely in Randall's face.

I was shocked, yet strangely relieved, that that was as bad as it apparently was going to get. Randall sat stone still, unmoving, and said nothing more as he just looked at Porter with dead eyes. Porter stood up.

"Listen, boy, never come near me again or I'll beat your scrawny little ass."

Porter stormed out.

After a few moments of stunned silence, I was finally able to speak. "Randall, we need Porter. We've got to get him back."

Incredibly, he ignored what I said and instead, laid into me for not backing *him*. I listened for a few minutes and left knowing I had some serious damage control ahead of me.

I met with Porter at his office a couple of days later after heads cooled. He let me know how disappointed he was in me for not backing *him*. As long as Randall was in the campaign, he was out, he told me. I apologized and finally got him to agree to stay on as campaign chairman and help however he could from the outside, with the understanding he would no longer have any contact with Randall. It was a toxic situation, but as long as their paths never crossed, it was the best I could hope for.

I also spoke with the volunteer scheduler, who affirmed her support of me in my effort to depose Chet. But she assured me that Randall was a major problem I had to eliminate. Unfortunately, she followed through on her threat to remove all her office furniture. Fortunately, other volunteers quickly donated furniture to keep things working. It was a sign that all was not well in the campaign hierarchy.

It's reasonable to expect the candidate to take responsibility for controlling the situation, and I *could have* resolved it better. However, some things are not in a candidate's complete control. The greatest asset of a campaign can be its volunteers, but the greatest liability can also be…its volunteers. They're all human and a volatile mix for any number of reasons. The key is to handle volunteers like they are your greatest asset and treat them as such. Randall was unwilling to trouble himself with such niceties.

As crazy as it seems, the campaign volunteers and I settled into an uneasy truce of sorts with Randall. As the summer progressed, we were getting more and more speaking events that I had to focus on. The volunteers manning the office understood the situation and focused on their duties. Randall was essentially pigeonholed to minimize potential damage and conflicts. That being said, he could also be charming and personable when he wanted to be, and, for the most part, he played nice.

As a testament to the odd relationship that I had with Randall, one strange situation did eventually have to be resolved. His habit of demeaning me continued, and not just when alone. I had never let the big brother/little brother dynamic bother me because I just didn't care enough. However, ever since he had first arrived, he had made a habit of being extremely critical of me and quick to denigrate me as a person to the volunteers in the office. It could be anything that I did or didn't do that might set him off, such as not wearing the right colored shirt that he had wanted me to wear, and then criticize me to anyone within earshot. He would go off about me to whomever was in the office--that I was a terrible candidate who wouldn't listen to anybody, and that I'd been like that as long as he'd known me. Volunteers noticed, and several came forward to voice their discomfort with his attitude. I realized that, although I didn't care personally, volunteers were a different story. The uneasy truce was going to have to be broken. It was the first time I would lose my temper with Randall.

Karen and I reluctantly agreed that it had to be stopped. We finally went to the campaign office one day, chatted with the volunteers for a few minutes, then I approached Randall while Karen retreated back to socialize with the volunteers. "Can I talk to you for a minute in your office?"

"Sure, what's up?"

As we walked in, I closed the door. "We've got a problem and we've had a problem for a while now. And it needs to stop right now."

"What are you talking about?"

"Look, you and I go back a long way, and you've always treated me...well, the way you've always treated me. I can deal with that, but you absolutely *cannot* badmouth me in front of the volunteers or voters," I said in a loud whisper to keep the conversation in the confines of his office.

"I don't know what you're talking about," he protested.

"We've had several volunteers come—reluctantly—to Karen and me saying how they don't think it's right the way you talk about me."

"I only say things when you don't listen to me," he said, quickly going on the offensive. "I tell you what needs to be done, and you ignore me; you spend more time at your business than you do here; you think you know it all, and you won't listen to me; you won't listen to anybody. I'm sick of your s***. If you don't want to do what needs to be done to win, then why am I wasting my freaking time down here?"

I snapped.

Three months of pent-up frustrations came out like a fury, but I still kept enough composure to remember there were other people in other parts of the office.

"Listen, you jerk," I whispered as forcefully as I could. "Do you not have a clue what's going on here?! I'm not just your stupid little buddy from up north. We're in the middle of an important congressional campaign, and, like it or not, I'm the candidate!"

He was taken aback by the ferocity of my verbal attack and settled back in his chair, staring at me.

"I don't care how you talk to me in private, but when you're in front of these volunteers or people who may be voting for me, you're talking to people who look at me as their potential congressman, not some stupid idiot who won't follow your orders. I don't care if you believe it or not, but in front of these others, you have got to show me respect. You can't badmouth me, cut me down, curse me, or blast me anymore in front of them. If you've got a problem with me, bring it to me. If you can't do that, then you need to just clear out of here. I mean it. I've had it."

He just sat sullenly, staring at me. He didn't say a word.

Still whispering, but more calmly, I added, "We've got good people here working to help us, and when you cut me down, they've got to start asking themselves, why bother showing up to work for a guy who's no good, according to his own campaign manager?! I mean it, Randall. We can't have this anymore. Are we good?"

He still said nothing, but his posture retreated. A new truce was enacted.

I went back to a normal speaking voice about some unrelated innocuous campaign question, just to bring it back to some sense of civility. We both continued on as if nothing had happened. In fact, he was downright pleasant the rest of the time we were there.

We settled back into somewhat of a normal campaign routine. Randall attempted to raise money and garner other support. He was at times congenial and seemed to be working hard, but not a lot was being accomplished. He was unable to raise a single dime on his own, which he had assured us, before coming, would be his strong suit. He adamantly proclaimed he would get us the money we needed to pay him for his work.

He once spent two entire days working on a critique of a speech I gave at a Right to Life meeting the Sunday before. The hundred or so people at the luncheon loved it and responded very positively, with us garnering a lot more overall support. But to Karen's and my surprise, Randall didn't like the way I had organized my extemporaneous remarks. He wanted me to start scripting out all my speeches, with his prior approval, so that I would only be saying the things he designated as our campaign "message."

Randall asked to go back home a few times, as we had agreed to cover his costs. We secretly hoped he wouldn't come back. He also asked for funds to cover certain personal expenses which, although not obligated, I agreed to, as he had raised no funds to pay himself a salary. At the time, we thought of it as just being gracious.

I compartmentalized the Randall situation as much as possible, so we could focus on the real task at hand—defeating Edwards. This campaign was not supposed to be about Randall, and looking at it from the outside, an observer might wonder why I would keep this man in the campaign. However, as we progressed through the summer, we came to the conclusion that getting rid of Randall could potentially cause more harm than good. Most likely he would not go quietly. At least, while he was in the campaign, we could exert influence over him. We determined that we had to move on as best we could, operating under the philosophy of letting sleeping dogs lie.

While something might seem like a blessing at the time, it can become a disaster. The campaign continued on, but it was handicapped with dysfunctional leadership. Even if my own field general was tangling up the strings of my sling, I had to focus on the approaching battle. Goliath was still out there, waiting.

CHAPTER 30

Financial Follies

Fundraising was our most pressing issue. We just could not get the traditional major Republican givers to come on board. Yes, we were raising small amounts from the faithful rank and file, but the big donors who can truly make things happen by giving the maximum federal donations just would not get involved. It was as if there was some invisible force field around us which would repel most potential major donors. It was truly heartwarming and gratifying to see the small donations coming in from the working-class activists and small business owners, but we needed the regular, maximum donors. We eventually made the decision to hire a professional fundraiser out of Austin.

It was my first glimpse into the real world of big-time politics. The lady we hired had a good reputation and we decided we had to spend the money to raise the money. I was one of several clients, but she was willing to take us on, as Edwards was still considered an arch enemy of the Texas Republican Party, and it couldn't hurt to see if possibly lightening could strike and I would pull off the upset. Besides, we agreed to pay her fee, so she had nothing to lose. I thought, *Finally, now somebody will make things happen. I don't know how, and I don't care, as long as we start getting some serious money in here.*

She sent one of her associates to Waco to meet with me and lay out how we would make it work. I was expecting big things to happen when he pulled out a thick stack of papers filled with hundreds of names, phone numbers, and addresses.

"These are all substantial donors throughout the state who make it a habit, and are on record, of giving maximum donations to various campaigns in Texas," he told me.

Alright, now this is what we're talking about!

I crashed back to reality when he started coaching me on things to say when I asked for money from these people.

"Uh, okay, that makes sense, but... I'm the one asking these people for money?" I asked, somewhat hesitantly, not wanting him to think that I was clueless as to how it's normally done.

"Well, yes, you're the candidate. That's *your* job," he said politely and with no hint of sarcasm.

"Sure, that makes sense, but I probably don't know any of these people, and they won't know me. Isn't that going to make it difficult?" I asked sincerely. "I assumed you knew them and would ask for the contributions with me standing by if they wanted or needed to talk to me."

"Oh no, we find it's absolutely critical that you're the one asking for the money. After all, you're the one who's running for Congress. They'll want to talk to you. They'll want to hear you speak. You need to sell yourself, just like you do with every voter you meet. Just from my short time meeting with you, I can tell you'll do fine. You've got a good personality and are comfortable talking to people. You'll be good," he said cheerfully.

"Okay, so how do--"

He cut me off. "Just start at the top of each sheet and work your way down the list. Here's the phone numbers and any pertinent information, like their secretary's name or their spouses' names. Do as many as you can. Set a goal, maybe ten or fifteen a day. Don't get discouraged if you don't get success right away. It's a numbers game, so you have to stay with it. That's part of your job if you want to be in Congress. You'd better get used to it," he laughed.

"Yeah, ha ha." My weak laugh tailed off.

"I can tell this is all new to you, but this is how it works. We're making this very valuable list available to you; that's what you're paying for. It's your job as the candidate to take advantage of it. Trust me, you'll do great. If you have any issues, just call me and I'll be glad to help. Why don't you try some with me here? It won't be so bad; you'll see."

I looked through the first page and was taken aback by what I saw. Half of the names on the first page alone were like a list of who's who in entertainment, business, and sports. I saw people on the list whom I'd heard about throughout my life: the quarterback I had idolized growing up, the guy who started one of the biggest corporations in America, a former governor of Texas, a woman whose organization was always in the news. I was staring at their home and business addresses, phone numbers, email contacts, and other private information. I was slightly intimidated and in awe.

"You want me to cold call?" I gulped with fear and true surprise. "They don't know me from Adam. Why would they even talk to me?"

"Rob, they do it all the time. They know they're on these lists, and they expect calls from candidates, but they won't give unless they hear from you personally. Go ahead; start with the first name."

I did what he said, but I was having flashbacks to my old single days when well-meaning people would attempt to set me up with a girl. I always internally rolled my eyes when someone would say, "You need to call so-and-so. She's *really* nice and you two would hit it off perfectly!"

"How do you know?" I would ask curiously.

"Because you're both wonderful and would make such a perfect couple together, and I absolutely know she'd like you."

"She's told you that?!"

"Well, no…but I've known her forever, and you'd be perfect together. Just call her and introduce yourself. Let me give you her number."

"So she doesn't know you're giving out her number? She doesn't even know who I am?!"

"Well, not yet, but that won't matter. You two would be great together. Stop being silly and call her!"

Yeah, right.

I wanted to be positive, but I sensed it was doomed. With my fundraising mentor sitting across the desk from me, I dialed the first number. No answer; the call went to an answering machine. With an approving nod from across the desk, I left a brief message stating who I was, what I was doing, and said I would call back.

"You'll get that. You handled it perfectly. Let's do another," he said.

I reached a real person on my third call. It took some serious explaining as to who I was and why I was calling. The man finally said he'd send me a check. I hung up and we were both pleased. "That's how it works. Just keep dialing and asking." With that, he headed back to Austin.

That was the high-water mark. It was nearly impossible to actually speak to anyone on the list. If I was lucky, I got an aide or possibly a spouse. But the vast majority of humans that I did talk to— while friendly—were skeptical and didn't understand why I would be calling them for a race in Waco. It was exactly what I feared.

It was an impressive list of names, but these were not the type of people you were going to get through to with a cold call. I was living my nightmare from my dating life. They didn't know me and had no reason to help me, unless someone *they* knew paved the way with a recommendation. Still, I soldiered on, not wanting to be perceived as a failure or unwilling to do what it took to successfully raise money. I never did get to talk to any of the impressive people upon first glance at the list. All told, I ended up with one commitment that actually came through with a significant check.

And that very first man that promised to send a check? It never came.

I called a couple of hundred names over the next couple of weeks before finally, reluctantly, giving up and focusing on campaigning. At the end of the day, I didn't even raise enough to cover the professional fundraiser's basic fee. So, sadly, I lost money and a lot of time on my first foray into big-time political fundraising. I don't know if it was me or the methods this particular professional fundraiser was using, but I wouldn't go down that road again.

Still, the financial pressure was building exponentially, and not just because we needed money to conduct campaign operations. At this point we were relying almost exclusively on volunteers and not yet doing any advertising or mailings. We were driving hundreds of miles in a day, and with gas exceeding four dollars per gallon, fuel costs alone were becoming a serious burden. I usually paid for gas myself, just to spare the campaign at least *that* growing expense.

I often joked with close friends and supporters that the only way I was going to raise money was if I started to wear a mask and carry a gun. It was my sardonic humor belying a real problem. We were at the point where almost all we could do was try and laugh about where things stood. It was mental survival. On a positive note, those who did give to us were absolutely committed to us. They weren't just writing a check and going on about their business. They bought into our campaign cause and that involved an emotional tie as well.

I reverted to raising money the way we had been doing it before. It wasn't extremely successful, but at least we were getting something. Still, the pressure to raise funds was intense, especially when you know you're soon going to be laid bare and open for ridicule by the Federal Election Commission and the local newspapers.

A congressional campaign is required by law to file a financial report every quarter. This report is made public and can make or break a campaign. It tells how much money you've raised and who's given it to you. That's why federal campaigns live or die with these numbers, which become a public record after each reporting period. A candidate's viability is largely determined by the amount of money raised as reported to the FEC. If your campaign can't show significant or successful dollar numbers, it becomes a self-fulfilling prophecy. In other words, if donors see that you've raised very little money, they assume something is wrong with the candidate or the campaign, and nobody wants to give to a candidate that's not viable. And it just doesn't matter why or for whatever reason. That's why the campaign fundraising numbers, in essence, become a contest of their own. Our political system has become fixated on the "competition" of who's raised the most money overall. And in politics, perception usually becomes reality.

Each approaching FEC reporting deadline was like facing a firing squad. The first overall reporting period in the cycle could be excused because we were just getting started, but by the second reporting period, we were in a dismal and embarrassing financial shape. And in this district, the major newspapers, which were in full protection mode for the incumbent, were almost gleeful in their front-page trumpeting of the current financial "race" for Congress.

"Edwards, the incumbent, is nearing $3 million with donations coming in from major PACs and donors from all over the country. Heck, he's even donating to other Democrat campaigns around the country! Curnock, the challenger, has raised almost (*snicker*) $40,000 from exclusively small donors, mainly within the district."

The papers seemed to be admonishing donor prospects in a not-so-subtle fashion: "Move along potential donors; there's nothing viable to see here." And if I was in their shoes, I'd think the same thing.

I have no doubt the Biblical Philistines had a good laugh when the small boy carrying only a sling walked out to face their giant champion. The problem for the Philistines was that they didn't know what that small boy knew.

Yes, we were devastated, but apart from the financial campaign, I was seeing something that no one else saw--not reporters, not supporters, and certainly not Edwards. At least, evidently, not until he did his own internal polling.

CHAPTER 31

Turning Tide

The official campaign calendar was increasingly filled with parades, meetings, forums, media events, and even a few rare fundraisers. On the surface, it looked like a typical challenger campaign. The powerful incumbent spent the bulk of his time just "working hard" at his congressional job, while the challenger ran around the district trying to get noticed and heard. Our paths never crossed until September, so voters would see me alone or in a few forums with an Edwards' surrogate. That scenario allowed me to concentrate solely on getting my message out without the clutter of rebuttal or denial from the incumbent. Eventually, we would have to be on the same stage.

The most common campaign events in small rural towns are parades. I've never been a parade person. I don't like watching them, and I certainly didn't want to be in one. But whenever one was coming up anywhere in the district, my lady volunteers were adamant that we needed to be there. They would throw themselves into the planning with full-throated commitment and joyful resolve, not only getting ready with candy and flyers to be handed out along the parade route, but they would gladly sign up to walk or ride along with Karen and me. To my chagrin, parades became a staple of the campaign, and I didn't relish the thought of riding or walking a couple of miles in 95-degree heat under a pounding Texas summer sun.

Over the July 4th holiday, the campaign had to make a decision on how we would work it. There were parades all over the district, and it would've been physically impossible to be in them all, so we wound up having surrogate volunteers present in some smaller parades in the southern part of the district, while I would participate in three larger parades in the northern counties. It would be hot, long, and tiring, but everyone on my team was committed, so we went for it. We actually had a great response, and I actually had a good time meeting people.

That being said, I have to admit I always dreaded the parades, right up until we got there. But once I got involved, I genuinely found that it was kind of fun. We never had any negative reactions, and, for the most part, most parade viewers were pretty supportive of our attempt to make a change in Congress. I had many opportunities to talk with a lot of people along the way because I made it a point of cheerfully engaging anyone who engaged me, or even appeared slightly willing to talk to me. I almost always got out of our various decorated vehicles and went on foot with our volunteer "walkers," working both sides of the street. I did it for a couple of reasons. First of all, if all my volunteers were on foot, I would be on foot. Secondly, I always thought sitting in a vehicle and just waving was kind of elitist—even if you were talking directly to people from your vehicle. Either way, I made it work and really did get a good reaction from the locals.

One unforeseen benefit of parades was a chance to campaign before and after them. That half hour or so in which you were expected to be early for purposes of lining up was a perfect opportunity to meet local residents. That included all elected officials from that particular county or town. It was during these times that I began to suspect something special was happening in our district.

On numerous occasions, in different small towns in various counties, it became clear to me that the congressional incumbent's hold on the local elected officials of *either* party was beginning to slip. To understand why, you had to understand the lay of the land. On the national level, Obama was moving steadily on to the Democratic presidential nomination, and Edwards was now firmly one of the top prospects as his potential vice-presidential running mate. These rural counties are the backbone of conservative Texas, and Obama might as well have been the Antichrist. These were exactly the people whom Obama would so casually dismiss and insult later on with his derisive attack on them for "bitterly clinging to their Bibles and their guns."

The Left wanted to claim that this dislike of Obama was race-based, coming from a bunch of redneck bigots who couldn't stand the thought of a black man in the White House. If that mindset existed, I personally never witnessed it. In this campaign, the only real animosity that I personally saw toward Obama stemmed from the fact that he was absolutely the most liberal candidate to ever seriously make a run for the White House. If there were any racial considerations, I heard virtually nothing along those lines. This man ran on the promise that he wanted to fundamentally "transform" America. He was a blatant Socialist who, although denying that label, accidentally admitted to Joe the Plumber, in a rare moment of unguarded honesty, that he wanted to "spread the wealth around."

These were the issues that had the average constituent in Central Texas scared to death of an Obama presidency. And Edwards was now tied to him.

That being said, Edwards was still the sitting congressman and, for many of the small, rural, and poor counties, he was the equivalent of the federal godfather. Many of these counties also represented the last vestiges of the days when Democrats held complete sway in Texas. In these rural counties, you still had to be a Democrat to hold office, so, amazingly, you'd have conservative sheriffs, justices of the peace, county commissioners, mayors, councilmen, county judges, all the way down the ballot to constables, who were Democrat. But even as the ranks of Republican office holders slowly grew, both Democrats and Republicans had to work with the congressman for federal funding and assistance in day-to-day operations. And for many of these smaller, poorer counties, those federal dollars were important, and the congressman was the bagman. That's why few local elected officials were willing to openly go against the incumbent.

And not by chance.

One rural county Republican county judge was brave enough to openly throw his support to me, but he explained from his own experience why it was hard for most county executives to take a stand. He related how that, shortly after he was elected, a congressional aide from Edwards' office came calling at his office in the county courthouse.

"He walked in like he owned the place, sat down right there in the chair you're sitting in, leaned back, folded his hands across the back of his head and asked me, 'What can the congressman do for you?'

"I was stunned by the blatant arrogance of this guy, but I asked him, 'What do you mean?'

"He smiled like he knew something I didn't and repeated it.

"'What does the county need? What can Congressman Edwards get for you from Washington? Just tell me and he'll get it done. That's what he can do for you if you work with him.'"

I could picture the pathetic scene. "So, what'd you say?"

"You'd a been proud of me, Rob. I leaned forward in my chair and looked him straight in the eye and said, 'How about giving me back some of my tax dollars that you all keep raising and taking from me. That's what I want from the congressman.'"

I laughed. "What'd he do?"

"He was stunned. I don't think he'd ever heard that before, because he didn't know what to say. He just quickly got up and told me that if I ever needed anything to not hesitate to call their office. I've never seen him since and I haven't called them either. But that's what's wrong with this country; everybody's got their hand out, and that's how congressmen like Edwards stay in office. Everybody's afraid to cross 'em, or they suck up to 'em, to get things they want. That's not how I work."

His anecdote perfectly mirrored my own experience in politics when it came to Democrat voters and their expectations from their elected office holders. It's the small-minded and selfish "What are you going to give me?" philosophy of politics. I left his office smiling because, I have to admit, I was extremely proud of that judge. He was a man of principle. This man was an elected official who could have used federal dollars for his own local community. The only thing that's going to save this country is for more people like him to be in positions of authority.

The judge was bravely willing to take a stand and publicly support the Republican underdog challenger in spite of the common wisdom that Edwards could not lose. For the first several months of the campaign, both Democrat and even some Republican local elected officials kept me at arm's length. Oh, they were polite enough when our paths crossed, but I could tell from experience that, even among most of these Republicans, there was no help coming for me or my attempt at getting rid of Edwards. Sadly, in some cases, their tacit support for Edwards was even poorly camouflaged.

But a funny thing began to happen all around the district at various functions. It may have been subtle, but I was beginning to suspect that some elected officials were making the decision to break free of the status quo support of Edwards.

The first clear evidence caught me by surprise as we were waiting to begin a parade in a small town in a rural county. While talking with several folks before lining up for the parade, a decorated car with magnetic signs announcing who was inside, pulled up nearby. It was a county office holder. I could tell by the reaction of the folks I was talking with that the people in the car were of some importance locally. An older man and woman were in the front seat, and the man called me over by name.

"Hey, Rob, just wanted to introduce myself to you," he said loudly past his wife who was sitting in the passenger seat. I left the little group I was talking to and made my way to the passenger side window, which was rolled down. He stuck out his hand to be shaken as he also introduced his wife, whom I was now standing over as I reached into the car and shook his hand. He lowered his voice so that just the three of us could hear the conversation.

"You probably don't know me, but I know you from television. I've been an elected county official for the last thirty years, and before that, my daddy was the county judge. My family goes way back in the Democratic Party. Everybody knows me and my family around these parts."

"It certainly is a pleasure to meet you and to know you were watching," I joked. "I know we're on the other side of the fence politically, but I sure hope you'll consider giving me at least a thought in the congressional race."

He then looked me in the eye and said, "Oh, we're gonna do more than that. Let me tell you something. I've been a Democrat all my life and I ain't lyin'. Even though the national party's lost its way, I've stayed a Democrat outta habit, but I'm darned sure conservative. I proudly supported Chet ever since he first got elected as our state senator all the way up to last year. I always thought he was a conservative, but now it's pretty clear he ain't what he claims to be. If Nancy Pelosi thinks Edwards would make a good vice president for Obama, then he damned sure ain't no conservative."

I was caught a little off guard, but I liked where this seemed to be heading.

"I can't do anything publicly because of the position I'm in, but you've got my support. No yard signs or bumper stickers, though."

"I understand," I said trying not to smile too big.

"I want you to know my word carries some weight around here, and when I tell certain folks that I'm supporting you, it means somethin'. I know it won't be easy but get out there and beat him. Hopefully, you'll get back up our way once you're the congressman."

"I appreciate that, and I'll do my best. I'm truly honored for your trust. It means a lot to me."

We shook hands again as he drove off to line up. Some of the crowd I had left earlier was still standing there. When I walked back to them, they were all excited.

"Did he say he was behind you?" asked one, as the others nodded in agreement and anxiously waited for my answer.

"It does seem that way," I said to their amazement. "But, unfortunately, probably just in private."

"Still, that's incredible! He's big in Democrat circles. That's huge for you to get him on board."

"That's great, but believe it or not, I'm getting more and more of that from around the district. I think Chet's in trouble," I calmly said to a now obviously more impressed group of people.

I was flying high. I didn't need to ride in the parade car; I could've pretty much floated around the parade route in that small town.

Although that long-time small county officeholder was the first Democrat to approach me in private, he wasn't the last. Over the late spring and early summer months, he was definitely one of a growing group of local elected officials jumping the Edwards ship. Always at a meeting, a parade, or some other event, it was the same clandestine routine. Both Democrats and Republicans would sidle up to me when there was no one else within ear shot.

Republicans would say, "I know Chet's a Democrat, but he's always been good to me, so I've been a supporter of his for a long time. But if he could even think about running with Obama, well, that's just too much. You've got my support." Then they would give a version of the same disclosure: "I wish I could help you publicly, or donate, but if you don't win, that would cause me a lot of problems. I'm sure you understand. But I'll tell my friends who I'm voting for."

Democrats were usually a little more discreet, even melodramatic in a cloak and dagger style. "Good luck to you," they would quietly say as they shook my hand, then lean in and quietly say, "I *mean* it. I want you to do well." A quick wink, an exaggerated nod, or a subtle pat on my shoulder, followed by a quick retreat back into the crowd or out the door.

A cynic would say they were just covering all their bases in case I might actually win. As a certified cynic myself, I admit that was definitely a possibility. But this just felt different. First of all, they didn't have to say anything at all, or they could just wish me the standard good luck. But there was a sincerity in the way they approached me. It was always discreet, like they were afraid to be seen with me. If they weren't sincere, why even take that chance?

I respected their wishes for discretion and never went public with any of their names or titles. And that's what was so frustrating and maddening. I was personally seeing this very real change and support happening everywhere I went, especially in Edwards' once reliable strongholds. But because I couldn't give any specifics, I just sounded like any other underdog candidate bravely trying to spin a positive outlook on the state of the race. In my heart and in reality, I knew Edwards was in trouble. Thanks to Pelosi and Obama, I now had a very real chance to win this race and pull off the miracle upset.

And, evidently, soon I wouldn't be the *only* candidate in this race who knew Chet was in real danger.

CHAPTER 32

Cold Calling Washington

The Curnock-Edwards congressional race still wasn't getting a lot of coverage in either the local print or electronic media. After all, everyone was sure I was nothing more than political road kill, and I hadn't done anything to change that perception. About the only thing that was being reported was that my fundraising was abysmal, while Chet was flush with millions. Also, the press was eager to report that Edwards was now a national player in the Democratic presidential campaign, who was busy being our congressman and dutifully taking care of his district.

When you add to that Chet's very real and effective strategy of completely ignoring me, I was having a hard time getting any widespread notice or respect from anyone outside of my supporters. And that included my own state and national parties.

While we continued to receive hints of a change in the mindset of District 17 voters, we had absolutely no money to do any kind of polling. What precious little money we did raise was being held back for TV and radio buys for later on in the fall. Another one of the benefits of having my own video company was the continued production of our own commercials for virtually no cost, as I was donating them in-kind after writing and producing them myself. This was, in essence, worth thousands of dollars that we did not have to raise.

But while we weren't able to afford polling, the fat-with-cash incumbent evidently did a standard, state-of-the-race poll sometime during the summer, and we got word through a roundabout source in early August. A supporter of mine revealed he had heard that I was causing heartburn for Edwards via an acquaintance in Edwards' camp, unaware of my supporter's ties to us.

"I ran into him the other day and asked him what he thought of the Curnock-Edwards race. He didn't know I worked for you, and I was pretty surprised at his answer. He told me that he hadn't been giving the race a whole lot of thought since Chet is so strong, but internal polling had this thing down to *single digits*—and without you even doing anything! He said Chet had better start taking this race seriously."

"Was *he* serious?"

"He was not happy, Rob. I'm telling you, they're worried."

"Well, I'm telling you—and I won't say this publicly—from everything I've been seeing out there, they oughta be worried," I said with complete candor.

At the time, I had no way of knowing for certain if this revelation was accurate. However, by the midpoint of August, I may have received a confirmation of the polling information by virtue of a major change in Edwards' tactics. That internal Edwards' poll, though, stayed just that, so it didn't do me any good in any official campaign capacity. We still had to soldier on with quiet perseverance in a virtual cocoon of widespread perceived irrelevance. As long as we continued in this vein, money struggles were a way of campaign life.

Even attempts at getting usually reliable conservative political action committees involved financially on our behalf were proving extremely difficult. Most major PACs operate on several levels when it comes to picking a side in a battle. Many PACs will come in only if they see a legitimate chance to make a difference in a given race. Other PACs only support incumbents if they can find any excuse to do so, rather than support a challenger who, while maybe more ideologically aligned with them, they perceive as unable to win. Some, like the National Rifle Association or the Texas Farm Bureau, support a single issue, regardless of the candidate's party affiliation. Ideological PACs like Right-to-Life or Anti-Tax groups will often step up out of principle, no matter what the odds. I was confident one or more of these would do something before it was all said and done. Still, it would've been nice to find *any* group willing to take a chance at this point in the race so we could build up some credibility, but it just wasn't happening.

When President Bush was governor of Texas, he appointed me to the Texas Commission on Environmental Quality's Small Business Compliance Advisory Panel, a task force overseeing businesses' responsible use of the state's natural resources. The appointment would prove beneficial. It was about this time that a well-connected member, and the other remaining Bush appointee to the panel, passed along my name to a woman who headed an influential small business PAC in Washington. He asked her to speak with me to explore the possibility of them throwing some support and money my way. She was skeptical but agreed to take my call.

I finally got a hold of her and laid out my case. She didn't know much about me or my campaign, but she did know of my opponent and his reputation as a Democrat who couldn't lose in a Republican district, and the fact that he was on the short list to be Obama's vice-presidential running mate. So, needless to say, I was talking on borrowed time when I gave her the particulars of myself and this race.

As I had nothing to lose, I held nothing back. I stressed to her that I wasn't a nut job trying to knock off a Democrat incumbent in a heavily Democrat district. I clearly and concisely laid out the case of why I could win and why Chet would lose. I surprised her when

I made a strong and cogent case that, for exactly the reasons that Pelosi liked him and Obama was considering him for vice president, he was now vulnerable in this extremely conservative district—no matter what all the pundits thought. I was calm and reasoned, and it seemed like she was impressed with my knowledge of the district, my opponent, and the race.

I could sense she was definitely interested—but definitely not sold—when she finally wrapped it up by pulling the rug out from under me.

"You are articulate and make a good case for yourself, but we generally only consider incumbents. I will, however, talk to my associates and will call you back if we want to arrange for a visit in front of the full panel. If not, I certainly wish you the best," she said politely before hanging up.

Oh, well, I probably won't ever hear from her again, I assumed.

At least I got my story out before being turned down. Besides, it doesn't matter. Help or no help, we're still fighting on. I know what's happening here, even if no one else believes me, I thought with as much defiant optimism as I could muster.

I was thrilled when, a few days later, she called back.

"Your passion draws me to your cause," she said. "Our board will be holding two days of meetings in a couple of weeks with all the candidates we're considering. It'll be up to you to make your case. I'm anxious to meet you."

I would finally get a chance to get the "powers that be" to at least hear me out.

The meeting was held in an upper floor of the elegant National Republican Congressional Committee headquarters in Washington,

D.C., just off the street surrounding the wide expanse of the Capitol Building grounds. I arrived over an hour early and waited for my name to be called for my twenty-minute presentation. While sitting in the hallway, I watched important-looking men with expensively tailored suits coming and going from the doors at the end of the hall with eager staffers in tow. It was like watching political celebrities on parade. I quickly recognized a number of senators and congressmen passing by in this rarified air.

Eventually a lady approached me. "Are you Rob?"

I smiled as I realized it was my phone friend. I was glad to see her friendly face.

"We're supposed to break for lunch, but since you're already here, we're going to eat in the meeting room and give you all the time we can. You'll get at most twenty minutes to win them over, so do what you do so well."

She ushered me into the large meeting hall with tables ringing the entire room and about thirty men and women seated at all the tables. My hostess warmly introduced me and turned me loose to tell my story.

When I wrapped up my thoughts, people around the room immediately began asking serious questions. I had serious answers with some humor tossed in to keep it from getting too heavy. After about fifty minutes, my original twenty-minute appointment was done, capped off with a warm round of applause. My phone friend was beaming like a proud momma who had just watched her son win an award. Once again, I was walking on cloud nine. I didn't know what they were going to do, but at least they didn't throw their lunch at me.

"That was wonderful," my host said as she escorted me out. "We'll discuss everyone after hearing tomorrow's candidates and let everyone know who we'll be supporting. But in the meantime, before you leave, I want you to head to the third floor and meet with some-one with the NRCC. I've already called and told them I was sending you up, and they're expecting you. Just tell them your story."

Somewhat optimistically, yet apprehensively, I headed where she instructed. Since that evening in the Republican state headquar-ters in Austin, this appeared to be my one and only shot to get the national party involved. I had to make it good. No pressure.

While waiting at the NRCC offices, I overheard a phone con-versation nearby that rose above the subdued cacophony of multiple, quiet conversations taking place all around me. A staffer in an open-door office was talking to someone in some far-flung congressional district. He explained that they had sunk enough money into that race and they weren't pleased with the results. He lapsed into the technical jargon of campaign dynamics. *This is where it all gets boiled down to the science of numbers, charts, graphs, and dollars*, I thought. *I'm in the belly of the big-time political beast.*

Finally, a young man in a suit walked up and apologized that his supervisor, the man I was waiting to see, was tied up in a meeting. He did want to hear what I had to say, and was relatively familiar with the race and district, so he would meet with me and pass all the pertinent information on to his supervisor. As I was, in essence, an unscheduled walk-in, this was probably the best I could hope for.

We went into a conference room and I began to tell him about the state of the District 17 race. He asked questions and jotted down notes as we discussed the Texas District 17 situation. He even had family connections to Central Texas, so I felt as if we at least had com-mon ground. But I also realized that he was firmly entrenched in this lofty political command headquarters and, like it or not, he and the NRCC were not truly aware of what was happening on the ground in Texas. I was frustrated by this, but in a sense, I could understand it. Even most people who were "on the ground" in the district didn't have a true sense of what was happening. Unfortunately, that knowledge was known only to me (and by this time, probably Chet), as I was the one experiencing it firsthand.

We talked for quite a while, and I tried to point out all the signs, events, and activity that showed how this race had changed and was, in my mind, now winnable. But then he politely put me in my place with his most damaging question.

"Rob, do you have any polling to show that there's been any real movement in this race?"

Bang! He popped my first balloon.

"No, we don't have any polling. All I've got is some general, yet apparently accurate, information about *Chet's* internal polling."

"But *you* haven't done *any* polling? Why not?"

Bang! There went another balloon.

"We don't have the money to spend on polling."

"Looking at the reports, it's pretty clear you haven't raised much money," he said with pointed, yet polite, understatement.

Bang! Yet another balloon, blown to smithereens.

"We've had an almost impossible time raising money. Very few people are willing to give to us because everyone thinks we have absolutely no chance of winning—including you guys." I was going to take the conversation in that direction, but quickly backed off from saying anything else. I didn't want to create an adversarial situation with the NRCC.

"I understand, that's definitely the hardest part of any campaign," he responded with a smile and genuine sympathy.

"I get that the evidence I'm throwing at you is anecdotal, but I'm telling you, things have changed on the ground here. Chet's in trouble. Isn't there any way you guys could do any polling to see for yourselves?"

Knowing the answer was somewhere between zero and none, I figured, *What the heck.*

"We rarely do anything like that. That's up to the candidate's campaign," he said, trying to be gentle in his rejection of what I assume he thought was my absurd suggestion.

Just about that time his boss arrived and said he wanted to meet me, but only had a few moments. We did a quick rehash of the most salient points, then I knew it was time for me to move along. I made one final plea. I owed the conservatives in my district at least that much.

"I sure hope you guys will take a closer look at this race. Not only is this the president's home congressional district, this is also a seat that we can actually take away from the Democrats. In reality, I'm not even sure what I want you to do, but any kind of support, in any form, would certainly help. I'm not detached from reality. I know my assessment probably doesn't hold much water up here, but as sure as I'm sitting here, this is an incredible opportunity to flip this seat and it won't take much. Just take a closer look and decide for yourselves. It's there for the taking."

They listened and then the boss responded.

"Rob, we sure appreciate you stopping in. It was a pleasure to meet a good candidate like yourself who's passionate and willing to take up the challenge no matter how great the odds. We sure want you to win. We'll keep an eye on your race, and if we feel like anything is changing, we'll give you a call. We wish you the best."

I felt like a child getting patted on the head by the bemused adult. *"You're so cute to think you can actually beat Chet. Now run along and let the adults worry about these things."*

On the positive side, they gave me almost an hour of their time, so I didn't feel as if I was brushed off and pushed out the door as quickly as they could get rid of me. And I did understand their perspective. All the NRCC had to go on was past results of election dust-ups with Chet, and for them, the most important hard evidence of all, the financial reports. I had very little money, and Chet had a lot. Who knows, maybe something positive would still come of it, but it didn't matter. I had a battle to fight in Texas. I *started* without them, and I would most likely *finish* without them.

After leaving the NRCC building, with a few hours to spare before my flight home, I made my way into the congressional offices across the street just to see what my future possible work area might look like if the voters of Central Texas decided to defy all the conventional wisdom and send a newcomer to represent them. I hoped to secure a pass to visit the gallery of the House of Representatives-- although I was unwilling to go to my own congressman to make the request.

Serendipitously, I soon ran into Congressman Sam Johnson from a neighboring district in the Dallas area just walking down a hall with some aides. He was a good conservative, a good man, and bona fide hero of the Vietnam War. He graciously stopped at my greeting.

"My name is Rob Curnock, and I'm hoping to be an ally to you in the next session. I'm the guy going up against Chet Edwards in 17."

"Oh, yes, I've heard about you. I sure hope you get it done," he said as we shook hands. "How's it looking?"

"Honestly, nobody believes me, but from everything we're seeing back on the ground in the district, he's in trouble. In fact, I just got back from the NRCC. I tried to get them to help, even a little. Unfortunately, I don't think they believe what I'm telling them. It's a little frustrating."

"Keep doing what you're doing and let's hope for the best. I'm on my way over to the Capitol, but is there anything I can do for you?"

"I was hoping to see the gallery before heading back to Texas."

He directed me to his office, and I got a pass, then I too headed to the Capitol. It was nice to get some encouragement after my frustration at the NRCC.

The House was not in session, so the lights were low with little activity on the floor. A few House workers and congressmen moved in and out around the floor, stopping occasionally to back slap or huddle for small one-on-one conversations. I recognized a couple of faces of Democrat House members. As I took it all in, it struck me that those would be the people I hoped my fellow constituents would allow me to do political battle with. I watched as they laughed and conversed. I was struck by the comfort they displayed in that massive chamber which seemed so impressive to me. I quietly thought, *If I get to come back here as a member, I'm one conservative who's not going to be afraid to mix it up with them.*

Several days after returning to Waco, I got a call from the lady at the small business PAC.

"We made a decision on which races we're going to get involved in and, guess what? Congratulations! You're one of them!"

"That's great!" I responded with enthusiasm.

"Out of those two-day meetings, *you* were a rock star," she declared.

"What does that mean?"

"After hearing from all the invited candidates, I put it out there to the full committee. 'Who do we like?' Several people shouted, 'The redhead from Texas!' Everybody nodded in agreement. Rob, they loved your passion and your fight. They said that's what they were all looking for in a candidate, and the country needs more men like you in office. On top of that, you're a small business owner yourself. I'm telling you, they were extremely impressed with you. In fact, several members said that they were going to send you money on their own!"

"That's awesome!" I was genuinely touched. It was a much-needed morale booster.

"I'm going to let you in on one other thing. You didn't know this, but you were the only non-incumbent office holder that we listened to over the two-day period. You really shined, but I knew you would after our first phone conversation. That's why I pushed to get you on the agenda. I know you're going to beat that Chet Edwards, and we want to help."

"I can't tell you how much this means to me. Thank you so much." I was thrilled at finally getting some good news on the financial front.

Of course, on the other hand, to bring it all back into perspective, no call would ever come from the NRCC. I determined that the next time I appeared in Washington, D.C., I wouldn't be visiting. I would be working—if Central Texas voters hired me.

CHAPTER 33

Ignored No More

I had felt like the forgotten man for the last eight months. Probably the most effective aspect of Chet's refusal to acknowledge my existence was when it came to our attempt to achieve some kind of equal footing as, at the very least, a candidate. My campaign manager, Randall, was constantly trying to arrange for debates as was standard practice in these congressional districts. In past races, various organizations generally held at least two debates during the course of the campaign, and Edwards would agree to participate. Understandably, for numerous reasons in keeping with his Rob-is-not-a-legitimate-candidate mentality, our requests for debates went unanswered, or else there were scheduling conflicts with the congressman's busy schedule as a high-profile mover and shaker in the Democrat Party. Some of it was surely warranted. After all, as a potential running mate for the now-victorious Democrat candidate Obama, he was being given an opportunity to make a prime-time speech at the upcoming Democratic National Convention. He had to prepare for this, so there was evidently just no time to give his basically irrelevant opponent any official face time with him for the voters to compare.

I had mixed emotions. I needed to be seen on the same stage as Edwards, if for no other reason than to send voters a subliminal message that I was a legitimate opponent. On the other hand, Edwards had been debating on this stage for almost twenty years and was a seasoned pro, smooth and experienced in this type of event. I had held a formal debate on *any* stage exactly...never. This could be a

250

disaster for me. I'd seen debate meltdowns with other challengers he'd faced. It might be safer to keep my distance and continue on as we were. Of course, Edwards had virtually nothing to gain from any debate. Although highly unlikely, he could get hurt as well. So why bother?

The Edwards campaign quit ignoring us in late August and suddenly changed the dynamics of the race completely. Evidently, the hearsay information I had been given concerning Edwards' internal polling must have been accurate. Without warning, the Edwards advertising juggernaut launched a mind-numbing commercial barrage. You couldn't turn on the radio without hearing an Edwards ad. You couldn't turn on the television without seeing an Edwards spot. You couldn't open a newspaper without seeing an attention-grabbing, full-page Edwards ad. This was throughout the district on multiple outlets, papers, and channels.

My supporters were shell-shocked. To them, the sky was falling. All the naysayers were ready to proclaim that I had awakened a sleeping giant. I, however, was not one of those people.

Admittedly, it was breathtaking to see the extent of his campaigning power. He was truly an awesome force to be reckoned with, just based on the sheer scope of what he was able to unleash with his money and clout. But I'm an old media guy who understands the power of a message and the potential effectiveness of advertising. I looked past the massive quantity of the commercials now pounding on voters by the day, the hour, and even by the minute. Instead, what caught my interest was the actual message.

Standard operating procedure in races of this type is for the candidate to put out ads describing who they are, what they've done, or what they stand for. Then come commercials perhaps dealing with specific issues. Usually, the last days of the campaign are reserved for the heavy lumber, the negative stuff. It doesn't have to follow any particular order, but, in general, this is textbook political advertising, especially against a weak opponent. In fact, a really weak opponent might escape the negative stuff altogether, if the incumbent and his consultants feel confident.

I was completely surprised to see and hear myself being named and attacked in every other ad.

Even though I'd been on television for almost a decade in Central Texas, it was a strange sensation seeing myself personally mentioned, pictured, attacked, and vilified nonstop in every medium available. Instead of making me want to run for cover, like that Waco newspaper primary hit-piece several years before, this was different. These were based on political issues. Sure, they were baseless, contrived, and hopelessly bogus, but, nonetheless, they were based on politics and not me personally.

Even more impressive and symbolic of the nature of my opponent's clout was the voice talent. We're talking the big leagues here. He didn't just get some local *schlub* to do the narration; he got the guy who once did the booming voice-overs for upcoming Hollywood features. If you've sat through previews in any theater during the past thirty years, you would recognize this voice telling you about the next great movie soon to be released.

The ad Chet ran the most concerned my qualified support of overhauling the currently flawed tax system and replacing it with the "Fair Tax." Never mind that the issue had not come up at all in this campaign. It had been mentioned years earlier on the radio when I was asked if I would support the Fair Tax. I answered that I could, "depending on the details."

So now, suddenly these spots appeared on both radio and television.

"If Rob Curnock has his way, the elderly will pay 30 percent more for their medicine; children, 30 percent more for food; and the price of a pickup truck will go up by 30 percent," And then it closed with the real stunner, "*Politician* Rob Curnock; he's failed us!" On the TV ad, they had the traditional bad picture of me, and then slapped a written "FAILED" in graphics across my forehead.

Politician Rob Curnock! That was pretty funny, actually. The career politician was trying to brand *me* the *politician*! Amazing. In fact, the whole thing was absurd if anyone stopped to analyze it, but, of course, that's not who Democrats generally direct advertising to. They target low-information voters, knowing that they will usually not question what they see or hear in any official media source.

Another negative ad mentioned troops in Iraq. It ran for one weekend before they pulled it. That was probably smart on their part, as this is a very conservative district and people were overwhelmingly behind the troops and what they were trying to accomplish in Iraq. The national anti-war Democrats turned themselves into some bizarre-logic pretzels, trying to claim that they were supportive of the troops—but they opposed the mission. That's about the dumbest thing I've ever heard.

When campaigning, I would point out to crowds that such an insipid mindset is akin to saying, "Oh, I really love the Dallas Cowboys, I just don't want them to win." I also understood that reasonable people could disagree with whether or not we should have been in Iraq. But the bottom line is, we were there, and the Democrats had voted overwhelmingly with President Bush to go in. The country should get behind the troops completely, until they achieve total victory. Once the fighting stops, then we can argue whether or not we should have ever been there—and if George W. Bush had done something wrong. If so, then he should be held accountable.

But here's the key to these negative attack ads. Forget the goofy message, forget the bad picture and fancy graphics. In Edwards' average radio spot, his name was mentioned once or twice, but my name was being repeated five and six times! That's the kind of opposition advertising you just can't get enough of. Talk about building up *my* name ID! I actually wanted to thank him.

The sheer volume of ads with their harsh negativity directed at me confirmed to me that his internal polling must not have been good. This is not the action of an overwhelmingly dominant candidate feeling as if he had nothing to fear from his inconsequential opponent. In a roundabout way, I took this as good news.

Still, the incessant drum beat of the non-stop pounding almost got under my skin, *only* when I was tired or fighting to stay positive. In the natural flow of a campaign, especially a long, difficult fight, candidates on both sides tend to have their ups and downs and their emotional ebbs and flows. Usually, toward the end of a long campaign, it can be easy to get emotional and worn out mentally. At that point, you begin to question everything you're doing and even why you bothered to get in the race in the first place. That's the time when you have to keep your eyes on the prize and continue moving forward. Sometimes, that's easier said than done.

One night after a long, full day of traveling and speaking, my wife and I finally made it home around 11:30. We were both exhausted and I was beginning to wonder what the heck we were doing: the long drives, the mental stress of giving speeches, the ongoing disquiet in my own campaign office with my campaign manager, the depressingly difficult time raising serious money, the total lack of support or any kind of respect on the part of the national party, the vitriolic sniping of the anonymous Democrats looking for anything to attack me on, and now, of course, the non-stop attack ads courtesy of Chet. Maybe I was just internally whining and feeling sorry for myself, but I knew Karen was feeling the same thing. And, hey, it happens. After all, I am a fairly normal human being.

I threw myself down on the couch and just wanted to unwind and forget about the whole campaign for an hour or so before going to bed. Karen sat next to me and we started airing our frustrations with some of the less-than-ideal things that were happening in the race. We caught ourselves and agreed to try and stay positive, and for now just watch some late-night mindless drivel on TV and forget about it all for the time being. We flipped on the TV.

It just so happened that some show was in a commercial break. Literally the first thing that we heard and saw was that now familiar narrator in mid-sentence, "…and raise the cost of a pickup truck by 30 percent. We can't afford Rob Curnock. *Politician* Rob Curnock: he's *failed* us." And there we were, staring at me on the screen, with that stupid FAILED graphic plastered across my forehead.

Neither one of us said a word and turned to each other. Then we both burst out laughing. The bizarre timing was so ironic that it was funny—we just could not get away from it. I have to thank Chet for raising our spirits, if only temporarily, and if only by the absurdity of his advertising effort.

CHAPTER 34

First Contact

With the advent of the commercial onslaught, the proverbial genie was now out of the bottle. For Chet, it was a little difficult to continue to treat me as a nonentity when he made it so obvious to anyone in the district watching television, listening to the radio, or reading the newspaper, that perhaps his Republican opponent did indeed exist. And for those who could read between the lines, maybe I was *possibly* a threat of some sort.

Whatever his thinking, the race now changed on the ground in the district.

Although ultimately not chosen to be Obama's vice-presidential running mate, Edwards had been given a slot to speak in prime time at the Democratic National Convention. This certainly gave him an extensive boost of notoriety, and it would have to be perceived as a great honor to any normal politician. But frankly, from my perspective, I wondered why Chet would want to do it. After all, he was not in a normal situation as a sitting congressman in a 64 percent Republican district which was, to put it nicely, not receptive to Obama and his socialist message.

Although he had still been given an incredible platform with a primetime speech at the Democratic National Convention, I think *I* was even happier than *he* was about it.

Edwards was now in the almost impossible intellectual position of having to get up on national television and declare to the world why *Obama* would make a great president of the United States. That message would be absolutely diametrically opposed to his carefully constructed persona back in Texas as that of a pragmatic moderate Democrat. Sure, I and other conservatives had been trying to unmask Edwards along these lines for years. It was usually dismissed out of hand by local conservative voters who just plain liked Edwards and wanted to believe his carefully crafted message.

But here we were, once and for all. If they didn't believe us, they would at least have to wonder about Chet's own words to millions of leftist Democrats and Obama supporters. I was absolutely thrilled with this great honor bestowed upon Chet, and we had our video recorders ready to share Chet's pro-Obama cheerleading with all the conservative Republican voters in Central Texas. If the opportunity arose, this would be our own campaign ad material.

Edwards did not disappoint the Democrats in the hall that night. Nor did he disappoint me and my supporters at home. He enthusiastically proclaimed the value of an Obama presidency. He was either lying or he truly believed it. Either way, he was now officially outed. There was absolutely no way to honestly and proudly proclaim Obama as the hope for America, while the vast majority of voters in our district knew just the opposite. This extremely liberal presidential candidate was a political disaster waiting to happen, and his subsequent vow to fundamentally transform America was code speak for forever dismantling traditional America. To conservatives, this was not a risk worth taking for this country, and if our own so-called conservative representative didn't understand that, then maybe, just maybe, he was out of step with his own district. Perhaps he wasn't truly representing the people of his district.

It was a powerful card and one of the very few we had to play against the incumbent. And we fully intended playing it, *if* we felt it would make a difference, or the timing was right with our extremely limited resources. I would be happy to, and did, play the Obama card in any live events or functions, but, in fact, I was conflicted on how or if to use this material on the air, as I just did not want to take a negative tack with Chet. I knew he was still well-liked on at least some level, so I wanted to be very careful about attacking him. Besides, I still personally liked him, and going negative about any opponent had never been my style. I may have been in the minority in my own camp.

The campaign finally took on the feel of a real campaign after the Democratic National Convention and his speech. The race now changed on the ground in the district. I think the incumbent knew he had damage control to take care of back in the district and needed to actually start campaigning, even if it meant we would be sharing the stage and I would be, at least symbolically, elevated to the status of a real opponent.

Our paths finally crossed in early September at an annual parade in the small community of West. Known more recently for an explosion at its fertilizer plant, this was a rural town north of Waco that was a predominantly Democratic stronghold and a reliable area for Chet. As we had been doing for months throughout the district, we organized another parade entry. We were now used to doing parades, and, as all these experiences had been positive, we had no reason to believe this one would be any different. We had about twenty volunteers to walk along the parade route beside or ride in our patriotically decorated vehicle. Being in what was considered Chet territory, I was thrilled with the effort of our volunteers.

Up to this point, we had always had the local annual parades to ourselves. At most, somebody on Edwards' staff would show up and drive a vehicle with his signs on the sides to give him a presence. As we were lining up and waiting for the start, I visited with various other parade participants like masons, firemen, or other elected officials. So far, I liked what I was hearing. The vast majority pledged their votes to me with the constant refrain that Chet "may've lost touch with us here in Texas."

Across the small street was Edwards' decorated convertible. We assumed it would be driven by a staff member, but then I saw Chet and his son up the block, walking toward his car.

My stomach fluttered. Not because I was stricken with celebrity awe; it was more like the shock of suddenly coming face-to-face with the focus of all our energies for the last nine months. This was the powerful incumbent I was persuading Central Texas voters to fire. This was the powerful Democrat congressman fresh off a national speech at the Democratic National Convention. This was presidential candidate Barack Obama's potential running mate. This was the man responsible for the barrage of ads blasting me for the past few weeks. We talked about him everywhere we went, even as we talked about what I stood for and wanted to accomplish.

That being said, he'd never been around, so it made it easy to campaign against him. Edwards finally showing up at an event gave me a momentary shudder. Of course, I wasn't going to let anyone else know of my internal trepidations. I turned to Karen and said calmly, "Look who's finally here."

To show how accustomed we were to *not* see him, Karen innocently asked, "Who?"

"Chet. That's him over there, coming this way with his son."

Karen turned and said, "Oh, wow. I wonder why he finally came to something? Now what?"

I wasn't sure myself, as this had never happened before. In fact, the last conversation I had with him was in my business parking lot so many years before. I was in a strange predicament of not wanting to talk to him because, on a very human level, I was trying to take away his job and was his political enemy. On the other hand, I'd known him for a long time, and a man of character would at least say hello. The easy and cowardly thing to do would be to avoid eye contact and wait for the parade to start. I made my decision.

"Do you want to meet him?" I asked, catching Karen off guard.

The idea was odd, in a way, as she knew all about him from months of campaigning. She had seen him attack her husband with negative ads and observed his elite congressional stature in the media. She had heard me talk about him for years going back to our long-distance dating days, when I ran in those earlier primaries. In essence, her entire personal life was now in turmoil because of this man. She felt like she knew him extremely well, but, ironically, they'd never been in the same room together. Since she'd never met him before, I decided this was the best excuse I had to break the ice. I knew she wasn't exactly thrilled, but she responded gamely, "Well,...sure."

We headed across the street where Chet was talking with his young son and the man who would be driving his car in the parade.

"Chet!" I called to get his attention as we approached. He seemed caught off guard a little, but quickly recovered.

"Hey, Rob. How are you?"

"Good, all things considered." We both laughed. "Glad to see you made it back from the national convention. I haven't seen you in a long time, and I just wanted to introduce you to my wife. This is Karen...we finally got married last October."

"Congratulations, and welcome to the area," he said pleasantly to Karen.

"Nice to meet you," she said.

He then turned and introduced us to his driver. It was kind of strange, but as we shook hands, he said, "Yeah, we've met before," without any emotion whatsoever. At the same time, he actually jerked my hand abruptly towards him, nearly pulling me off my feet. *That's weird, what's his problem?* I thought. *Was that intentional? I guess someone other than Chet is taking this race personally. What a jerk.*

Chet then introduced us to his son, who was around eleven years old. "Do you remember Mr. Curnock? You were a lot younger when we were at his business," he said, bringing up a time years ago when they had come to Dub-L Tape. The boy obviously didn't remember, but Chet continued. "Mr. Curnock is running for the same job I have," he explained in a nonthreatening, polite way.

At that point, I decided to have a little fun with him and try to loosen things up after the bizarre handshake episode.

"Hi, I'm Rob Curnock, and I would appreciate it if you would consider voting for me," I said in my best mimicry of a candidate talking to a voter. My wife and Chet laughed, as the very confused boy looked first at me, then his father, with questioning eyes.

"He's just having some fun. You don't have to answer," he said, laughing.

"Well, I tried," I said to Chet. Karen, the former teacher, then locked into a conversation with the son about school.

The handshake guy drifted off, so I was able to briefly visit with Chet alone. "So, you were almost the vice-presidential candidate—that's pretty heady stuff. Was it serious? Did you almost get picked?"

"Yes, actually, it came down to me and Biden," he said, referring to Joe Biden, the long-time senator from Delaware, and Obama's ultimate choice for running mate. "I was told they eventually went with Biden because of all the John Edwards mess going on right

261

now." He was referring to the newly released allegations that former Democratic presidential candidate John Edwards had an illegitimate child with a mistress, while his cancer-stricken wife was fighting for her life. It was not pretty, even by Democrat standards.

"They didn't like the idea of the possible confusion of an Obama/Edwards ticket, thinking that people would assume I was him. That just wouldn't be good right now."

"Oh, wow, that's unbelievable. Who would've seen that coming?" I honestly hadn't thought of that as a reason for him not to be picked.

"It was an honor to be considered, but it's okay. I'm fine with it."

"Well, welcome back to this race," I said with a wry smile.

"Thanks, we'll see you around," he said, and Karen and I headed back to our volunteers down the street. They were all anxious to know what was said after they got over their shock of seeing Chet and me talking together.

At that point, the parade began. In this traditional Edwards stronghold, we got a lot of positive response from the throngs of people lining the parade route. Chet was too far ahead on the parade route to gauge the response he received. No matter. I just walked the long route under the hot Texas sun and shook as many hands as possible. In my mind, as long as people in this Edwards stronghold didn't throw things at us—or hiss and boo—we were doing okay.

A few weeks later, in the last parade of the campaign, we got a chance to clearly see what others outside the district could not: Edwards was definitely in trouble.

Although in a small town in the center of the district, the parade was part of a county-wide annual festival which drew people from all over the area. This small town was also just emerging from under the control of old "yellow dog" Democrats. In other words, this was another part of the district that Chet could always count on for solid continued support.

We had a good group of about a dozen volunteers along with a decorated truck. We were doing our standard pre-parade assemblage and politicking when I was approached by a parade official who asked me to fill out an information card. He explained the card would be used by the official parade emcee, who would read the cards over the loudspeakers in the center of town at the grand stand as each parade participant passed. The information card had a spot for our official title and room for a brief description of who we were, or some sort of catch phrase. It needed to be brief and descriptive, and certainly not controversial. The title was easy: Rob Curnock for Congress. Now I needed a simple description, like "Republican congressional candidate for District 17."

As I started to write that description, I thought, *What the heck, that's too boring*, and changed it.

We had been getting great reaction from all the people around us lining up for the parade, and fresh on almost everybody's mind was Chet's recent convention speech in which he extolled the virtues of Obama and why he should be president. To virtually every person in this crowd who spoke up, Chet was dead wrong on that issue, and most were not pleased with where their "formerly conservative" Democrat congressman stood concerning Obama. So, feeling in a bit of a giddy mood and wanting to make a statement of some sort, I asked the official, smiling but harboring a little concern, "Would this get me in trouble if I submitted this?" After all, I didn't want to come off as a jerk.

He looked down at the paper, read what I wrote, and burst out laughing. "I don't know, but I'll just leave it in and see if they announce it or not. I heard Chet was supposed to be here, but I haven't seen him. He's probably the only one who wouldn't like it. But I couldn't tell you for sure if they'll read it or not," he said, chuckling as he walked away, shaking his head.

Karen saw what I wrote and laughed nervously. "You didn't really put that down; they probably won't like that. You don't want to get in trouble," she said, the teacher in her always afraid that my thinking outside the lines could cause people to get put out with me.

"Look, if it's inappropriate, they just won't read it. It's fine either way. It's not like they're going to kick me out of the parade," I said, trying to probably reassure both of us.

Just then I saw Chet drive up in a lightly decorated vehicle. It only had a couple of magnetic signs on the doors, him and a driver. I thought to myself, *I'm sure they won't read it now. That kind of ticks me off. It would've been funny.*

Chet's car pulled into line literally moments before the parade began moving. However, this time his car was only three vehicles ahead of us, so, for the first time, we would be able to see what kind of reception he received. When you don't have any polling and it's getting late in the campaign, any bit of information can help.

I stood in the back of the pickup truck with Karen, a few volunteers, and a couple of decorated veterans who were supporting me. We also had walkers hurriedly working the people along the winding parade route, handing out candy and literature to any who wanted it. Standing behind the cab, I could see all the entrants in front and behind. I could also easily talk to people on either side of the street as we drove slowly by. It was a good crowd of thousands for such a small town, and most were eager to interact with us, give a thumbs up, or applaud when they saw who I was.

I also had a perfect view of the incumbent just ahead of us— and it was thrilling. Every time I had a chance to glance his way (which really wasn't that often), I saw almost nothing happening. The contrast couldn't have been starker. He was waving as he rode by, but I saw little response. Some politely returned his wave; most would just watch with little or no reaction to their congressman. On the other hand, as we went by, people burst into applause for the decorated vets or shouted encouragement to me and yelled for me to beat Chet Edwards. It boosted the morale of all of us.

We didn't know it at the time, but this parade was a little different than most. Toward the end, the parade culminated in a reviewing stand, surrounded by large bleachers set up in the middle of the town. The announcer would read each card that parade entrants had submitted over loudspeakers. This was all out of sight until the parade turned a corner and moved a block into the grandstand area. The route then took a hard right away to the end of the parade route. Still interacting with people along the streets, we began to hear the loudspeakers announcing each float, vehicle, or band walking by. As we got even closer, although spectators thronged the parade route, we realized, *Holy cow, this is where the vast majority of the people were!* Nearly a thousand people filled the stands and were packed all around on both sides.

Soon we heard them announce, "This is Congressman Chet Edwards, running for re-election to Congress." There was a smattering of polite applause as Edwards' vehicle passed through the crowd, then the next entry was announced. "I guess we're about to find out whether or not we're going to get run out of town," I told those around me in the truck. "After all, this is Chet territory."

By this time, everyone in the truck had heard about what I had written, and they were all taking bets as to whether or not it would make it over the loudspeakers. The consensus was—it would not.

We approached the huge crowd and knew we were next. The loudspeakers blared, "Next up is Rob Curnock, Republican candidate for Congress." There was a pause. I put my head down, thinking, *wait for it, wait for it*...and after a slight moment, which seemed like forever, the announcer broke the silence. "He's the one who *doesn't* think Obama should be our next president!"

The place exploded, like the moment when somebody has just scored a last-second, game-winning touchdown for the home team.

People cheered, whooped, hollered, applauded, and jumped up and down, pumping their fists in the air. I was stunned. As we rolled into the center of the grandstands, all I could think to do was my best Richard Nixon impersonation, as I shot both arms in the air pointing at the sky. It sent a chill up my spine as the crowd just kept roaring until we had passed well out of the square. Everyone in our truck was totally stunned—and pumped up. Our walkers had nothing left to give away, and they rushed through the cheering throng.

As we passed, and the cheering subsided, one of the vets in the truck asked, "You think Chet heard that?"

Still on a bit of an adrenaline rush, I answered, "You know he did. How could he not?"

I looked ahead and the place where his car had been was empty. They must have just kept driving and left town. He sure didn't stick around. We, however, stayed and joined with the county Republican's booth set up as part of the festival, now in full swing. We met a lot more people and soon ran out of both yard signs and bumper stickers.

This was incredibly encouraging. We essentially had an *entire* town cheering us. If this was what was happening in the small rural counties that *always* tilted for Chet, he had better start spending even more of his huge campaign bankroll.

He was going to need it.

CHAPTER 35

Shared Stage

The campaign was now moving into the final months. My opponent, meanwhile, was operating in a netherworld of incongruity. For personal appearances, he continued to conduct a strategy based on the concept that I did not exist and was inconsequential to the congressional contest. On the other hand, he spent hundreds of thousands of dollars on radio, TV, and newspapers demonizing me for my qualified support of the Fair Tax, all the while branding me as a FAILED politician. That's pretty strong stuff for someone so irrelevant.

While I made it a habit to avoid consuming any news reports on the election, someone showed me an article with a quote from Chet responding to an issue. The reporter informed Chet about something I had said about the issue, and he was asked for his response. Chet prefaced his answer with, "I don't really know much about Rob Curnock." I found it amusing that he would go to such lengths to marginalize me. Though we would never have been considered friends, we'd known each other for more than twenty years on multiple levels. Nonetheless, I understood what he was trying to accomplish. He had started down that road of me as *persona non grata* and was committed to it.

In the meantime, my campaign manager was still trying to line up a debate with the congressman. Over the course of several weeks, he was eventually able to extract a commitment to a single debate in Bryan/College Station. That was considered a victory at this point, and that was the extent of the somewhat good news. The bad news was that Edwards' campaign would never commit to a specific date. Time slipped away, and we were quickly running out of possibilities. It was the political equivalent of a rope-a-dope or four-corner stall. The strategy was working.

On the campaign trail, we were still being invited to various candidate forums. Up to this point, Edwards himself had always been a no-show. But in late September, a group of veterans scheduled an event, once again, in the small town of West, and, coincidentally, where Chet and I had recently come face to face. In an effort to maximize the importance of their event, and to convince us to attend, the organizers told us that Edwards had already accepted and they expected him to be there. I would have been there regardless.

It appeared that I would finally and officially share a stage with Edwards. I knew from recent history this was his audience and West had been his territory. Traditionally, the veterans had been his strongest supporters going back to his days representing Fort Hood and sitting on the Veteran's Affairs Committee in Congress. So, while I relished the opportunity to test my political skills by going face to face with him, I was also slightly nervous about what I might be walking into. In my campaigning experience, I found that most people are polite and respectful in these types of situations, but now, for the first time, I would be taking on the favorite son of many of these veterans groups. And, realistically, I wondered how I would do against this smooth and experienced, professional politician. *Is it possible that I'll be intellectually outmatched and overwhelmed?*

The crowd in the VFW hall was modest, maybe sixty people, mostly groups of two to four veterans sitting with their wives scattered around round tables. The vets sported brightly colored canvas hats common with active veterans, multiple pins, and some even wore the old service status bars on their chests. Making my way around the room before the event, I found most knew me from my television days, or from Edwards' ad bombardment, which had turned me into a well-known entity. Almost everyone was polite, but it quickly became clear to me that this was going to be a mixed room. I estimated the crowd was about half for Edwards and *maybe* half with me. Not too bad, considering this was 'captured' territory that Chet had held for years.

Notwithstanding, ideologically, the vast majority of these veterans *should* stand with me. After all, these folks were usually very conservative, but that just went to show how well Chet had worked these guys over the past sixteen years. Many didn't fully comprehend that they didn't agree with Edwards or his party on virtually all cultural, fiscal, or military issues. All they knew was the mantra that, as vets, Chet took care of them. In fact, the catchiest and most popular bumper sticker seen around the district for years was, "Vets for Chet." And truthfully, in many ways, he *was* attentive to their needs. Of course, I maintain that was just what he was *supposed* to do. That was part of his job and *any* good congressman should be responsive to the needs of their constituents.

Chet and I would address the audience last, following speakers from other contested local races. We would speak from the podium that was in the middle of a line of tables on a raised stage at one end of the hall. And, although I prefer to go last to get in the last word, I was told I would speak before Chet, being the challenger. At this point, there was no sign of Chet.

When the meeting started, to ease the standard pre-event jitters, I jokingly whispered to Karen, "I guess I'll have it all to myself after all. I'm beginning to wonder if he even exists. Maybe the man is just afraid of me!"

She quietly laughed at my bravado, but just then, with impeccable timing, Chet and an aide came through the door at the back of the room.

"Oops, never mind; he must've heard me. Finally, this is it," I said to her under my breath. "Game on."

With no prepared remarks, I started formulating what I would say. I wanted to touch on military and veterans' issues, but not focus solely on those things. Seeing a candidate hammer away at a single issue to the exclusion of most everything else seems to me like pandering, and it doesn't let those people know who you are as a whole. For me, after an introduction of who I was, I would focus on my immersion in veteran's issues as the son of a World War II veteran and career VA hospital staffer, why we needed to support the troops in *our* war effort, how that differed from the Democrat leadership, why I was running, and why we needed a change in our congressional representation. It was my standard campaign message with more emphasis on the veterans' aspect.

I also wanted to be careful not to attack the incumbent. It just seemed like common sense to avoid offending half the people in the audience whom I guessed were Edwards supporters. Why antagonize them unnecessarily? On a personal level, I didn't want to attack my opponent out of a sense of simple courtesy. It may seem strange to admit, running a high-profile political race to get elected into one of the most divided governmental chambers in the country, but I've never had an in-your-face confrontational personality, especially with someone I knew on a cordial basis. I'd rather calmly reason with someone, as opposed to descending into the chaos of an emotional verbal assault. That being said, I will vehemently stand for what I believe and defend my core values to the death. My plan was to stick to my candidacy and shared values with the audience.

When it came our turn, we made our way on to the stage and we both nodded to each other. He sat down at the table a few feet away, and I made my way to the podium. I took a deep breath and began to speak.

This time there wasn't a lot of response from the audience, other than a few nodding heads here and there. But I also sensed that I needed to give them specific reasons to differentiate between the two of us. I closed my talk with a plea to the audience for reasonable thought on their part, as to why they should consider a congressional change.

"I understand you all have a clear choice in this election. If you like the job the incumbent's been doing, then you'll probably stick with him. And that's okay. Even *I* don't take issue with the basic job he's been doing. He's been decent with constituency services, but that's his job. That's what any congressman is supposed to do! But that's only half of his job. Where we differ completely is on the issues that define who we are as a people and where we're going as a nation.

"And along that line, right now, the most basic issue of all is, who should be our next president. I vehemently disagree that Obama should be our next commander in chief."

There was finally a smattering of applause and nodding heads. In all honesty, there were also a few stone faces and a couple of angry glares looking back at me from the audience. I pressed on, looking at Chet sitting nearby.

"In fact, my opponent was on the short list to be Obama's running mate. I'll admit that's probably a great honor, but it also shows that we have very different values when it comes to running this country. I want you to know I approve of Obama picking my opponent. I think Chet would be a great choice for him."

I then spoke directly to Chet. "In fact, the Obama people were probably getting sick of hearing from me. I called them every day, urging them to pick you. I'm sorry they didn't listen to me."

At this point the room burst out laughing, and even Chet had to smile at that one.

I wrapped up my talk with the standard plea for their vote, acknowledged the applause, and turned it over to Chet.

As I sat down within a foot or so of the podium and Edwards, I apprehensively wondered how hard he would hit back. He would probably refute my talk, point by point, on the key issues I had raised. It's what I would've done. I also knew that, while listening, I'd have to show no emotion, as that wouldn't be professional or polite. I knew the audience would be watching me as well as him.

As Chet approached the podium, I was pleasantly surprised to see there would be no refuting, rebutting, or defending of anything I had to say. He opened up a notebook and laid it on the podium. I realized he was going to read his speech. It was an *aha* moment. He quickly finished his perfunctory, unscripted welcome and thank-you's, and sure enough, began reading his speech.

I sat calmly and appeared to be listening attentively, but my mind was racing. *This is the man who was fresh off a speech to a national audience, on a short list to be vice president of the United States? He hobnobbed with President Clinton, was tight with Speaker of the House Pelosi, has been an elected congressman for sixteen years, and a state senator before that? He was on powerful committees in Washington, had millions of dollars in the bank, and had easily dispatched all of his previous Republican opponents? Yet here we are in a little forum in West, Texas, in his first head-to-head political encounter with his unfunded, unsupported, and over-matched irrelevant challenger—and HE WAS READING HIS SPEECH! And I've been afraid of him? Are you kidding me?*

I sat there in stunned disbelief, as I knew my impression of him had now changed dramatically. I was no longer in awe. Maybe Goliath wasn't so big after all.

I continued to listen as he read his way through a standard laundry list of his accomplishments as a congressman and all of the good things he had done over the years for vets. He refuted *none* of my pronouncements and had no counters, or even attempted spin, concerning my more salient points. Even if he was ignoring them because they were coming from his weak challenger, these points had solid merit on substance and did resonate with many voters in this district. Personally, I would never have let those things go unchallenged. I thought, *You fool, you ignore these things at your own peril. Thank you!*

I was jostled back to the moment when I heard him wrapping up his remarks. As I looked out over the audience, I thought, *Well, that was uneventful.*

Then, as he closed his notebook, he asked people to support him because, "Unlike my opponent, I would never try to destroy Social Security."

I had been looking out over the audience at that moment, but I whipped my head around. At the same time, I forgot about my plan to just politely and stoically listen. I demonstratively raised my eyebrows in shock, shook my head, and mouthed silently but very visibly to both him and the crowd, "Excuse me?"

He immediately backed away from the podium to polite applause. I was still in shock as he shook my hand, and, without saying another word, he walked off the stage. I stood there up on the stage for a moment and looked at my wife and supporter. In front of everyone, I just shrugged my shoulders and turned my hands up to the sky, while giving them an I-have-no-idea-what-that-was puzzled look.

The attack was out of the blue, and totally disconnected with anything that had ever been discussed or brought up by anybody so far in this campaign. This was the first time it had even come up in *any* form whatsoever, and he just threw out the incendiary accusation that I wanted to "destroy" Social Security.

It was straight out of what radio guru Rush Limbaugh calls the Democrat Playbook. Edwards was scaring senior citizens with the notion that I wanted to take away their Social Security but doing it in such a way and at a time when I had no opportunity to refute it or push back. It was outrageous. It was as if he was acting out a parody of what Democrats have been accused of doing for the last fifty years, playing dirty in campaigns. Those accusations of Democrats playing dirty evidently have a very real basis in reality. Afterwards I spoke with as many of the remaining veterans in the room as possible to refute his Social Security accusation.

Overall, I believed this first joint stage experience went well, and I had certainly held my own. More importantly, I now personally felt there was no longer any real reason to fear my opponent. However, it was now clear to me that evidently, he would be working out of the traditional Democrat Playbook. In a way that was comforting—I now pretty much knew what to expect.

Looking on the bright side, at least he hadn't accused me of being a racist.

CHAPTER 36

The Grind

We were in the last and crucial stages of this endeavor. Everything I was experiencing affirmed my growing feeling that we had a real chance to win this.

This was also the time that I was being called to meet with the editorial boards of the district's major newspapers. They would be making their recommendations and endorsements for the race, so it was a campaign rite of passage that candidates went in front of them and faced a withering fire of questions on various policies and issues that they deemed important to the race. As the main papers were in lock step with the incumbent, I was very tempted to skip these exercises in utter challenger-futility.

I told my horrified wife that I honestly was questioning why I should even give them the satisfaction of rejecting me. There was no way in Hades that I would ever get their endorsement over Chet, no matter what I said. At least, this way, I could legitimately claim that I refused to take part in their charade.

I was never truly serious about skipping the meetings. In reality, it was more about me letting off steam to her. But deep down, I knew I was right. I went to three meetings with three newspaper editors, all three of which had always endorsed Chet in the past. It was a case of going into a room with one or two editors and maybe a reporter. We would spend an hour or so, with them peppering me with various questions. As a former reporter myself, this activity was no big deal to me. The exercise itself was just a matter of answering questions. If you have basic core values and know what you believe in, it can actually be kind of fun. At least I think so.

The Bryan-College Station editors were pleasant enough, although very thorough in their questioning. We actually had a good discussion and covered a lot of ground. But I knew at the end of the long meeting that there was just no way they would endorse me over the longtime incumbent. I confidently told my wife, who was anxiously waiting for me in the lobby, that, although it went fine, "That was a total waste of time. They'll stand by Chet. But maybe I at least made them think a little and see the other side of this thing. Who knows, perhaps I made some new friends."

The Waco *Tribune-Herald* editors were longtime partisan liberal Democrats and, as expected, the most contentious. For the most part, everyone was cordial, but it was clear from the get-go that I was not going to be their friend—or congressman—at least if they had anything to say about it.

On my way out, I stopped off in the newsroom downstairs and said hello to a couple of beat reporters I had gotten to know over my years as a television reporter. I expected both of them would be voting for me in spite of their employer's stance.

It was a working news room and full of reporters. In low voices, my friends asked how it went. I laughed quietly and, in a stage whisper, said, "Oh, I'm positive they're going to endorse me...right after hell freezes over."

They both laughed quietly. "Well, you never know. You might be surprised," one said quietly, earnestly trying to offer some hope.

The other columnist and I just looked at him and said nothing. There was absolute silence for a moment, then we all burst out laughing. All around the newsroom, heads popped up, as all eyes were suddenly locked on us to see what this loud outburst was all about. We quickly quieted down, I said my goodbyes, and headed out.

For the most part, down the stretch, I went about the business of campaigning, while at the same time tending to my personal company. I had no choice; it was still my main source of income. Of course, this was another source of irritation to Randall, who felt that my first commitment needed to be to the campaign, and I should spend all my spare time in the campaign office. I understood his point, yet there was no way I could sequester myself in the campaign office. But I always made darn sure that I was available for any campaign duties.

Although Randall had failed at raising any funds whatsoever in spite of his early assurances, numerous donors graciously gave us small donations throughout the campaign. Several wonderful people stepped up and threw fundraisers over these last months, but it was just never near what we needed. We were down to the last month of the campaign and had just barely passed the $100,000 mark, with much of that in-kind contributions.

Edwards' attack ads continued unabated, but by now the district had been so saturated with them, one began to sense that they lost any real effectiveness as they just became part of the overall background of the political landscape. I produced several radio and television campaign ads for our own media assault but, due to lack of funds, we would be settling for targeted electronic media buys in the last three weeks of the campaign.

One of the self-produced ads responded directly to the Edwards tax attack spot. This came as a result of one of my volunteers talking to a young "low information" voter who liked what she knew about me and normally voted Republican, but she was very concerned that I might really want to raise everybody's taxes by 30 percent. "I just couldn't afford that," she said. I was surprised that anyone could possibly believe the Edwards' tax ad because, to me, it was so outrageously ridiculous. Perhaps the sheer quantity of the ads was getting through to some people. We decided it wouldn't hurt to publicly refute the ad in a spot of our own, but I didn't want it to be defensive.

I wrote the response and delivered it myself on camera. Addressing the viewer, I said, "By now, you've probably heard that I want to raise your taxes by 30 percent. It's absolutely not true, and I have no idea where that comes from, but I can tell you something that *is* a fact. There's only one candidate in this congressional race who *has* actually voted to raise our taxes—and it ain't me."

As I said, "…and it ain't me," Chet's face appeared full screen.

It was a simple production with just me on camera talking to the viewer, but the message was two-fold. First, I wanted to use a little humor to refute his wild accusations, all the while keeping things from getting nasty. Secondly, I wanted to get the point across, without whining that, although I was the one being accused of raising taxes, Chet was the one who had actually played a role in raising our taxes. So, in essence, I was doing a mild attack ad, but presented it in a friendly manner. When we finally did run it, we got a lot of positive feedback, with many people even making it a point to mimic my "it ain't me" line.

The point in time where we needed to start running the various radio and TV spots was approaching rapidly. We had a number of both produced.

It was also about this time that the truce with Randall began to crumble, mainly because of a misunderstanding. As a former media guy himself, he wanted to be the one to voice all the radio spots in which I wasn't doing any on-camera work. I thought that would be fine, but some of them just needed to be done quickly. I wrote and voiced several myself, just to show how I wanted them to sound.

Evidently, though, I wasn't clear on my intent with my office production manager at Dub-L Tape, so when Randall called to ask when he should cut the audio, she thought they were done and told him I had already recorded them. Randall was extremely upset that I wasn't allowing him to do what he was good at. He threw a fit and furiously denounced me as someone who wanted to do everything myself and angrily hung up the phone.

When my manager told me of his reaction, I immediately did what I could to clear up the misunderstanding and apologized to Randall. I told him that, of course, he would be the voice, I only wanted him to get an idea of the tone and pacing of the narration. My production manager had just misunderstood. I then had her call him to set up a recording session. He appeared to be temporarily placated, but it would soon be evident that he was not happy.

While we had developed a strong nucleus of volunteers from all over the district working closely with us on various aspects of the campaign, Randall alone was responsible for the critical TV and radio advertising placement.

The problem was, he wasn't getting it done. Every day I asked him to get the air time bought *that day*, then I left for other campaign events. The next day I would ask Randall, "Did you get the commercials placed?" And every time his answer was along the lines of, "I got tied up. I'll get it done today." Again, the next day he would have some reason for not placing the ads. Days passed. I was getting frustrated and, yes, irritated. We were now moving into the time when we had to get something on the air or it would be pointless.

"Randall, I don't care about these other things, get the time scheduled, *now!*"

To this day I don't know why he was dragging his feet. Some key people in the campaign who were aware of what was happening began quietly grumbling that they weren't sure whose side he was on.

One woman in particular, Wynne, had been driving down to Waco almost daily from the northern part of the district in an effort to do whatever could be done in these hectic last days. She knew that Randall was complaining that he had too much to do, so she approached me about becoming his assistant. At first, I declined; an hour-and-a-half drive every day was too much to ask of her. But, after she insisted that she wanted to do it, I accepted that it would be a wonderful solution to our problem. I approached Randall with the proposal as a way to take some of the load off him. He agreed, and it actually elevated his mood, as he was now getting his demand met for some personal help.

For me, giving Randall an assistant would be a double bonus. From her past efforts on behalf of our campaign, Wynne was well aware of the internal turmoil that had surrounded Randall over the past six months. She was willing to act as a buffer between Randall and all other volunteers. The second and biggest benefit was that she would hopefully push Randall to get things accomplished on multiple fronts. Sadly, it had become apparent to many of us in the campaign that Randall was in over his head, and just wasn't accomplishing much.

The overall mood throughout the campaign leadership was elevated. Unfortunately, it didn't last long. Wynne stayed in close contact with me while I was out campaigning, and she was pushing Randall into buying the media time. A few days after taking on her new role, I got a call from her soon after she had arrived at the campaign office that morning.

She said bluntly, "Randall is quitting. You may want to talk to him."

"Now what?" I was totally done with dealing with the drama that had surrounded Randall from the very beginning, and my frustration was clearly evident.

"He said he's tired of not being respected, and he's through."

"He's quitting *now*—at this late stage of the campaign?!"

"He says he'll stay on as a volunteer, but he's through being campaign manager."

"That does it! I'm done with him." I was angry and venting. "He's doing this now just to try and hurt us the most. I've had it. We'll figure something out."

Without missing a beat, Wynne responded, "If you want, I can take over for him. We've all got too much invested in this, and right now you're our only hope at beating Chet. If you say the word, I'll run things."

"Can you handle it?" I asked part hopefully, part skeptically.

She laughed, "I've never done it before, but I'm confident I could do it. We all know Randall wasn't getting much done anyway. I still don't know what he's doing all day in his office, but I'll do the best I can. We've got to have somebody working with you."

This was a big decision, but I knew there was about three weeks left until Election Day. I had no time to dither.

"Wynne, if you're willing, the job's yours. Of course, you understand we can't pay you anything other than to help with your expenses at this point; we just don't have the money."

"I understand. We just need to win this."

"Awesome. Thank you. I'll come right over. Don't say anything; I'll handle it."

When I got to the headquarters Randall was in his office. I nodded hello to Lynn and another volunteer and went straight into his office. I had been stewing on the ride over. In the past, when Randall had said he was quitting, we would talk him back down, apologize, and basically beg him to not quit. This time, there would be no such performance. He was pulling this nonsense at a time when, I was assuming, he thought he could do the most damage, and, therefore would have the most control over the situation. I'd had enough. I didn't know whether he was thinking—or even hoping—I would do my usual pleading or not. I didn't care.

"What's going on?" I said tersely, not really caring what he answered. "I understand you've got a problem?"

He looked at me like he'd been severely wounded, but quickly started lashing out. "Yes, I can't take it anymore. You don't listen to me, you don't treat me with respect, I don't think you understand all that I'm trying to do, but I'm done. I'll stay on as a basic volunteer, but I'm not campaign manager anymore. You can do it yourself, since you want to run everything yourself anyway. I'm just not going to put up with it anymore."

I looked at him for a moment, searching for the right response. I could feel the rage building in me, but I finally just responded with an even keel. "Okay, I understand. It's your call. This isn't the best time, but if you need out, then we'll work around it."

He stared and made no visible reaction.

"What do you mean when you say you want to be a regular volunteer?"

He was no longer aggressive. "I'll help with the media buys the rest of the way, because that's what I know best, and that's what I like doing."

I wavered as I studied him for a moment. I really just wanted him gone, but I honestly wondered what kind of trouble he might make if we ended it like this. I determined it would be best to keep him in the campaign as long as he was pigeonholed. Besides, it would actually help us if he focused on the media buys.

"Okay. If you want, you can make the media buys. Wynne will take over as campaign manager."

I stepped out of the office and said loudly enough so everyone could hear, "Wynne, you're now the campaign manager. We appreciate your willingness to take on that role. Thank you."

And that was it.

After seven months of turmoil surrounding Randall, I was relieved that it finally ended as well as could be hoped for. Wynne wisely and graciously made a point of declining Randall's office, so he was even spared the indignity of having to clear out. It went very smoothly. As for our relationship with Randall, there was almost nothing left. I just felt, at this point, doing anything could cause more harm than good and, quite frankly, we had no idea what he might do if we asked him to leave. We basically let the sleeping dog lie.

However, I did tell Randall to make the commercial buys immediately. The radio spots he bought quickly, yet it still took him several days to finally work out a schedule and buy the TV time. Unfortunately, early voting was already occurring when our first TV ads finally made it on the air. While the radio spots he did were bought quickly and were probably effective, for some reason, he just wouldn't get on the TV ads.

CHAPTER 37

Ready for Battle

Wynne wasted no time in making things happen. Within three days she secured a two-thousand-dollar contribution from fellow Texas congressman Ron Paul. It also turned out that my chance meeting in Washington months before had made an impression. I was genuinely shocked and grateful that Sam Johnson also came through with a lot more than just a House Chamber pass. He sent us a significant donation similar to Paul's.

Wynne was also responsible for pledges of support from other elected officials, and aggressively pursued various other PACs and organizations in an effort to get endorsements and donations. She organized and coordinated other aspects of volunteers throughout the district. No one ever verbalized any negative comments to or about Randall, but sadly, to those of us in the know, in three days, it seemed like she had accomplished more than he had in seven months.

Randall's other main task had been to coordinate the debate. With all the delays, stalling, and cancellations, the debate date was finally set for a Tuesday late in October in Bryan/College Station, the home of Texas A&M University. The only problem was early voting began that Tuesday, and many votes would be cast *before* the debate. Randall was pleased with the date, and, in fairness, he had probably done about as well as could be expected considering Edwards' mind-set. Hopefully it would not be too little, too late.

It would be on radio, but not televised, and it would take place at the Hilton next to the Texas A&M campus. It just so happened that Chet was a graduate of A&M, whose students and alumni are known as Aggies. As a whole, Aggies are unusually loyal and supportive of one of their own, so I'm sure it was no coincidence that Edwards insisted that the debate be in the heart of "Aggieland." The only thing working in my favor was that Aggies are also notoriously conservative, so I felt that Chet certainly had no lock on their universal support.

In the end, Chet's rope-a-dope stall had virtually worked, and he also had the venue he wanted. These are the advantages of being the incumbent. But the bottom line was that we now had a formal debate. This was my title bout and I had to be ready. I was slightly nervous, but overall okay. I wish I could say the same for my wife and key campaign staffers. The big fight with the undefeated champion was now on. Once again, this could be a disaster—or a moment of triumph. We would soon find out in a couple of weeks.

As we drew closer to the debate date, my new campaign manager Wynne and key volunteers were focused on getting me ready for my rhetorical battle with Chet. Ironically, they were more ill-at-ease than me. We all knew the potential stakes, so it was understandable from their perspective that I be ready. I tried to assure them that I'd be okay, but we all agreed to meet the weekend before the debate for a prep session. We gathered at campaign headquarters and eight of us sat around the room, including Karen and me. I could see the concern in everyone's faces. I could also see they were nervous—for me. Chet's debate reputation was renowned, and everyone in the room desperately wanted me to succeed.

They took turns grilling me on various issues, postulating what questions might arise from the panel, and how Chet might go after me. They were all pleasantly surprised that I had no trouble formulating responses. Still, they would diligently offer suggestions of various possible responses, or changes in wordings, or emphasis on different things. They urged me to memorize various facts, just in case things went in a specific direction. For the most part, there was little disappointment with my mock performance.

There was no way to know what specific questions I would get, so my interrogators insisted I make notes and memorize facts on myriad issues. The collection of notes grew and expanded the longer we went. I soon found myself stressing in a futile attempt to adequately foresee what was coming. More importantly, I began to see the possible difficulties of trying to refer to or wed myself to notes and memorization. If I were to try and look up information, or struggle to remember a fact while in the middle of the debate, my performance would suffer. Looking unprepared or ill at ease were the worst things that could possibly happen.

Still, I continued to go along with what I was beginning to sense was an exercise in futility. I knew it was important to these wonderful supporters trying to help me out. It felt like David being offered the king's armor. He preferred to trust in God and his sling. I appreciated their hard work and investment in this endeavor. I didn't want to come off as not understanding the gravity of the situation or being so arrogant that I wouldn't listen to help from others. But after an hour and a half of this growing tension, and even talk of a second prep session, I saw my opening to tell them the strategy *I* wanted to employ.

Someone asked hopefully, almost pleading, "Rob, are you ready for this?"

All eyes were now on me in an effort to gauge the truthfulness of my response.

I said, "Guys, seriously, I know you may not believe me, but I'm good. I truly appreciate what we're doing, but there's no way I can try to memorize answers. I either know what I believe in or I don't. Yes, I admit, if it gets down to a contest on the workings of Congress or intricacies of government, I'll lose. I'm not the career politician, he is. I'm just a small business owner who thinks we need more people who *aren't* professional politicians in Washington. And guess what, *that* would be my answer, if it comes up in the debate."

I could see relief slowly creeping across everyone's faces.

"I've got to trust my instincts on this. I'm not trying to be cocky, but I live by a core set of values and beliefs. Those values guide everything that I do. Unlike Chet, I know what I believe in, and it doesn't change depending on which audience I'm in front of. Am I nervous about this debate? Sure, but that's just because I've never debated before in my life. And, yes, I'm going up against an old pro. But I honestly believe that if I trust my instincts and don't over-think things, I'll be fine. I either know what I believe or I don't. And I do."

There was silence as everyone digested what I said. Finally, one person broke the quiet. "You said exactly what I wanted to hear. That's good enough for me. This is why you're our guy."

There was sudden unanimous consent as the stress of the afternoon disappeared like a burst bubble. All agreed, ready or not, I was ready! And that was it.

On our way home, Karen, who had been the most concerned, was now my biggest convert. She assured me that she was now absolutely convinced that I was ready to go into battle.

Deep inside, I hoped she was right.

CHAPTER 38

Mano e Mano

The debate was sponsored by the Bryan/College Station Chamber of Commerce and was to be held in the main ballroom of the Hilton, not too far from the Texas A&M University main campus. It was to be broadcast live on the local talk radio station and videoed for re-broadcast or archive. My mission was to hold my own and make as good of an impression as I could on as many voters as possible as we neared Election Day.

As debate day drew nearer, for the benefit of my wife and supporters, I was calm and ready. Inside, though, I vacillated wildly between a mild, controlled panic and a quiet determination to make my case as best I could. I only had one debate to make my case. The stakes felt enormous, and the pressure built within accordingly. Everything I'd been working toward over the last sixteen years was finally coming to a head.

This was my opportunity to defend my conservative values and publicly confront someone representing much of what I thought was destroying America. This was my chance to tell a leader of the liberal Democratic Party exactly what I thought of his governing philosophy. This was my opportunity to finally make an official, personal case to my opponent on why we needed him to find another job. And, most importantly, I would have my opportunity to confront my accuser, who'd been very publicly misrepresenting my values over the last couple of months on every medium in the district.

On the other hand, this actually *would* be my "first rodeo." I'd never even done a formal debate in school, so this experience was uncharted territory. In spite of the fact that he hadn't impressed me all that much in our first encounter at the veteran's forum, I would be going up against a politician who had been debating, or at least speaking in legislative bodies, most of his adult life. I had to make a concerted effort to quell my fears that there was a chance I could get destroyed and be publicly humiliated. It's one thing to have opinions and espouse them; it's another to do it face-to-face with someone you assume to be a solid pro. When combined with the fact that this was all going to be a completely new experience for me, it was easy to spend more time in the controlled panic mode.

Panicked or determined, it didn't matter. Either way, I would be the man on the stage. There was no way I could or would turn back.

A volunteer drove my wife and me to the debate so I could be as fresh as possible following the hour-and-a-half drive. They talked in the front seat while I quietly collected my thoughts in the back. We arrived a little more than an hour before start time. Supporters and debate organizers had already begun to arrive, and I presented myself as jovial, calm, cool, and collected. Inside, my stomach was in a top-of-the-hill-and-starting-down rollercoaster sensation.

I needed to change my mental dynamics or this could be a mess. I'd come too far and represented the hopes of too many people to let that happen. I had a few minutes before I was supposed to meet with Chet and the debate organizers to go over the official debate ground rules. I excused myself from my wife and supporters to go to a restroom away from the commotion. Splashing water on my face didn't relieve the stress.

Remembering pre-event warm-ups from my athletic days, simply jumping up and down helped quell pre-game jitters. I thought, *What the heck? I've got to do something or I'll be a mess.* Of course, jumping up and down before a volleyball match is one thing, but doing the same thing in a dress suit before a formal debate would probably be construed as odd. But I had to do something. I glanced down the long, virtually empty hallway and saw no one nearby. I retreated into a secluded alcove and did some pre-game hops, complete with a body shake for a few seconds. Incredibly, it worked! I suddenly calmed right down. I quickly straightened and smoothed everything and headed back to the ballroom for my date with destiny. I was now ready to do battle.

The Chamber of Commerce leaders, including the president, asked me to join them in a private meeting room to go over the format and rules. We sat at a round table with the moderator, who was a personality on the local talk radio station and hosting the broadcast event. Chet showed up a few moments later with a couple of aides who stood in the background, eyeballing me as we went over things. We flipped to see who would go first and last overall, and I was pleased that I would get to close out the program with the last word.

As we were wrapping up, I decided to have some fun. I knew from supporters in the area that, like the *Waco* Chamber of Commerce, the Bryan/College Station Chamber was known to support Chet. It amazed me that a business organization would support a Democrat so closely aligned with the greatest enemies small business could ever have. It was clearly a case of wanting to be on the "good" side of the congressman, no matter which policies he pushed.

This was my first time meeting Teddi, the president of the BCS chamber, who was perfectly cordial, but it had been clear when Chet walked in that they all knew each other, and I was the odd man out. Just before we broke to go to the debate, I said in all seriousness, "Teddi, I just wanted to let you know how much I appreciate your decision to support me. I know it wasn't easy for you."

The look on her face was one of abject horror, shock, and confusion. She was dumbfounded as she searched for something to say.

On the other side of the table, Chet went ashen and shot his own look of confusion at her. It was priceless and, frankly, made the whole episode worthwhile. I brought it back to reality quickly and broke the sudden tension smothering the room.

"Just kidding," I said with a laugh and looked toward Chet. "Don't worry, Chet. Teddi's not supporting me. I'm just joking," and everyone laughed. Teddi let out a deep breath and laughed as well.

For me, it was a way to lighten my own mood, but it also sent a subtle message: I knew the lay of the land in this race, and I wasn't afraid to deal with it.

Volunteers at the doors handed out stickers signifying support for either Edwards or Curnock. As I worked my way through the gathering audience, I was happy to see that the vast majority of people, if they were wearing stickers, sported Curnock adornments. The room was set up for about three hundred people, and from the looks of the growing crowd, it would be a full house. Chairs were filling up fast, and people stood around the fringes. I had a piece of paper with handwritten notes to use in my opening talk, but I hadn't decided if I would use them or not.

I sat at a table to the right of the stage; Chet was positioned at his table on the left. We both faced the audience and a table with the moderator and two other questioners flanking him. Directly behind them was the first row of audience seats, which cascaded all the way back to various elevated levels in the room. We were positioned in a sunken area, with a clear view of the audience, now sitting and standing all the way to the back walls. My wife and a few supporters were seated in the front row off to my right.

A little to the left, behind the moderator, sat four A&M college students, all wearing Curnock stickers. So far so good. As we counted down to the start of the radio broadcast, I looked over the sea of faces anxiously awaiting the start of this rhetorical battle. I felt strangely at ease, and all the trepidations of the last month or so were gone. I glanced over at Chet, who was intently going over his notes in an open notebook.

The moderator reviewed the format for the radio audience and the live audience. I wondered how Chet would handle his opening statement. I soon found out. As in the veteran's forum several weeks before, he again read his comments. I confidently set aside my cheat sheet and thought, *I'm just going to talk to everyone, and I'm going to listen intently to whatever Chet says and respond accordingly.* I'd watched a few other televised Edwards' debates in past races and was disappointed to see opponents clearly clinging to their talking points. I determined this was going to be a real conversation, at least on my part. Besides, what did I have to lose? Nobody was expecting anything from me, and, if I wanted to convince people to fire their congressman, I had to make it very clear there were real differences between us. I wouldn't get nasty or angry, but I wasn't going to let him throw out unchallenged statements, like his parting shot in the veteran's forum. If he said something controversial or inaccurate, he was going to have to defend it.

Chet spent his two-minute opening statement touting his Aggie connections and how many millions of federal dollars he had brought to the district, in particular, Texas A&M University. It was standard Democrat boilerplate fare. The moderator turned it over to me.

As I began, a young man I recognized as an Edwards campaign aide hopped up in the second row and began taking pictures of me. Because I was speaking directly to the audience rather than from notes, when I looked side to side he would lean to his left or right as I did and snap a flash picture. I assumed he wanted a full facial shot and had positioned himself accordingly. If I looked left, he stepped right and flashed. It was *just annoying enough* to catch my attention. This occurred throughout my entire opening statement. *I wonder why Chet's people want a good picture of me so badly?* I thought.

After offering my background and what I stood for, I informed the audience that I knew they had heard I wanted to raise taxes by 30 percent and also to privatize Social Security. So, I admitted that, as a result, "I'm going to make a little news tonight. I just want you all to know that I've decided to vote for Chet myself—because I wouldn't vote for anyone who would do something like that."

Of course, I was pointing out the absurdity of the charge. The audience got it and laughed, and that opened up the tax issue for discussion. We spent several minutes talking about taxes and the IRS after the moderator took over.

After Chet had answered the first question, they turned it over to me to get my response. As I began talking, Chet's aide jumped up again and started snapping flash photos. And, once again, he kept trying to get the camera in my direct line of sight whenever possible, even to the point of just holding the camera out to his side with his arm fully extended. I'm not normally a conspiracy person, but now I was getting suspicious. Fortunately, I was able to keep my train of thought, and he sat down as soon as I finished. Believe it or not, my first thought was that Chet's guy was simply being rude to the people behind him.

I led off with the next response and once again he jumped up and repeated his flash photography as I talked. I now realized that perhaps—unbelievably—he was trying to distract me! It was working just enough so that I wasn't quite as smooth as I normally would be. While Chet responded to my last answer, I tried to get Karen's attention in the front row, pointing at Chet's guy and mouthing at her to tell him to stop. She and my other supporters couldn't figure out what I was saying.

It came back to me for rebuttal, and, like clockwork, he began flashing again. I'd had enough. *How pathetic is this, that they have to resort to this tactic? Man, they must really be in trouble.* I finished speaking and motioned to my biggest A&M student supporter in the front row, who was actually a *big* man, while pointing directly to the photographer. I had already determined that if this happened again, I was going to ask Chet to call off his guy. It would've been embarrassing for all concerned, but if they were going to act like sixth graders, then they should be embarrassed like sixth graders. My supporter looked at me quizzically and mouthed "Huh?"

By now the whole auditorium could see me pointing at this guy while Chet and the moderator spoke on. At that point, even this political paparazzi punk looked at me and our eyes met. While angrily pointing at him, I demonstratively mouthed, "I know what you're doing. KNOCK IT OFF!" Evidently, he was the only one around who could read lips, because he immediately looked down, lowered his head, and slunk back into his seat, much like a kid who just got caught being bad. Maybe I needed a Dirty Tricks Squad after all.

Fortunately, he didn't resume his antics. Now I could give my full attention to the debate and concentrate on Chet's propaganda.

We battled over Edwards' tax ads as he pushed hard to defend them. In reality, he was quoting statistics from an anti-Fair Tax group. I refuted his numbers and insisted that I had never touted any percentage, leaving that up to the legislative process, if it ever was seriously discussed in Congress. Amazingly, from Chet's point of view, in his Washington Democrat power position, it was almost unthinkable to want to change the tax code, other than to raise taxes on the wealthy. He genuinely thought he was scoring major points by continuing to accuse me of being for the Fair Tax. In response, I kept proudly insisting that, yes, I was for something like the Fair Tax because the current system is a complicated and corrupt mess.

The more we got into the debate, the more confident I became. It was encouraging to see people in the audience respond to my message. In what I thought was a tactical blunder, Chet kept playing to the Aggie crowd *ad nauseam*, constantly talking about all the fiscal benefits that he, as a fellow Aggie in Congress, kept bringing to the school. It was right out of Politics 101.

While most of the audience in the room was connected to Texas A&M in some way, they were also, by far, conservatives with a traditional view of what America stands for. And that's a view that is diametrically opposed to the agenda of the Democrat Party. If Chet believed in the things his national party stood for, then he had to defend those values. If not, he'd made his political bed with the likes of those national liberal Democrats, and now he had to lie in it or disavow it. And, frankly, either way, that's what I was going to come back to and hit him with—at every opportunity.

Only two people in that large ballroom could see the entire audience and gauge their reactions throughout the debate: the congressman and me. Once the flashes from Chet's aide stopped, it had to be clear to both of us that this audience was reacting enthusiastically to virtually every point I made. Fist pumping, over-the-head applauding, exaggerated head nodding, and the verbalization of things like, "That's right!" and "Tell him!" could be heard from the room. Or the converse, as Chet made his points, people all over shook their heads with obvious disapproval or rolled their eyes. It was clear to me which way the vast majority of this Aggie audience leaned. His home court advantage was, in fact, mine.

At the outset of the debate, during his welcome and introduction, the moderator had emphatically insisted that there would be no audience participation allowed, and he meant to enforce that rule to the best of his ability. Several minutes into the program, he had to hold up his hand to the audience and say, "*Please!*" when the audience began to make a little noise for me. That made me feel good, but I certainly wasn't trying to orchestrate anything. Like most hard-pressed conservatives in this political process, evidently, I wasn't the only one eager to have the congressman hear my voice and get pent-up frustrations off my chest.

It finally came to a head about twenty minutes into the debate, after a back-and-forth about the mortgage bailout. I insisted it was the direct result of policies enacted by prominent Democrats from Bill Clinton to Barney Frank to Obama, many of whom actually made personal or political money from the whole mess while the taxpayers were left holding the bag. The moderator then switched gears and gave me a question that I could have only hoped for.

He began, "There are liberal, conservative, and libertarian segments in this district. Tell me how Rob Curnock lines up with the District 17 electorate?"

It was the proverbial fastball right down the middle of the plate, and I swung for the fences. Obviously, this would not have worked in many districts, but this wasn't *any* district. This was right smack in the heart of Texas, the state to which many people ascribe as the last best hope for the survival of traditional America.

I responded with enthusiasm. "You said there're liberal and conservative; for the most part, this is a very conservative district. We went 70 percent for President Bush. I think I am more in tune with the values of Central Texas. I have consistent, conservative values, and I've always lived by those principles. I disagree with my opponent in many respects. We have a situation here where *Nancy Pelosi* has more representation here than we do as conservatives in Central Texas. Again, that's where I disagree with my opponent.

As the audience became more animated in their body language approval of my thoughts, I continued stoking the fire I saw burning in front of me, as well as within me.

"If Nancy Pelosi wants him to vote for a bill, he votes for a bill. If she wants him to do something, he does it. Now, I understand that's how Washington works—if he wants to move ahead with the Speaker of the House."

I interrupted myself. "There's an example right there where we disagree. Not only would I not vote for Nancy Pelosi to be Speaker of the House, I wouldn't vote for her to be 'cleaner' of the House."

Before I could continue on, I was interrupted by the audience, as the room erupted into widespread spontaneous applause. The moderator jumped in quickly with a stern, "*No applause please!*" The audience was admonished, but I didn't care at that point. It was the equivalent of a judge instructing a jury to disregard what they've just heard. It ain't gonna happen! In my mind, we, on the stage, were the jury. And we *both* heard what the majority of the audience thought. I finished with my point--that I wanted to bring our values to Washington, not bring Washington's values here.

All Chet could do in response was to profess his desire to work with all sections of the political spectrum, while tossing out a list of "conservative" groups that backed him, like the Chamber of Commerce and the Texas Farm Bureau. In other words, divert attention from the substance of what was on the table while disingenuously implying that, because these so-called conservative groups had endorsed him, well, draw your own conclusion. He never once denied his eager willingness to work with uber-leftist Pelosi, et al. So yet again, he didn't address the substance of the argument and decried partisanship. All in all, it was probably the best argument he could make, considering the position he had put himself in over the years.

The more the audience encouraged me, the more politely aggressive I became. The fear and pre-debate jitters were gone. It was time to make a stand.

The tone of the debate was definitely a notch above routine. With this being my one and only chance to get some things off my chest, I took every opportunity to go on the offense. With Obama at the top of the Democrat ticket, there was definitely some material for me to work with. A question was later posed about the "Joe the

Plumber" incident the week before, in which Obama was famously heard admitting in an unguarded moment that he wanted to take Americans' wealth and "spread it around a little bit." To every conservative in the country with any semblance of common sense, this was a tacit admission that Obama truly was the Socialist he had been accused of being.

When Chet was asked for his thoughts on this incendiary comment, the skilled politician in him knew he was in trouble with this one, and he did his best ignore-and-misdirect routine in his answer.

"I'm not here to speak for Barack Obama tonight, but I will speak for myself. I think we need a tax policy that is fair to middle-income working families. I voted ninety-five times in Congress to cut taxes."

It sounded like a good political speech to a low-information voter. Sadly for him, I and most people in the room were not low-information voters. I bought none of it and couldn't wait to pounce, even after the moderator took Chet's bait and wandered off into a give-and-take about what constituted middle class.

"The term is 'spread the wealth.' That's what the Democrat nominee has said, so your point of view?" the moderator eventually inquired of me. I wasn't going to let the congressman off so easily.

"First, Chet Edwards *does* speak for Barack Obama in Texas." Turning directly to him, "You were his point man after you endorsed him in the primary, so you definitely *are* speaking for Barack Obama. You think he should be the next president of the United States. I strongly disagree with that, of course, but if you won't speak for him, I will. Barack Obama is an unrepentant Socialist and that's what 'spread the wealth around' means. He wants to take from those that produce and give to everyone else."

Audience members pumped their fists, enthusiastically shook their heads, and some even ignored the moderator's earlier admonishment, softly clapping. I was just getting started.

"I disagree with it. It's fundamentally unsound, fundamentally un-American, and fundamentally unfair. This country does not need socialism. I spent a month in the Soviet Union before it collapsed, and socialism does not work. It scares me to death to see a major presidential candidate trying to drag us into socialism."

Knowing I had the congressman backed into a corner, I kept on the attack as many people were starting to bounce out of their seats in vehement agreement. "You can't separate yourself out. If you believe that Barack Obama is the best man to be president of the United States, then that means you're supporting his positions or his politics. Now, if you don't support his politics and positions, we need to know which ones you don't support. I personally think he would be a disaster for America, and I believe most people in District 17 agree with me."

I made sure I didn't ignore the original question and annoy the moderator. Besides, as a former reporter and political junkie, it irritates me when political candidates of any stripe don't answer questions put to them.

"From that perspective, I don't care what his definition of wealthy is. He wants to spread the wealth around so that no matter *who* is making money, he just wants to take it from them and give it elsewhere."

I knew that I had put him into a box and confronted him like I had never heard him confronted in his eighteen-year congressional career. He was in trouble on this issue and he had to know it. As a practical matter, he couldn't defend Obama without offending most voters in Central Texas. As a congressman on the national Democratic stage, who had just very publicly promoted Obama to the nation, if he now tried to distance himself from the man, I would be very quick to point out his phony hypocrisy for the voters to see.

I was confident with the cards I had just dealt Chet. As the moderator doggedly returned to me to get my definition of middle class, I wondered how Chet would try to wriggle off this hook. The jig was up. He had finally, publicly, been caught, and I and the vast majority of the listening audience knew it.

I answered the question to the moderator's satisfaction and quickly learned what Chet was going to try and do to save himself from this mess that he had actually self-constructed over his entire congressional career. He chose to go the old tried-and-true menu of the left. He pulled out the personal outrage appetizer, complete with a side order of the dramatic wounded, *How could you?* entree, followed by the haphazard construction of a straw man dessert, all the while completely ignoring the substance of the topic on hand.

He intoned, "I just can't let this go unanswered. For my opponent to call Barack Obama un-American, an unrepentant Socialist, is beyond the pale. That is exactly the kind of sharp-edged, partisan attack that is wrong with Washington, D.C. The kind of change I'd like to bring to Washington, D.C. is to have more Republicans and Democrats be more respectful. To call Barack Obama—who eight days from now may well be our next president—un-American, is absolutely wrong. I drive by Arlington Cemetery on my way to work every day and see the graves of men and women who died for us to have the right to disagree. I don't think the questioning of the patriotism of a major candidate gives anything positive to our Democracy. It's wrong."

Waving my pen in the air, I vehemently made a point of wanting to respond, and the moderator acquiesced before moving on to another planned question.

"I absolutely did not question his patriotism, I questioned socialism. Socialism is un-American. Socialism is unpatriotic. I'm not questioning Barack Obama's patriotism; quite honestly, I don't care about Barack Obama's patriotism. He doesn't represent the values that I represent. I question his mentality on what he wants to do to this economy."

The moderator stopped the fight. "Let's move on."

We finished out the debate with some spirited exchanges, but in my mind, the damage was done. I felt confident that somebody had finally pinned him down on his political values and forced his hand on the game he had been playing with the voters concerning what he was doing in Washington as opposed to what he was saying in Texas.

It felt good to know I had friends in that room. I found out later that I was making friends in the radio audience as well. I heard from several people who hadn't been listening to the debate, until they got phone calls from other people who were listening. They were told, "You've got to turn on the radio and hear this guy who's going up against Chet. It's awesome! He's pounding him!" One man told me he was burning up the local phone lines calling all his friends to get them to listen to the program. Whether they actually knew who I was or not, or whether their assessment was accurate or not, it was the type of thing that might give us a chance come Election Day.

Immediately at the end of the debate, we stood up and shook hands while posing for a few pictures. I have to admit, for me, it was extremely uncomfortable having to come up with some sort of small talk to get us through those awkward moments. All I could manage was some sort of comment along the lines of, "Man, I don't know how you get used to this every two years. This sure isn't easy." I was actually being sincere on that point.

I had debated the old pro and survived. I knew I had at least held my own, if not outright beat him. I would leave that for others to decide. All I knew was that somebody had finally confronted him with things that had him on the defensive all evening. He surely wasn't used to being in that position. Ironically, it was the *non*-politician in me who didn't like the idea of having to go after somebody really hard, someone I'd known and genuinely liked on a personal level for a lot of years. I was glad I had held my own and even felt that I had scored major points, but I didn't want to go through that again.

The question now was, how many people actually heard what had happened? Was it too little, too late? Would it change any votes and help us pull off the political miracle?

We would know in a little over a week.

CHAPTER 39

3:10 to Election

In Texas, we have early voting, a two-week period prior to the official election Tuesday, when voters can cast their ballots at a few consolidated precincts throughout each county. The majority of voters still wait for Election Day, but a sizable number of voters cast in this two-week window. For a candidate, it means that you've, hopefully, made your case two weeks *before* Election Day.

Edwards' team made a good move by stalling the debate until after early voting had begun. As the longtime powerful incumbent, he had little to gain against his unknown, underfunded, and unsupported opponent. Virtually every person that I talked with in the Bryan/College Station area that heard the debate or attended it was exhilarated with my handling of Chet. No one knew what to expect, so when I came out swinging, they were thrilled and convinced that I had Edwards on his heels the whole night.

The next day we contacted the radio station to get an audio copy of the debate, and that's when I found out I lost at least one vote due to the delayed debate strategy. The woman helping me said she would vote for me because of my impressive performance, but her husband, who had engineered the debate for the radio station, had already voted that previous morning in early voting. He voted for Edwards because he didn't know anything about me, but after hearing the debate, he told his wife he'd made a big mistake. They agreed *she* should offset his vote. I wondered how many other people in the Bryan/College Station area had done the same thing. Of course, I didn't have to worry about that happening anywhere else in the district, as they did not even have the chance to hear the debate. It got little or no coverage. My impressive debating debut was like the proverbial tree falling in the forest--no one heard it, or it didn't make a sound.

The political science pundits prognosticating and handicapping the race were matter-of-fact that Chet would likely surpass his vote total from the last cycle and finish up with close to 70 percent of the vote. After all, I was on my own with almost no money or support from the national party. Chet destroyed the last opponent who had almost matched him dollar for dollar, and that candidate also had support from Washington. Their analysis predicted Edwards would do no worse than last time, and most assuredly better, against a much weaker opponent.

I didn't blame these "expert" pundits for diagnosing it the way they did. On paper, they were right, but they didn't know what I did. Even though I couldn't prove it, I just knew this thing was close! Could we win? Yes, deep down I honestly believed we could, and I even dared to surmise that we would, but I kept that mostly to myself and my wife.

Those final last days of the campaign were brutal. Physically, I was worn down from being on the go all the time. Even though I was a former broadcaster used to speaking for a living, doing it at length every day, sometimes more than twice, began to wear me down. My voice was on its last legs and lacked any kick.

On an emotional level, it was also getting dicey. I consider myself to be fairly strong mentally and loathe showing any kind of emotion that connotes "weakness." Maybe it's a guy thing, but it's just the way I've always been, and I don't apologize for it. I don't like showing that side of me to anyone and have always been adept at shoving it back down within me if I ever felt it coming to the surface.

304

But as any candidate in a tough campaign will tell you, there almost always comes a point where you're just plain tired and, yes, even discouraged, no matter what face you put on to the public. In my case, it was ten months of non-stop campaigning, which, in and of itself, is highly stressful. Ten months of knowing that your finances were woefully inadequate, and every reporting period proclaimed your failure to the world. Ten months of people politely urging you on and even supporting you, but deep down you knew that they knew you didn't have a chance. Add to that the fact that many of those who pledged support also pledged their silence to the public, giving you that Biblical thrice-cock-crowing-denial type of feeling. On top of that, your own national party completely ignores you and turns its back on your efforts. Then cover it over with a non-stop barrage of negative personal attack ads and you've got yourself a perfect recipe for a self-pity party of immense proportions.

About this time, I got a call from an A&M newspaper reporter wanting a response from me on a claim by Chet that even the national Republican Party was no longer backing me. The reporter said that Chet claimed I was so extreme and irrelevant that even the Republican Party was unwilling to get involved in this race and had now rejected my candidacy. I was surprised that Chet would go down that road.

I thanked the young reporter for being thorough and fair by giving me a chance to respond. Some mainstream network reporters could take a few pointers. I then laughed at the notion that the national party thought I was too extreme.

"The national party isn't distancing themselves from me; they were *never on board* with me in the first place! The very first night I filed, they told me they were no longer going to challenge Edwards until 2012 and redistricting. They thought he couldn't be beaten and wanted nothing more to do with him. They told me they were focusing on other races, like Tom Delay's old seat. They politely wished me good luck in my endeavor."

"So, they didn't back off of you and take away their support?" he asked, beginning to get a sense of what Edwards had tried to pull.

"No, that's ridiculous. It's true, they've never helped me, but that's the only thing he's said that's true. I don't know why the congressman would make this nonsense up, but it's a total misrepresentation of what's actually been going on. At this point, why would he throw this out there? I wonder if he's worried?"

"It does make you think..." he answered before moving on to ask me my position on several issues concerning Texas A&M.

I laughed about the lack of support to the reporter, but inside it stung. I knew that lack of support led to a lack of funding, which contributed to our inability to do a lot of things that would have made for a powerful message. Plus, it was frustrating to know that nobody was giving me a chance. I was beginning to feel myself slipping into a dark place emotionally.

During the last week before the election, Karen and I escaped to a movie to forget about politics. It was a newly released Russell Crowe movie--*3:10 to Yuma.* It was a remake of an old western, but other than that, neither one of us knew what to expect. It turned out to be the perfect therapy.

Christian Bale played a rancher trying to get the outlaw Crowe onto a train to prison. Crowe's cutthroat gang, however, had other plans: rescue him with no qualms about killing Bale to get what they wanted. Although things start out positively enough, by the end of the movie, Bale is standing virtually alone as everyone else had been killed or ran away as the odds got worse.

In the scene that hit me right between the eyes, Crowe told the now-alone Bale to walk away, that nobody would blame him or even know. The response from Bale? *He* would know. It was something personal and from within. He had to do what was right, no matter what it cost, no matter who was watching.

At this point, I was holding back tears as I turned to Karen. "I totally get it. I can absolutely relate to this character." It was stunning how cathartic this movie turned out to be. It was only a fictional character, but it had the very real effect of bringing me out of my doldrums and elevating my mood and drive to make it through to Election Day.

Ironically, unbeknownst to us at the time, the movie remake was written by a couple of Baylor grads. Years later, one of the writers was back at Baylor speaking to students about the industry. Being a life-long movie buff, I had the incredibly unique opportunity to thank him for the inspiration and pick-me-up at a pivotal moment in my life. That's something that's never happened to me with any movie before.

On Election Day, Wynne insisted that I visit as many key election sites as possible for last-minute politicking. Even though it went against everything I'd ever believed about Election Day, I agreed. It got our minds off that final day, and we stayed busy until the results were made public that evening. Wynne, Karen, and I went from polling place to polling place in and around Waco. I heard many well wishes from voters planning to vote for me or that had just voted for me. It was rewarding emotionally. By the time we rolled back into Waco, after the close of the polls at 7:00 p.m., I was ready for something to happen. In fact, I was ready for anything to happen. I took a quick break at home to wash up and change clothes before heading over to our watch party, which volunteers had decided was extremely important and were going to do it up right.

We arrived at the hall after dark and it was already filled with cars, including live vans and news units from all the local TV stations in Waco. Many people were already inside. This felt completely different from any other election night I had ever experienced as a candidate. As we got to the door, I held back to let Wynne and Karen enter first, but Wynne insisted that, as the candidate, I lead the way in. It dawned on me that this may be a big deal for not only me, but a lot of conservative voters as well. I took a deep breath, opened the door, and rushed in, not knowing what to expect.

Someone immediately spotted me and squealed, "Rob's here!" and the entire room of more than a hundred supporters broke into spontaneous applause. Hugs and handshakes followed, and even a few quick conversations with members of the press. Unlike in the primaries, these reporters were here to stay until the final vote verdict came in.

About this time the first results from early voting came across on all three TVs arranged around the room. I was neck and neck with Edwards in several counties, and slightly ahead in the two most northern counties! *Could this really happen?* I asked myself. I was quietly and cautiously optimistic.

I was chatting with supporters, in between results being announced, when an enthusiastic supporter ran up. He was ecstatic after seeing the first major results come in.

"Rob, have you heard the latest? This is unbelievable! You're only down by six points!" he genuinely gushed with joy.

"We're down by six? Crap…" I said, visibly disappointed. My positive vibes were shaken.

My supporter was surprised by my response. "But, Rob, this is incredible! You're right there with him! You're only down six points. That's excellent!"

It suddenly became clear to me. Although badly wanting me to win, he had bought into the widespread prediction that I would be lucky to get 30 percent of the vote.

I responded with a smile to weakly masquerade my annoyance at this latest turn of events.

"No. It would be excellent if Chet were down by six points. *That's* what I want to see."

He walked off still happy and still insisting that this was great news, and he hoped things kept up this way. Obviously, sadly, he and I had completely different expectations for the evening.

Normally, a presidential election would be the focal point of election night. Depending on the winner, America would either continue its slide headlong into socialism as the liberal Democrats continue to push for a clone of the European systems, or, if we were lucky, get a Republican to at least forestall what seemed to be inevitable, to one varying degree or another.

But this evening I had bigger fish to fry. I had a personal stake in the outcome of this congressional race. If I won, Karen's and my life would change forever. Even though, periodically, we would notice one state after another drop into the Obama column, we focused on the local congressional numbers. Besides, in my mind, the moment we, as Republicans, nominated John McCain, we were in deep trouble. When asked, during the campaign, if Obama would make a good president and McCain answered with complete sincerity, "Yes, I think he'd make a fine president. We just disagree on most issues," I knew in my heart the presidential race was over. At that point, I kept my attention firmly on District 17.

As far as I was concerned, the news just never got any better. Ironically, a lot of my supporters were actually quietly satisfied as the numbers really just didn't budge after the first reports. Many would put on their best displays of disappointment for my benefit, but you could tell that, for them, their real reaction was a satisfied surprise—surprise that we had made it a race. After years of seeing Chet dispatch other much "stronger" candidates with relative ease, for most of my supporters, this was a huge moral victory.

By the time the race was finally called late in the evening, I reluctantly conceded to my opponent by way of live television. I then made a personal call to Chet to congratulate him. It was almost as awkward as the end of the debate, but he was gracious. I took the opportunity to find out what his plans might be, as a result of Obama's victory and his close association with Obama. Rumors had been flying around the last days of the campaign that, even if Edwards won, he would probably get appointed to a post in an Obama administration, if Obama won. If that happened, Republican Governor Rick Perry would then appoint a successor to the District 17 congressional seat. Of course, many in my camp predicted that would, or should, be me. Those were a lot of ifs, but that scenario had to be considered.

After congratulating him on yet another defense of his seat, the former reporter in me couldn't resist the opportunity to try and get the information straight from the horse's mouth.

"I guess you're pleased about the Obama victory. I bet you'll have some big decisions ahead of you."

"What do you mean?" he asked, genuinely unaware as to what I was alluding.

"I'm assuming that, since you were almost his vice president, they'll offer you some position in his administration. It makes perfect sense."

"I haven't heard anything to that effect, but if it did happen, I don't know that I'd take it. Believe it or not, I really like being in Congress. I like what I'm doing."

"Good luck, no matter what happens," I said. "Obviously, I'm not thrilled at the results, but you definitely are good at campaigning, and I'm glad things stayed relatively civil."

"Thanks, Rob. I appreciate it."

I don't know if he knew something or not, but he was holding his cards close to his vest. Or maybe he was letting me know that this seat was his—and would be—as long as he wanted it. Either way, I was left with a feeling that there were more cards to be played in this political tragedy. It just felt like the story wasn't over.

But for Karen and me, this ordeal had made for one long first year of marriage. We were ready for some down time with just her and me and no politics. We thanked our friends and supporters, shut down the campaign organization, licked our wounds, and prepared for some rest and relaxation. *Rob, what are you going to do after being defeated in a head-to-head battle with the powerfully entrenched incumbent Chet Edwards?* An iconic trip to Disney World was the only thing we could see in our immediate future, and, boy, was I ready for a departure from reality.

No matter how brief.

PART IV

End Game

CHAPTER 40

Finishing the Job

Barack Obama's presidential candidacy cut like a two-edged sword in my battle to unseat Edwards. The fact that he was at the top of the ticket, extremely unpopular in Central Texas, and tied to the congressman turned out to be a gigantic boost to my campaign. It leveled the playing field as much as I could have hoped. But the greatest damage came as we were getting reports in from the minority precincts in Waco and Bryan/College Station. County chairmen from those precincts reported that black voter turnout was double and triple from the norm in a presidential election. Obama brought out those votes, and virtually every single one went to the Democrat congressional incumbent in the form of straight-ticket voting.

The final tally brought us in at 45.5 percent of the vote, Edwards at 52.9 percent. The Libertarian got the rest. Another four and a half percent falling our way and we would have won. Out of more than 250,000 votes cast, Edwards won by a little over 19,000 votes. It was darn close, and it caught the attention of the national party. Edwards spent $2.1 million to defeat his poor, helpless, and unsupported challenger. Unbelievably, we spent a little over $79,000. On a cost-per-vote basis, Chet was forced to pay $15.60 for each vote he got. We got the most for our money at $0.68 per vote. That's bang for your buck!

Overall, 2008 turned out to be a horrible year for Republicans in general. Months later, an analyst from the state party came to

Waco to speak to one of our Republican clubs. He debriefed us on the state of the party nationwide and in Texas in the wake of the Obama election. Most of what happened was troubling for the party, but he talked about one set of numbers that caught my attention and planted a seed that would germinate. According to the numbers, in *every* congressional race in Texas, except in only one district, Republicans suffered a significant decrease in the vote totals. Even solid incumbents who handily won their races saw their margin of victories tighten up. *I can believe it*, I thought. *I saw the Obama effect first hand. It cost me the race.* He then surprised everyone in the room by informing us that we should be proud, because the one district that did not lose Republican strength was us, *District 17!* In fact, we were the only congressional district in Texas that significantly *increased* our percentage from the previous congressional cycle. He added that the national Republican Party was now targeting this seat, making it their number two priority congressional race in the entire country for 2010. Many in the room turned my way and smiled broadly.

That fact went a long way to salving the gaping wound of the surprisingly close loss. At the same time, it cemented my lack of respect for the leadership of the Republican Party, both state and national, for their lack of respect for anyone that is not of their choosing—in this case, me.

But the party bureaucrat never acknowledged my presence in the audience and moved on to another subject. It was an ego check for me. If I was doing this for recognition or self-satisfaction, I would be disappointed. There would be no recognition, thank-you's, nor anything else from the Party leadership. Confirmation of that came courtesy of a county Republican chairman, a friend and supporter, who relayed a brief conversation he had with none other than my old buddy Karl Rove while attending a national meeting. My friend asked Rove if the party would back the guy who almost knocked off Edwards in the next go-around, if he ran again, as I had run a good race and came so close.

According to my friend, Rove's curt response was, "Frankly, I wasn't too impressed with the candidate who ran that race. He raised virtually no money and clearly didn't know what he was doing. We need to find somebody who can win." My disappointed friend didn't respond as Rove moved on.

Although, as a human being, I was troubled by Rove's assessment, I tried not to take it personally. I'm confident he didn't even know who I was, and besides, it wasn't anything that I hadn't experienced throughout the race. It was just something I had to deal with. My wife wasn't happy when she heard about this incident, but we had known all along that, like David, if we were going to win, we had to do it alone, and without the help of the "establishment."

Just like David in the Bible, we had gone up against incredible odds with absolutely no help or weaponry from our side. The close results of the race also affirmed that, just like David, we had taken down Goliath. I knew with every fiber of my political brain that he was done. Politically, he was mortally wounded. But, unlike David, I had yet to complete the monumental task. According to the Bible, after David brought down Goliath, he took Goliath's own sword and, well, finished the job. I had no doubt that, whether I liked it or not, I had unfinished business ahead of me.

The rumor that Edwards would be given a post in the Obama administration turned out to be just that--rumor. For whatever reasons, Edwards never publicly acknowledged that he was ever contacted to join the Obama administration. It was interesting to note, and a little irritating to me, that although it never happened, some people began quietly jockeying for position behind the scenes with Governor Perry, in hopes that they would be appointed to the seat if Edwards should move on to work for Obama. And, incredibly, at least one of these people had actually worked closely with us from the beginning. At least we thought he had. In politics, you never know for sure. In my mind, it was pretty audacious to think that you should be appointed to a seat that another candidate had just spent the last eleven months fighting for. It seemed to clearly be just one more example of the lack of respect that some people evidently had for me. More ominously, it was also a sign of things to come.

Several weeks after the election, Wynne called. She wanted to know if Karen and I could come to a meeting at our now almost empty campaign headquarters with her and key volunteers from all over the district. She was vague about her intentions. When we arrived for the meeting, we were surprised and thrilled to see a dozen of our key volunteers who had traveled to Waco from all over the congressional district. Chairs had been arranged all around the room in a large circle so we could face each other. Wynne thanked me for the effort I had made in almost pulling off the miracle, and they all wanted to know how I was holding up after the defeat. But everything they asked soon led to one central question: What were my intentions?

"I'm a competitor that hates to lose," I said. "No matter what all the pundits, even many of my own supporters predicted, I feel that this was an incredible missed opportunity."

"Chet outspent us by $2 million. He hammered us with negative ads nonstop. He had all the major newspapers on his side. We couldn't get anyone from the national or state Republican Parties to help us. In fact, they worked against us by telling contributors not to waste their money on us. No one believed we could win."

"We had all these negatives going against us, and yet, at the end of the day, if we could've gotten four and a half more points, we would've won. In fact, the only thing that saved Chet was the minority turnout, courtesy of Obama. That, and only that, is the reason he held on to his seat for another session. But I'm telling you, it's over for Chet. He *will* lose in the next election. Chet is done."

It wasn't bravado. I wasn't trying to pump anyone up, I wasn't trying to brag. I was merely stating what I knew was a matter of fact. I gave what could be considered the last speech of the 2008 campaign—or, as it later turned out, the first speech of the 2010 campaign.

Somebody spoke up and said, "And that brings us to you, Rob. What are your plans? We're all wondering if you'd be willing to consider going again and finishing the job?"

Everyone around the room nodded in agreement. Karen and I had talked about the possibility of going again to finish the job, but up until that moment, it hadn't been definitive. It was an oblique desire to win the race we now knew we could win. However, we absolutely couldn't afford to do it on our own financially. And quite honestly, the idea of going through all that hard work and aggravation again was just not appealing after our nearly one year on the road. The bottom line, we were still emotionally and physically spent. But, if there was ever a way to light my fire and get me going, this was it. Knowing that I had a group of quality people counting on me and wanting to go into battle with me was a shot of adrenaline.

I gulped hard to swallow my emotions. They had no idea what they meant to me in that moment.

"I've been trying to get this seat in the hands of a conservative for twenty years, any way I could," I answered, "and I really don't want to quit now. We came extremely close, but I'm confident we could finish it. I believe if we went again, there would be immediate changes in the dynamics of this race, all in our favor. The critical factor of not being considered a legitimate candidate should now be completely off the table. That would definitely boost fundraising and assure us of having more weapons to work with. It also would give us credibility we didn't have this last time around. The upside is tremendous. I'm not saying it would be easy, but for Chet, the writing's on the wall."

I looked around the room at everyone listening intently and nodding their assent. "What are you all thinking?" I asked.

One volunteer spoke. "If you're willing to go again, we all want to help. We believe that we can win this, and we're ready to do whatever it takes to make you the congressman. We pledge to work with you."

I struggled to control my emotions. I glanced at Karen and there was no doubt she was on the same page. I looked around the room and, with a total peace, said, "Okay, let's do it. I'll pledge to go again, if you're all in. I'm humbled and honored that you'd put your trust in me, and this time, we'll win this thing."

For the first time, I had an organized group of like-minded people pledging to stick with me. Wynne would stay on as campaign manager. She was enthusiastically ready to accept the challenge and continue on the trajectory that she had begun in the last weeks of the race. With the next campaign still over a year away, Wynne, with the help of this squad of volunteers, began laying the groundwork for the distant campaign to finish the job. The idea of running again seemed daunting, and I won't say I didn't have any trepidation about living in the fish bowl and getting publicly pounded again, but if this was what I was called to do, I was not going to argue. Once again, I locked my eyes on the prize.

CHAPTER 41

Shadows of Randall

If I had any allusions that this time around would be painless and without difficulty, that was erased four months later when I got a visit at my office from Sean, the key volunteer who had helped us secure our campaign office and a house for Randall, the campaign manager, to live in while he was running the campaign. Sean walked in for what I thought was just a social visit to say hi and catch up, as we hadn't seen each other since the campaign. Nope, I was wrong.

It turns out Randall was still casting a shadow in my life and causing problems from out of the past and all the way up in the Northeast.

"Hey, Rob, I need to talk to you about some outstanding bills from the campaign for expenses that Randall ran up," he said.

"What expenses?" I asked with annoyed alarm.

"Evidently, Randall ordered all the most expensive cable packages that you can possibly get and who knows what else. The owners of the donated house got the exorbitant bills and called me to see about getting your campaign to pay it off. I just hadn't had a chance to get with you until now."

"You're kidding me?" I said, even more annoyed.

"Yeah, and on top of that, he had unbelievably high electric bills. I don't see how he could even get them this high unless he was like turning the AC up to full blast and leaving the doors open or something. Anyway, these are all bills that the campaign should be taking care of. I don't think it'd be right to stick it to the people that own the house and let us use it for free."

"No, I totally agree. But of course, this is the first I'm hearing of any of this. Randall certainly never turned anything in for us to pay. I can't believe this. How much is the total bill?"

"All told, it's around $1,300. I've got all the statements and receipts to document everything. Do you have any money left in the account to pay for things like this?"

"No, we actually came up a few thousand dollars short as a result of some late invoices that came in for last minute media buys. I just personally paid those off to make sure we never stiffed anybody. The campaign account is empty and in mothballs."

Sean pressed on, "Well this needs to be paid. It's just not right to stick…"

"No, I know," I interrupted, extremely irritated at the mess Randall had left me. "I'll have to take care of it. Freakin' Randall. What a jerk. What about the guy that lived there with Randall for a while? Is any of this his?"

"No, he gave Randall a check for his half of utilities at one point. I thought Randall turned it in to you."

"Wait a minute, are you kidding me? Was that a check from Steve *somebody*?"

"Yeah, Randall said he gave it to you."

"Now I remember; he did. But he had handed it to me and bragged that he had gotten us a nice donation. He was very pleased with himself. I remember it now because it was the only money that Randall had ever actually brought in on his own! And now you're telling me it was just this guy's portion of expenses and Randall never told me while passing it off as a campaign donation?! Unbelievable! What a colossal jerk," I fumed.

"I'll just have to pay it since we're not going to stiff anybody, but man, this makes me mad." I was truly upset, but there was nothing I could do about it. This mess was dumped in my lap, and I had to clean it up.

"I still don't see how he could've even spent that much on this stuff. Who knows what he was doing," Sean wondered, then laughed. "Maybe he was ordering pay-per-view every night."

I didn't respond, laugh, or care. I was too angry; six months after the fact, and Randall strikes again. Sean offered to call Randall for me to try and get him to pay the bills off. I said no, he wouldn't ever agree to pay up, and there was no point in even trying to get him to. I just decided to pay it and be done with it. I reasoned that, in reality, it was a small price to pay to get him out of my life once and for all.

I found out later that there are many times in life when you don't always get what you pay for.

CHAPTER 42

Circling Buzzards

We knew that this race had attracted the attention of the national party powers-that-be in Washington. They were now willing and ready to go after this seat after all. There was no more talk of waiting until 2012 and redistricting. But the Washington Republicans weren't the only ones. Opportunists with illusions of grandeur and a gleam in their eye for an easy congressional seat came out of the woodwork. Chet Edwards was now very publicly wounded, and anybody with any political savvy knew he was ready to go down. Like hyenas sensing an easy meal they don't have to work for, suddenly lots of opportunists from all over Central Texas and beyond were 'bravely' ready to take on the wounded and weakened Chet. Their end goal: an easy road to Congress.

As the man who had fought and given Edwards his mortal wounds, this was not pleasant to watch. It probably wasn't realistic on my part, but I couldn't help being mildly disappointed that not a single potential candidate did the courteous thing of calling me to see if I would be going again. I never got any contact from the party leadership to thank me for running when no one else would and showing them that this was, indeed, a winnable race, or to see if they could now help me finish the task. I'm no Pollyanna, but the idealist in me can still always hope for a world that's fair and just.

About this time, on the national political stage, a new phenomenon was materializing across the country. An organization called the Tea Party began to appear and represent a growing sentiment that Washington was out of economic control. The election of the extremely liberal Obama, who actively sought and promoted a larger role for government, galvanized and fertilized this nascent movement. Although—never officially joining the ranks of the Tea Party, I, nonetheless, agreed with almost all they stood for. It appeared to me that the average Tea Party member was overwhelmingly for lower taxes and less government, two staples of my congressional campaign mantra. Politically, they were conservative but with a focus on economic issues. It was also obvious that many in their ranks were new to the world of political activism. I thought this was a positive thing for the American political system and wanted to do everything I could to encourage them. I was happy to see the movement grow and prosper.

I got my first taste of the Tea Party later that spring in Waco. A local chapter had arisen and was becoming active. The Waco chapter organized a rally on tax day, April 15, to highlight their opposition to the onerous tax policies being forced upon citizens by an overreaching government. I was approached to be one of several speakers to give a two- to three-minute speech. Wynne thought it would be a great opportunity for me to get back in front of voters and remind them of who I was. I wasn't completely sure about the situation because, although I had been active in politics in this area for a long time, I'd never heard of this lady who was now the leader of this group. Still, I couldn't think of any good reason not to, so I agreed to follow Wynne's lead. She contacted the local Tea Party leader and got us a spot on the agenda.

When we arrived, it was clear that most of the people there would have been, or had been, my supporters in the political spectrum. We worked our way through the crowd with most people recognizing me and encouraging me to run again to "finish off that Chet." We made our way to the makeshift speakers' platform. The Tea Party leader explained the ground rules to us, and made it clear she would not allow any partisan rhetoric or political campaigning. We should stick to tax issues.

As we moved over to wait my turn, we all looked at each other like, *Okay, so what can I say?* I quickly had to figure out what would be acceptable, and what would not be just a repeat of what was already being said speaker after speaker after speaker.

When it came to my turn, I introduced myself to the enthusiastic crowd as Rob Curnock, the guy who had just narrowly lost to the incumbent congressman in November. I talked to them about tax issues from the perspective of a small business owner who was sick of losing half of my income to taxes. Then I evidently made the mistake of veering into partisan politics. I began to challenge the crowd that, if we wanted to change the tax policy, "we had to change our congressman," to solid appreciative applause. The Tea Party leader from below the platform reached up and tugged on my pants leg. "No politicking!"

I continued on with my thought but cut it short by saying that we would "finish what we started in November and make that change happen in our district by getting rid of Chet Edwards." The audience cheered and applauded, but the Tea Party lady made it clear that she was not amused as I stepped down. She tersely reminded me that she had specifically told me that there was to be "no politics." I apologized, and we moved away.

As we made our way through the crowd, all three of us were perplexed about what was exactly happening here. Almost everybody we ran into was clearly pleased with what I had said and urged me to run again and win. We also recognized many in the crowd as my supporters from last year. Yet the leader didn't want any mention of the political realities of trying to change tax policies. In my mind, it was a little bit of a disconnect from political logic on the part of the leader.

I chalked it up to what I saw as the only flaw in the Tea Party movement: it wanted to present itself as nonpartisan. The Tea Party overwhelmingly attracted conservatives, and conservatives are overwhelmingly Republican. The reality is the Tea Party philosophy had absolutely no place or following in the Democrat Party. Also, many of these new activists had no experience or knowledge of the working realities of the American political system. That's positive in many ways but likely the reason for the friction between the Republican establishment and the upstart Tea Party.

While working our way out through the crowd, as others continued speaking, we got our first hint of things to come on the congressional campaign front. We suddenly came face-to-face with that political consultant who had tried to talk me out of running against Chet the evening that I filed in Austin. She wore an "Atkins for Congress" button and held a handful of cards touting more of the Atkins for Congress message.

Atkins?!

I introduced her to Karen and Wynne, then asked, "So what are you up to?" ignoring the obvious.

"I'm helping Eddie Atkins run for Congress."

I told her good luck and cut it short before I said something I would later regret. As we got out of earshot, both my wife and Wynne asked the question we were all thinking. "Who the heck is Eddie Atkins?"

"I have no idea. Never heard of him before. Maybe he's from somewhere else in the district."

Here we go again, I thought with a sense of disappointment.

A few minutes later we ran into another supporter from the last campaign. "Have you seen the guy who says he's going to run against Chet next time?" she asked. "I assume *you're* going to be running again to finish off Chet, since you're the one who came so close last time. But I'm afraid this means you're going to have competition."

"Just what we need, another contested primary," I said sarcastically.

"I met him, and I don't think you have a whole lot to be worried about. I wasn't impressed," she said. "Besides, I'm sure that most people, like me, will stick with you since you're the one who proved that he's vulnerable."

"I hope you're right."

This was something we didn't want, but there was nothing we could do about it. However, if he had the consultant working for him, he had enough money to pay her fees and, at least, had the connections to even know to call her, even though he was unknown himself in local political circles. She was considered a hired gun with a loaded Rolodex filled with potential active donors, and she definitely did not work on a voluntary basis.

We all had questions, but at this point, no answers. It was still very early in the political process and a long way from the filing date, so things could possibly change as nothing was official yet. We only knew that there would now probably be no straight shot back at Chet. We'd better brace ourselves for another primary. If this indeed turned out to be the case, it would definitely not be good news to anyone...but Chet.

Shortly after our first brush with the Tea Party, my good supporter Sean called to see if I planned to run again. "Yes, we're planning on running, but it's still too early for anything official, so we're just getting our ducks in a row," I told him.

"Keep me up to speed," he said. "I still want to be on the team, so let me know if there's anything I can do to help." Then he asked me something that told me we would probably face a primary opponent. "Have you heard anything about some guy from Waco getting into the Republican primary? I've heard rumor of that."

"I think his name is Eddie Atkins," I said. "I have no idea who he is, and I'm not sure of his plans. A lot of people talk about running for office, but few actually do it. I'm hoping that'll be the case with this guy."

"I agree. I'll do some digging and see if I can find anything out about him."

Deep down it galled me that someone who had no idea of what was going on in this district in our efforts to win that seat and had apparently never been involved in any previous activity to remove Chet, would suddenly come along and unilaterally decide to run. Of course, he had every right as an American to do it, so there was really nothing to be done about it.

A few weeks later I got a call from a man who wanted to talk with me personally about something related to the congressional race. I didn't know him, but he assured me that he had supported me against Chet. He showed up at my business at the appointed time with a handful of official-looking documents. After introductions, I asked what was on his mind.

"Do you know Eddie Atkins?" he asked pointedly.

I rolled my eyes. "I've heard of him. The only thing I know is that he's thinking about getting into the congressional race."

"He *is* running for sure, but there is no way we can let him win the nomination," he said with increasing agitation. "I'm a former business associate of his, and he has serious skeletons in his closet.

I'm afraid that if Eddie somehow beats you for the nomination, Chet will be able to blow him out of the water by exposing his past business activity—and Chet'll win again."

"I don't know anything about him or his past business situation. Unfortunately, there's nothing I can do about this Atkins guy running."

As he opened up his stack of papers, he said, "Let me show you what I'm talking about."

I listened as he explained his past business relationship with Atkins and how some of the things that were done were not only unethical, but, in his mind, illegal. He handed me several official documents from a state agency and related how a number of Atkins' past business practices had clearly violated state law. He also told how he was personally ripped off in his past dealings with Atkins. He finished his presentation by imploring me to get the state agency involved and deter Atkins from even running.

I politely handed the papers back to him. "I'm sorry but I can't do anything with this. Even if I could, it would look like nothing more than a political attack coming from me. On a legal level, I know absolutely nothing about any of this. If you have proof of illegal business practices, you really need to take this to the state yourself and get them to do something."

He was obviously disappointed at my reaction and unwillingness to get involved. It was not what he wanted to hear or had expected.

"His business partner told me that Atkins is going to be the next congressman, and that if I wanted to ever get any money, I should drop any thought of a lawsuit and accept a pennies-on-the-dollar settlement. If you ever have any dealings with this guy, watch out, he'll screw you," he warned.

"What's his name?" I asked, more out of politeness than curiosity.

"I can't remember exactly. It's like... Watters or...maybe... Sam Winters."

A light went on in my head and a quick knot formed in my stomach as he had struggled to come up with the name.

"Was his name *Weathers*? Sean *Weathers*?" My supporter who had been such a big help in our race against Chet.

"That's it. He's in finances. That's how he works with Atkins. Do you know him?"

"Yes, I know him." I said with complete, nonchalant understatement.

We wrapped up our meeting, and I said nothing more about Sean Weathers to the man in front of me.

Later on I thought, *Man, Sean was one of our most trusted and early volunteers last year. Could he really be that cold-blooded of a traitor?* I decided to not say anything. I'd let him think I was unaware, to see how far he was willing to take his audacious betrayal.

I got my answer a week or so later. Sean showed up at my shop one night just as I was about to close up. My staff was all gone for the day, and he came rushing in, seemingly agitated with a flyer in his hand.

"Have you seen this? I got it in the mail," he said, handing me the paper. It was an announcement for an Eddie Atkins fundraiser barbecue at a local ranch. I glanced over it and handed it back to Sean.

"I guess this guy Atkins is having a fundraiser," I said, hiding my disappointment at seeing this. It meant that there was now little doubt that we would have a contested primary. Several names on the host list were quasi friends of mine.

"Did you see the names on this?" he pressed. "These are the heavy hitters on the Republican money side around here. This means they're with him. We've got to find out who this guy is and what kind of support he really has. Why don't I go and see what I can find out?"

I played along. "Sure. Why don't you do that."

My question had been answered. Sean was a traitor and, worse, thought he was playing me for a fool. I let our key people know that Sean was no longer with us and would, therefore, be getting no more useful information from me or anyone else connected with our future campaign. Several weeks later Sean dropped by my office once again.

"This isn't easy, but I wanted you to know that I've decided to support Eddie. I didn't want you to hear it from anyone else. I feel I at least owe you that because of our past."

"Really?" I said, feigning surprise.

Then he dug in and went to work apparently trying to demoralize me. "There's just no denying it: all the big money in Waco is now lining up behind Eddie Atkins. In fact, I just came straight here from a major donor's meeting, and all the heavy financial hitters were there. I personally saw at least $60,000 change hands."

I was about ready to explode.

"I'm your friend, but I don't see how you're going to be able to raise any money. They've all picked Eddie, and I've got to go along with them."

I couldn't contain myself any longer.

"You're going along with them because you've been with Eddie all along. So, stop lying to my face like I'm some kind of a stupid idiot," I shouted at him angrily.

His mouth dropped open and it took him a good moment to recover. "What are you talking about? I don't even know Eddie…"

"You're not former business partners with Eddie?"

"Well, uh. I know him from business, but we're not really friends."

"That's a lie," I shot back. "Somebody came in here months ago who knew both of you. I've known since then that you've been working with him. I really just wanted to see how far you'd take this…so knock it off. I know what's going on, and it's pathetic. I'm certainly not going to quit because you say the "big money" has chosen Eddie. They're free to do what they want. Nobody knows who the heck Eddie is, so please, just do me one favor…"

I began to calm it down…and pushed on with a little sarcastic bravado just to tweak him.

"Talk to these money guys and ask them to please support me *after* the primary. I know they're probably going to be ticked off about throwing their money away on someone who's going to lose… but we'll need them in the fall if we want to finish off Chet.

I don't want them to be mad at me in any way and then refuse to get involved in the real fight."

He soon recovered his composure from the initial shock. He then went on the offensive.

"Rob, they all want Chet out, but I'm going to be honest with you. A lot of people don't like your style. It's how you come across.

My wife tells me that she agrees with most of what you say, but she thinks you're just too harsh. That's the knock on you."

"That's the first time I've heard that criticism, but *I am who I am*," I told him. "I'm not trying to be somebody I'm not. Most people tell me that the thing that attracts them to me is my passion."

He finally walked out visibly subdued, while I just tried to remain calm as I went home. I learned later, via someone attending the fundraiser, that Sean was actually one of the *organizers* of the event!

So, then the obvious question becomes, just how deep was Sean in the Atkins campaign, and why would he help someone else run from Waco, which, in the grand scheme of things, helped only Chet? There may have been a lot more going on than meets the eye. As the actual primary progressed, we began to harbor some serious suspicions about this whole situation and who was really working for whom, going all the way back to 2008. But we never uncovered any definitive proof.

Yep, this was politics at its finest. And, oh, it would get even worse.

CHAPTER 43

First Attack

It's hard to describe the mindset at work in the district once the long-time incumbent was seen as vulnerable. Opportunists from all over began contacting various county chairmen in the eleven counties to make it known that they intended to run for Congress in District 17. In fact, since there's nothing in the Constitution about residential requirements for Congress, a few from *outside* the district saw an easy opportunity to knock off what they saw as a lame duck congressman living on borrowed time. It was quickly turning into a mad scramble with the district's political leaders put into a difficult position. Legally, they couldn't forbid someone from running, but the sheer number of interested candidates was growing at an alarming rate.

In response, an informal group of concerned activists, working with several county chairmen, formed a congressional coalition to get a handle on the situation. Although they had no legal standing, the group organized a forum in Waco for all known interested candidates, with a plan to listen to each potential candidate and assess their ability to run for Congress.

Never mind the legality, for us, quite honestly, this was difficult to stomach. We had spent the last year doing everything we could to unseat Edwards. We'd been in the battle giving it everything we had and dealing with all the attacks that came with it. Almost all of these 'wannabe warriors' had stood on the sidelines and watched us struggle without offering any help. It seemed laughable that, after what we'd just been through, we'd be "required" to let others dictate to us how or if we could even campaign. But we now knew, beyond a shadow of a doubt, that our dreams of an uncontested primary were long gone. This meeting would, at least, give us a chance to see what the level of competition would look like and how many challengers there might be.

We reluctantly agreed to attend.

There was a pretty good crowd of about 40 people in the room with some county chairmen and club presidents in the audience. Before speaking, we were asked to sign the organizers' newly-crafted campaign pledge. The pledge was an attempt to avoid the nastiness that normally develops at some point in most contested primaries. I hastily read through it and, without comment, signed it. Deep inside, from real world experience, I knew that the paper, although well-intentioned, was virtually worthless and unenforceable. Since we would not be allowed to hear the other "candidates," I sat outside with the others and waited to be called in.

When my turn came, I pled my case as to why I was the best and most logical choice to take on Chet Edwards in the fall. As I was the only one in the building that had been down this path before, I spoke of the closeness of the race and my unique perspective as the only one who'd actually been in battle with the long-time incumbent, even though I'd had little money and absolutely no support from the national and state parties. This next time around would be different, because we now had credibility, which we knew would translate into successful fundraising and should result in help from the national party. I closed by asking for a chance to finish the job. "I'm already tested and proven. Why take the chance with someone new who hasn't been vetted?"

Over all it was surreal. I'd just been through the wringer with Chet and came respectably close to winning, but here I was on an equal footing with other potential candidates who we'd never seen in any kind of political setting before, waiting to be given some sort of unofficial seal of approval from a group of people, many of whom had done little or nothing to help in the last campaign.

I wholeheartedly agree that this was actually American politics at its finest, with average citizens calling the shots. But on a strictly personal level, this event was a very real lesson in self-control and humility. I'd even been told by one organizer beforehand that they hoped my talk would focus on how I could win in the next election cycle, while keeping in mind that people "really don't care that you ran last year."

Later, one of my supporters in the audience reported on what he had seen and heard. He said that I was the most compelling speaker of the bunch, and in his mind, along with those in the audience he talked to, I was the logical choice and would probably have the best chance to defeat Chet. However, he warned me about two other candidates.

"Eddie Atkins tried to make the case that he would have support in Waco that you didn't have when you ran, and he would definitely raise more money than you did. He also claimed that he was a former federal worker. I think a few people were positively impressed.

"But the one you're probably going to have the most problems with is this oilman from College Station, Bill Flores. He claims he's been asked to run by the party leadership in Washington because he also has the money to self-fund the campaign. He argued that he was the only one who had the financial ability to run a credible race against Chet Edwards. A lot of people were impressed with that."

"This is the first I've heard of him."

"On a personality level, he's not a good speaker, and he doesn't seem dynamic. But people were impressed that he could afford to run. Rob, he's the one you're going to have to look out for."

Any time a candidate can self-fund a primary race, you have to take them seriously. He may or may not have been recruited by the National Republican Party to run—that could be hyperbole designed to impress—but the money aspect was easy enough to confirm and would be a problem. I called Wynne and asked her to check him out.

The next day, Wynne reported he was, indeed, extremely wealthy, but he would also be carrying some serious baggage for a congressional candidate running in a Republican primary. A Republican registry called *Texas Voter Vault,* supplies data based on voting history. It then rates all voters on a scale from Strong Republican to Weak Republican or Strong Democrat to Weak Democrat. Wynne was surprised to discover that a Bill Flores from the Houston area was listed as a "Weak Democrat."

"A weak Democrat?!" I exclaimed. "He's listed as a Democrat? Are you sure it's the same guy?"

Wynne, who was quite good at opposition research, responded, "I don't see how it could be anyone else. Besides, I'm assuming that this is the same Bill Flores who's on record as having donated to other Republican candidates. I guess he's listed as a weak Democrat because he voted in the Democratic primary in 2008."

"Why would a guy who voted in the Democratic primary turn around and run in a Republican congressional primary—in another district? If it *is* the same guy, he's going to have a lot of explaining to do."

"That's not all," Wynne continued. "He's evidently made his fortune from an oil company he started, but get this--one of his major funding partners was George Soros."

I was stunned. As any good conservative knew, Soros was like an open bank account for all the radical leftist organizations plaguing and, in my mind, destroying America.

"Yes, *the* George Soros. He evidently put up a lot of money into Flores' company. I don't think he's still tied to him, but he definitely made Flores successful," she said.

"That can't be right. Why would this guy be running in the Republican primary for the congressional seat in District 17? Once this all gets out, I don't care how much money he has, he'll get blown out of the water. How does he possibly think he can win this primary?"

I got my first impression of Flores when we met in another early forum in Waco. He seemed pleasant enough when we first met, but after sharing the stage with him, I agreed with the assessment of my supporter who said Flores was not a strong speaker nor did he have a dynamic personality. Afterward, with aides in tow, he made a show of giving a large monetary donation to the organization putting on the event. That told me all I needed to know about how he would be running his race. When he bragged at that first organizing meeting that he had the money to win this race, he was going to make a point of proving it at every chance. And, sadly for me, that can be a tough strategy to overcome.

Since the end of the previous campaign, we were joined by a retired businessman named Bob, from the northern region of the district, who wanted to be our volunteer finance chairman. After coming to a few campaign events with us, Bob determined that, because of the money situation, Flores was the one we needed to be most concerned about. Bob was a sharp businessman, but he wasn't exactly an old pro in politics. After seeing Flores a few times in forums, he believed we should meet him and urge him not to run. I didn't think that was realistic, but, on his own, Bob approached Flores to see if he would meet with me. I was surprised when Flores agreed.

Other than his aggressive and gregarious personality, one thing I liked about Bob was that he was an avid pilot with his own plane. Because we were operating in such a widespread district, I was pleased that Bob volunteered to fly us to different events throughout the eleven counties, with fuel to be reimbursed by the campaign. This would save us from the constant and draining long drives. Flores had just finished building and moving into a new, large, and impressive home in the Bryan/College Station area. Bob flew in from his home in the northern part of the district, picked me up in Waco, and we headed down to the south where another volunteer met us and let us use his car.

Flores showed us into his study. His home was beautiful, and it was clear that he had done well in life. The plan was to talk about the race and see what the other was thinking. Flores pointed out that running for Congress wasn't his idea, but he had been approached by political leaders to help unseat Chet. He also felt he had the economic expertise to understand complicated fiscal legislation that most people didn't possess. Flores reiterated to me that, although I had done a good job of running against Chet, I didn't have the resources needed to win such a race. He assured us that *he* did. At that point he waved his hand toward the back of the house, which was adjoining an exclusive private golf club, and said, "I could raise a hundred thousand dollars from just my friends on the golf course if I need to. That's the type of money I'll have no trouble getting." Sitting in the midst of his luxurious home, his point was well taken.

I countered with the arguments that I only had a little way to go to finish off Chet, I'd already been vetted, this time around we'd have no trouble being taken seriously by the party, and I was sure we'd get the support we needed to get it done. Bob tried to impress him with the fact that we already had a large and dedicated cadre of volunteers working for our campaign. Ironically, Flores quickly and dismissively replied that he had plenty of money to get all the volunteers he would need. "That's not a problem."

Before we were done, I threw out one last, "You know, if you really don't want to run, like you've been saying, you could always just help me financially to finish this off, and we'd definitely win it.

Once in Congress, if you are, indeed, an expert on economic issues, if you helped us get there, you would be the guy I'd call if I needed advice or help on financial and economic issues. I'd much rather us work together than against each other."

He opened a door ever so slightly. "I hadn't thought about that. I haven't entirely made up my mind yet. You've given me some things to consider."

At that, we took our leave and walked down the long curved drive to our parked car. When we were out of earshot, Bob broke the silence with his declaration that Flores was "the most arrogant son of a bi**h I've ever met."

On the way to the airport, I told Bob it was obvious to me that Flores didn't want to bother with a campaign or running for office. "He's more interested in buying the seat and parachuting into Congress," I said. "Think about it; I've got to get ready for a parade in McGregor tomorrow morning. There is no way Flores wants to have to walk down the middle of a hot street in a small-town parade, stepping over cow patties."

"You might be right."

"We'll see what happens. Maybe lightning will strike and he'll change his mind."

A few days later, Flores sent out a blast email to announce that, for business reasons, he was suspending his campaign. Bob thought that maybe our trip had paid off after all. While I took it as a positive sign, I also noted that his statement pointedly left the door open for him to get back in the race if things changed.

The innocuous meeting with Flores subsequently became the basis for the first attack in the primary race, even *before* the race had started. For whatever reasons, it seemed to us that there were those who did not want me facing Edwards in November again, and would go to extreme lengths to get me out of the race.

Weeks later, echoing a past primary, a reporter with the Waco *Tribune-Herald* called to get my reaction to the fact that I had violated campaign laws by flying, courtesy of a donor, to a campaign function. The reporter wanted to know how many flights I had taken and for what reasons. Unbeknownst to me, a newly enacted and little-known campaign rule severely restricted the use of private planes in congressional elections. The *Trib* jumped at the chance to once again "get me" and expose me as a callous violator of campaign law.

Unlike years earlier in my dealings with the *Trib* on their "Curnock Ads Violated Campaign Law" story, this time I wasn't stunned or scared; I was angry. I expressed my ignorance of the rule to the reporter but did confirm I had taken one flight to Bryan/College Station to meet with Flores. I would have nothing further to say on the matter until I talked with the FEC.

I immediately called the FEC, and the official's initial reaction caught me by surprise.

"Technically, you may have violated that new rule, but it's so *new*, it hasn't even come up yet. I can't tell you if you're in violation because we haven't even had a chance to formulate the official interpretation of this particular statute. Our agency is still working on trying to implement what we think the Congress intended with its passage. We're not experts on this one yet."

"So, what should we do? Are we in any kind of trouble?"

"No, just make sure you reimburse the pilot for his fuel and declare it on your expense reports. If the media has any questions, they can contact me." Then he added with a chuckle, "And for now, I would strongly suggest that you don't take any more private plane rides for the campaign. Driving would be a lot less trouble."

Several weeks later, the FEC did put out an official notice concerning the private-plane-ride statute, and nothing more came of it regarding a possible violation. The Waco *Trib* did run its story with the implication that I may have done something in violation of the rule, but at least they reported the FEC's ambivalence at the time and that there was no official determination to hang on me.

More ominously, the night before the paper was even released, the head of the local Tea Party, the same one who had tugged on my pants leg, put out an email blast declaring that I was irresponsible and could not now be trusted and so on. We wondered how she knew about the article before it was even out in print. This was a clear indication that we would face more than just other candidates in the upcoming primary.

The entire incident alerted us that someone was trying to come up with anything, no matter how trivial, to hurt us. The question was, who? The only person who knew of our flight was Flores. But he wasn't even in the race, right? And on top of that, who would even know of this statute, which hadn't even been officially codified by the bureaucracy charged with enforcing it? Sure would seem like the work of some kind of wonk out of Washington, D.C. Could it be Chet? Maybe the answers would eventually turn up. They almost always do if you know what to look for.

So here it was. A dreaded contested and crowded primary was now a reality. The question for me was, Could I come out of it unsullied, while not getting drawn into the seemingly inevitable personal destructive nature of the standard contested primary? I knew for a fact that the higher the stakes, the better the chance for acrimony between candidates. In fact, the whole plane ride incident was merely a portent of uglier things to come.

CHAPTER 44

Sizing Up the Pack

With the filing period growing closer, the number of prospective candidates grew as well. At one point, about a dozen people had publicly committed to jumping into the race. In our campaign, we joked that I had created a monster by showing that Chet was indeed vulnerable. As my campaign had the most structure and many loyal volunteers held over from the previous run against Edwards, we decided to make a show of strength by submitting petitions in lieu of a filing fee. Besides saving us over $3,000, we hoped to warn others off by showing we had a good base of grassroots support. It was encouraging when our volunteers easily collected the required number of signatures from all over the district. In spite of the whirlwind of candidate activity leading up to the filing deadline, when the dust finally settled, five primary candidates remained.

Flores was one. My suspicions about him not truly quitting turned out to be well founded. He made it official late in the filing period and came back into the race after missing the long summer of parades and forums. Now all he had to do was money-bomb the district's primary voters and take his chances that he could knock off the incumbent nominee. Information was also put out implying he had been recruited and chosen by the national Republican Party to take on Chet. In other words, he was *the* chosen one.

In the meantime, Flores had amassed a fully paid campaign staff complete with a speech coach and a hired gun out of Washington to manage the campaign. His D.C.-trained campaign manager turned out to be someone who evidently liked to play hardball and practiced a scorched-earth brand of campaigning. Looking back, we took an educated guess that he would be exactly the type who would know of a new, obscure, private-plane rule.

Eddie Atkins from Waco made his campaign official, as well as two others from the Bryan/College Station region: A military veteran and professor at Texas A&M University, as well as a young male nurse. Chet Edwards couldn't have asked for a better scenario.

Our focus was to build on the success we had in the last general election. We knew some supporters would likely float off to other candidates, so the key was to keep defections to a minimum and give our supporters a reason to let us finish the job. On a very positive note, new volunteers joined in leadership positions. These were skilled people in the real world who brought energy and expertise to the campaign: professionals in public relations, advertising, media, social media, administration, and sales. This gave us a full complement of skills needed to run a successful campaign. Although everyone on our team was a volunteer, this was the equivalent of the "professional" staff that someone like Flores was paying a fortune for. Incredibly, we soon had four headquarters throughout the district with three of them completely donated. All were manned by volunteer staff and operating under full extended hours. This was the epitome of a grassroots operation.

Organizationally, we were a force to be reckoned with, but finances once again proved to be stubborn in the coming. Although I was now perceived as a legitimate candidate, the "donor" class remained resistant to get involved until after the primary. Nonetheless, with the reputation and relationships made in the prior election, more often as not, when I visited potential donors, I would come away with some sort of a check. That rarely happened two years before. Bob, our campaign finance chairman, was a go-getter too. His aggressive fundraising paid off with contributions and in-kind donations coming in from donors all over the district. It wasn't the large, maximum donations, but he was successful with moderate-to-small donors. This buoyed all of our spirits, especially those of us who had clawed our way through the last battle with little money. We soon surpassed our entire contribution total from the 2008 general election.

We knew we had to get enough money to do limited television and radio, and we did, but we still didn't have nearly enough money to reach every Republican primary voter with direct mail. And, unfortunately, even with the limited success of the fundraising, any money brought in had to be spent fending off other Republicans. It was disappointing that we couldn't save every penny for the main event.

Leading up to the primary election, the nation was struggling with the notion of "Obamacare," President Obama's push to enact nationalized healthcare. The Congress was getting a lot of heat from upset citizens who wanted no part of this government takeover of the private medical sector of the American economy. Congressmen and senators all over the country were getting hammered at town hall meetings by angry constituents demanding that Obamacare not be made into law.

As expected, Congressman Edwards tried to remain publicly noncommittal, and pointedly refused to schedule any town hall meetings. Our media director came up with the brilliant idea that, if Chet wouldn't give citizens the chance to talk to their congressman, we would give them a chance to talk to their Republican congressional challenger. We organized town hall meetings in three parts of the district and gave voters a chance to voice their opinion at open mikes. We'd then take their thoughts, transcribe them, and officially deliver them to the congressman's office.

It was exceedingly successful as people took advantage of the opportunity and showed up in droves. After *our* first meeting, the congressman's hand was forced, and he suddenly agreed to several carefully controlled conference calls to let people have their say on the issue. We noted with great interest that his "call" meetings fell on the exact same time and dates as our final two scheduled events.

For us it was a great chance to show we were serious about representing the people and getting their input on such an important and controversial topic. We dutifully did what we said we'd do and made an important point. But for us, the best by-product of this exercise was that we gave people a chance to officially sign up and volunteer for our campaign. The vast majority of those who attended these meetings were impressed that our campaign actually seemed to be doing something, and they wanted to be part of it. The number of volunteers who signed up began to swell exponentially. By the time we were several weeks out from the primary Election Day, we had an official volunteer tally of more than 1,600 volunteers.

Of the five candidates remaining, it was soon apparent where everyone stood on the political spectrum. Although everyone called themselves conservatives, for purposes of the Republican primary, we all represented various loosely organized factions. The nurse from Bryan, was a fire-breathing ultra-right-winger who held nothing back in his pronouncements of a very limited view of government and was quick to call out other candidates whom he felt lacked conservative purity. The former military man-turned-professor was an intelligent thinker with an intellectual approach to conservative politics. He knew his stuff but seemed to have a no-nonsense personality. Atkins from Waco appeared to make a conscious effort in the early forums to carve out a niche as a moderate, but the cool response from Republican primary voters apparently made him abandon that strategy quickly. He tacked to the right by playing up conservative beliefs and his time in a federal agency.

Flores also started out as a moderate conservative, but his political philosophy evolved even as he spoke. It seemed to me that he had no real defined set of political values and was being coached at every point as to what would be the best response to given questions in various situations.

Several weeks before early voting, the McLennan County Republican Party held a candidate forum to be broadcast live on the radio and internet, with some coverage by local TV. For me, this was an important event. We would answer questions from various sources and would have specific time limits for responses and fol-low-ups. However, this one had a new wrinkle: we would each have the opportunity to ask one other candidate a question of our own.

This presented a dilemma. As the "incumbent" Republican nominee, perhaps I was playing out a subtle variation of the *persona non grata* strategy against my new challengers that Edwards had used on me. So, I had to come up with a question that wouldn't help any-body else and, at the same time, I didn't want to single anyone else out as a presumptive threat. However, I knew that Flores, with his huge bankroll, was my real competition.

Late in the debate, the moderator told us to ask one other can-didate a question. It just so happened that my turn would come last. The other candidates took the opportunity to hit hard at their chosen target, getting issues off their chests that had been festering from any number of minor skirmishes which had taken place at earlier forums. All the exchanges got a little heated. For whatever reason, I came off untouched, hopefully leaving me appearing to be above the fray.

When my turn came, I spoke to the audience. "I'd like to lighten things up a bit," I said. "All I want to know is, who did the others vote for in the last two general elections for Congress?" People around the room grasped my point and chuckled. "Can I ask them all?" I asked the moderator.

"You have to pick one."

"Okay, then… Bill. Since you're sitting next to me, who did you vote for?"

Flores understood my point, he thought, and was willing to accede with as little fanfare as possible. "I voted for you, Rob. I wanted you to win, and I thought you should win, but it just didn't happen."

"That shows good judgment on your part," I said, with more laughter from the audience. "I'll put that down on our website as an endorsement. But I asked who you voted for in the last *two* general elections."

"I wasn't living in this district for that election."

He fell right into my trap without realizing it. I had gotten my point across by having him level a key accusation at *himself*. I wanted to let the voters know that he had moved into the district to run for this seat without me having to be the one to say it. At the very least, even if he didn't move into the district specifically to run, he'd only been here a brief time and didn't have any deep roots in the area.

With a few weeks to go, we began running limited television and radio spots throughout the district. We had no polling data, so we had no sure way of knowing how things looked between the five of us. We just had a strong sense that the race would come down to myself and Flores. We knew there was no way we could keep up with him in either the mail or media fronts. Money was trumping everything. Although he now denied it officially, Flores' campaign continued to slyly intimate that Flores was the candidate the national Republican party backed. He was the one the national Republican leadership had recruited and thought could win. Unfortunately for us, to a lot of voters, that's a very powerful voting motivator.

Although the nurse candidate had brought up some of the negative things about Flores, he was the only one to do so. I still opposed going negative on principle alone. We decided to just hunker down and hope that the activist conservative Republicans would carry the day.

It seemed like Atkins from Waco had dropped like a stone. A contact close to his camp revealed he was confused and depressed that all his early money donors and support—for some reason—suddenly went away. Perhaps it went back to the old question of, "Who was really working for whom?" Whether Atkins understood it or not, once other candidates jumped into the race and forced a contested primary, Chet Edwards didn't need a candidate from Waco to be in the race. So, who convinced Atkins to run for Congress and what were their real motives for doing so? Based on personal experience, I guessed that person was likely working both sides of the aisle.

We figured the nurse had no chance, so it came down to the professor as the only potential threat for that second spot. He did limited advertising and a mailing, but we sensed that wouldn't be enough. Besides, he'd be fighting for votes from the Bryan/College Station area with Flores. We wanted to win it outright, but at the very least, we had to finish in the top two.

CHAPTER 45

Get That Vote

At this point, our campaign continued the very core focus of any campaign for any office: meeting as many people as possible and trying to get them to pull that lever for you.

Although, after many months of this, it can become monotonous for some candidates, I actually enjoyed meeting voters and accepted the challenge of trying to win over everyone I could.

A truly dedicated candidate will go to great lengths to get that vote. For me, I determined early on that as long as it passed my moral, legal, and ethical test, I'd go to almost any length to shake a hand and talk. Even when passing that test, there were times when I had to go one step further than expected to make that contact and secure support.

One of our volunteers in the northern part of the district wanted me to meet with a very influential member of their community. He assured me that a visit with this gentleman could yield solid electoral dividends since he was very well respected with people, and if he supported me, many others would most likely follow. Because this kind of math was the main focus of all my campaigning, I thought it was certainly worth the effort and made the drive up to meet him.

Since this was no official event, I went alone and connected up with my contact, and the two of us would head out to this man's farm for an impromptu meeting. My supporter assured me that this was a really big deal for this man to take time out to meet with me, and, if it went well, it would be well worth the effort.

We headed up the long drive to the area where his agricultural equipment was housed in several metal buildings. As we came into view we saw a man standing just outside one of the buildings with another man, a little ways off, tinkering with a farm implement parked nearby. As we got closer, my supporter said, "There he is... the guy on the left."

He had his back to us and never even really looked up as we approached, but as we got closer, it was clear that he was relieving himself. I said with a laugh, "You mean the guy taking a whizz?"

"Well, hey, out here there's nobody around to offend," he said as we both laughed.

We pulled up and got out of the car, just as he was finishing his business, and it was at that moment I had to make a quick decision. As his friend said hello and introduced us, he turned around and did the normal polite thing and reached out to shake my hand.

Oh boy.

I'm no prima donna or germaphobe, but really?! Determining that a wave was now out of the question, and I certainly didn't want to be rude, I stared down at his outreached hand.

'*Crud, how bad do I want this guy's support?*' I asked myself in that split second of decision-making. '*Suck it up,*' I thought to myself. '*If this is the worst thing I'm facing, then I'm doing well.*'

I reached out and shook his hand and introduced myself.

Okay, I'll admit I didn't squeeze as hard as I normally would. This is a perfect example of why campaigning in a bathroom is never a good idea.

He was as nice and as friendly as could be, and we ended up having a really good conversation. As we drove off, my supporter was happy with the way things went and was convinced we had accomplished our mission.

Welcome to the pitfalls of basic campaigning 101. In the end, you just do what you gotta do. That also includes doing some things no matter how futile it may seem at the time.

We were at another function up in the northern part of the district and had some extra time before heading back to Waco. We were with a black couple who had become loyal volunteers in our effort. They took us to the main park in town, and off in the distance, we saw a stage had been erected and preparations were being made for a Juneteenth celebration concert in the park later that evening. In Texas, Juneteenth marks the day that word reached Texas during the Civil war that Lincoln had signed the Emancipation Proclamation. It's largely celebrated in the minority community.

As such, when our friends suggested I go over and talk to the people beginning to gather, I was fairly skeptical.

"You really think there are going to be many Republican primary voters over there?" I asked somewhat bemusedly.

"No, but you should at least make an effort." Deborah challenged me to go over and campaign. "Who knows? Maybe you'll open some minds."

I saw absolutely nothing wrong with her logic although I still didn't think it would yield much results. We headed over to a group of about ten people sitting in the front seats of an otherwise empty large collection of chairs facing the stage.

As we walked up, I greeted the first man who made eye contact sitting in the front row. I shook his hand (squeezing normally) and introduced myself.

He was a middle-aged distinguished-looking man dressed in a shirt and tie, even though it was getting to be a warm afternoon.

"Hi, I'm Rob Curnock, and I'm running for Congress, I'd like to ask you to consider voting for me, if so inclined."

He was friendly as he shook my hand and then asked the logical question. "Are you a Republican or a Democrat?"

"I'm running in the Republican primary. We came pretty close last time around in the general election, and I'm hoping to finish the job in November," I said, handing him some literature as my volunteers gave cards to the others now listening.

"Thank you, but I really only vote Democrat," he said affirming what I had assumed when we headed over in the first place.

"I understand, but if you ever change your mind, I'd appreciate it if you'd give me a look," I responded as I was ready to look elsewhere for the votes I needed. I started to move along.

My supporters were not as willing to let it go as I was. Deborah went straight for the jugular and firmly but politely asked why he only voted Democrat, since they supported abortion and were wrong on all the other social issues.

It turned out he was a minister and he said, with a significant amount of discomfort, "I honestly can't think about where they stand on those...uh...social aspects. I really can't. I don't agree with those,"

He looked off and shook his head. "So, I have to just think about financial issues. Otherwise, I'm just not comfortable when I think about it."

The conversation between us went on for a few more minutes and stayed very cordial. The Reverend even seemed to open the door a crack as we discussed several key issues in both the fiscal and social arenas. Surprisingly, those gathered around him made it a point to ask for more material.

Did we gain any converts? Probably not, but it was a good exercise in thinking outside the box and at least reaching out. Even more importantly, Deborah and her husband were proud that I was willing to take the challenge, and it reaffirmed their belief in what our campaign stood for and their reason for actively volunteering.

For me, it was yet another sad confirmation of what my roommate had shared with me so many years before. From our conversation, it was clear that this influential pastor and I probably agreed on 90% of the issues, yet he was still firmly wedded to the party which was actively working against all the values that he espoused from the Bible and his pulpit.

This misguided lockstep loyalty with the Democrat Party is extremely frustrating to witness, but again, as a good campaigner, my goal would be to at least make him think, even if I wouldn't get his vote.

In that regard, it appeared: mission accomplished.

CHAPTER 46

That's Extortion!

With the primary drawing to a close, on a light campaign day, I was back at my shop taking care of business. A FedEx driver came in with a letter delivery. I signed for it without giving it too much thought, but when I looked down to see who it was from, I suddenly got an uneasy feeling. It was from Randall, the bane of my 2008 campaign.

What on earth would Randall want, and why would he be sending me a "costly" letter via FedEx? We had always emailed or talked on the phone. This seemed out of character. In fact, the last time I had any verbal contact with Randall was two Christmases ago. Karen and I were visiting her family for the holidays, and I gave him a call just to be cordial. The following August he sent an email to see if I would be interested in opting into a football pool for the upcoming season. Not that I wanted anything to do with Randall after the last campaign, but I attempted to let bygones be bygones.

So why would Randall suddenly contact me out of the blue via FedEx?

With a little apprehension I opened up the envelope and read his letter. I was stunned. It was a brazen demand for $20,000. He stated that my campaign owed him that much for all the work he had done in 2008 as per our agreement. Then he ominously warned that if I didn't pay him the money, he had contact information for all the local media outlets, and he would be calling all of them with the story. Then he warned that he had also hired a local Waco attorney, and I had until Tuesday to meet his demands—or he would go to the press.

I'm sure it was purely coincidental that Tuesday was the first day of early voting.

I stared at the letter, not believing what I was seeing. I've experienced a lot of things in my life, but this was my first brush with being the target of what was clearly an extortion attempt. For a brief moment, I thought about calling and confronting him. Fortunately, common sense prevailed, and I realized that a phone call would go from bad to worse quickly. With an emotional mixture of shock, anger, fear, disappointment, sadness, disbelief, and a very tangible desire to beat the crap out of him, I immediately called my lawyer, who happened to be a former assistant district attorney.

After going over the story, my lawyer, *without* emotion, laid out our options. My desire to physically pound Randall was taken off the table. My thought was to go to the media first and put out the story that my former campaign manager was trying to extort money from our campaign. The lawyer cautioned me about publicly using that exact term, in that it could give him fodder for a potential liable suit. We could pay him, but that would give the impression that we did owe him money, and there was no guarantee he wouldn't make trouble in the press anyway. And quite probably, he would demand more money later. Another option was to do nothing and let him go to the press. Most likely, most news organizations would not even hear him out— but there was always the possibility one would run the story. A last option would be to go on the offense legally and attempt to prosecute him criminally. That would be a slow, difficult process, and he would still be free to wreak as much havoc as possible. Again, there was the possibility that he could damage us enough to cost us the election.

This wasn't the type of thing we needed in front of voters on the first day of early voting, which is exactly the desired effect and what makes an extortion attempt possible.

We decided that we would go on the offense legally and attempt to prosecute. My lawyer would run it by his contacts in the FBI. In the meantime, I called one of our key volunteers, who just happened to be a sitting prosecutor in one of the northern counties. He agreed it was a clear-cut case of extortion, but for the time being, we would let it sit over the weekend and let my attorney take the lead.

I was left to let my mind wander and think of all the possible ramifications of this incredible turn of events. The most difficult aspect was to wrap my mind around how this man could be so despicable. I've been fortunate to have never been in any situation remotely similar to this in my life. This was a guy who had been a friend, and now was actually trying to extort money from me. At the very least, he was attempting to destroy my campaign, which was poised to win the congressional seat if I could get out of the primary. I spent a difficult weekend of vacillating between fear and fury.

If there was any doubt this was indeed happening, that doubt evaporated the following Monday morning. Checking my personal email, I saw one from him. I hoped maybe he had come to his senses and was calling the whole thing off. Just the opposite. He was doubling down in his effort to make a bad situation worse.

His email was short and to the point. He said that he knew by now that I'd gotten his letter and that if I did the right thing and pay the money, "…this can be resolved very quickly and quietly…".

The man was creating a textbook example of extortion. Was he unbelievably stupid or supremely confident in his quest for a big payday and his assumption that I would crumble like a stale cookie? I contacted my lawyer with this new evidence. Later that day, he got a call from a man representing himself as Randall's Waco lawyer to see if we were ready to meet his demands. If not, how much would we be willing to pay? He then tossed out the trial balloon that Randall might be willing to accept as little as $16,000. My lawyer relayed my affirmation that we owed him nothing, and I wouldn't pay him one penny.

Early voting started the next morning, so we focused on somehow removing this cloud over my head, wondering if it would turn out to be nothing more than a bluff. The answer came later that morning when I got a call on my cell phone from a reporter at the Waco *Trib*. He wanted to know if we could talk about this situation with my old campaign manager. Randall had already made his call and was going to do his best to blow up my campaign. The media protectors of all-things-Chet at the Waco paper dutifully swung into action.

"You guys are actually going to run this garbage?" I asked with little regard for niceties.

"We're not sure, but he has contacted us with his side of the story, and we want to be fair and let you tell your side. But we do think that this is a legitimate story."

Being careful to not outright accuse Randall of extortion, I tried to hit all around it.

"You understand what's being done here? We absolutely owe him nothing, and he'd never even made any demands until suddenly *five days before the start of early voting!* If we don't give in and pay him, he threatened to call you and other media outlets to hurt our campaign—just as voting begins. He also sent me an email that said that if I paid him this money, it could all go away 'quickly and quietly.' Doesn't that sound a lot like what a lot of people, including a county prosecutor on our team, might consider something illegal, seriously close to what many people would consider, you know, *extortion?*"

The reporter countered with, "Maybe, but you could also look at it from the perspective that he's using the only leverage he has in a financial dispute with your campaign. It may be his best and only way to get money that he believes he's owed."

"He has nothing to do with the current campaign, and he's made no demands for any money from the 2008 campaign before now, because he knew we had none and that we didn't owe him anything. In reality, he never raised any of the money he was supposed to raise so that he could pay himself. So now, suddenly, this is just somebody trying to force us to pay him for something that he's not owed. We're not going to give him a penny. And we're turning everything over to the proper legal authorities for them to determine what's going on here. But I think it's pretty obvious to most people what's happening."

I hung up knowing the paper would yet again run another hatchet job on me. I let my lawyer know that Randall had already gone to the press. Strangely, a couple of hours later, my lawyer called me back to report that Randall's Waco lawyer had called again to get our answer on whether we would pay the money or at least some portion of it. When my attorney informed him that his client had *already* gone to the press, Randall's attorney was clearly blindsided by this information, and informed him that Randall was no longer his client as of that moment.

We had an event down in Bryan/College Station later that afternoon and, after discussing it with my campaign brain trust, we decided to do a preemptive strike of our own and put out a press release stating that a former disgruntled campaign chairman from 2008 was making baseless demands on our 2010 campaign, and that we would not be paying him under any circumstances. We described the scenario under which the demands were made and explained that we were turning over all pertinent information to the proper legal authorities. Unfortunately, that was as far as my lawyer would let us go.

The CBS affiliate in Bryan/College Station, and sister station of my old TV station in Waco, asked me to come in for an on-set interview for the 10 o'clock news. They would then feed the video up to Waco for use in Waco. I was not happy about having to go on television to carefully and cautiously put out the story, but at the time it was our best option to short circuit the story that would be coming out in the Waco *Trib* the next morning.

Before going on set, the anchor and I discussed what was happening and why it was happening the first day of early voting. When I told him the full story of how this thing came up and how my lawyer was handcuffing me with what I could say, without any prompting from me, the anchor said, "This sure seems like extortion."

I just nodded and, being very careful to not use the term myself, said, "That's what it seems like to us as well."

The next morning the *Trib* ran an article that was told from Randall's perspective and was as close to a true hatchet job as one could imagine. They didn't leave out any of my quotes or get any of the quotes wrong, but as I had to follow the advice of my lawyer, there wasn't a whole lot I could say.

Two other TV news outlets called later that day wanting to follow up on the story that ran in the *Trib*, but after a brief conversation in which I read Randall's email threat, the reporter and producer, who had called from different organizations, both said without prompting, "That's extortion!" I again agreed. Both immediately expressed their displeasure that I had to go through this. Both also said that they would talk to their news directors and recommend that nothing be done with this story. However, they did want to follow up if the legal authorities went after Randall. I assured them I would keep them posted.

Eventually, my lawyer did turn the email and letter over to a retired FBI agent he knew, and the agent agreed that, in his opinion, this was textbook extortion. He took it to the local U.S. attorney to see if they would take the case. The U.S. attorney felt that since this was a dispute based on a workplace agreement, it could be construed as a civil dispute, and pressing a criminal charge would be too difficult to prove in court. Every legal and criminal expert, including a judge or two connected with our campaign, disagreed with the assessment of the U.S. Attorney. One wonders if the fact that the U.S. Attorney worked for the Obama Justice Department might have played a role in the decision not to take the case. Unfortunately for us, there was nothing more that could be done as it was a federal matter, so we just went on about our business and waited for Election Day.

Over the next couple of weeks, Randall got a new lawyer in Waco. His demands through his new attorney began to shrink. Our answer of "No way in Hades" did not shrink.

At the same time, our campaign brain trust began to smell a rat; someone from Waco was helping Randall. It was obviously someone who knew Randall, so that narrowed it down to people from our 2008 campaign. Then, who still had contact with Randall out of state and didn't despise the guy? The list just got very exclusive, especially in light of the fact that the person heading up that extremely short list had earlier been embarrassed by being exposed as a bald-faced lying double agent in his jump to another primary candidate at the start of the 2010 campaign.

The "why" was fairly evident. One of the other candidates was likely hoping that he would be the beneficiary of me somehow being weighed down with a scandal just before the vote. Once again, we had solid suspicions of the person throwing gasoline on Randall's fire. But no hard evidence.

The damage was done. The biggest question, of course, was, how bad? Would the voters care? All we could do was keep working to get in the top two on Election Day. We ignored Randall the rest of the way.

The results of the primary were not all we hoped for, but they were good enough. Flores and I were the top two vote getters. The professor finished third, with Atkins and the nurse far behind. I was disappointed because Flores was the top finisher, and we were now forced into a runoff with him. On the pragmatic side, I was pleased that I was still alive.

It was now a two-man race. I was confident that I would beat Chet if I could get past the runoff. In fact, I was fairly certain that whichever of us came out of the runoff would inevitably beat Chet, even though I thought Flores had baggage. In my mind, I just had to get past this heavily financed and connected opportunist, even if he was a complete political neophyte.

CHAPTER 47

Question of Character

In the month and a half of the runoff election, it appeared the Flores campaign would pull out all stops. At first it was stupid, irritating little things that, on their own, were harmless, but taken in their totality, they began to slowly and subtly lower the overall civility of the campaign. For me, this was new territory.

Although I never prepared speeches, I had certain catch phrases or statements that I invoked whenever a given issue came up. In most cases, these were phrases that I had been using since my very first primary race, and if I got a good reaction from my listeners, I would continue to use them. An example might be in reference to the nomination of John McCain for the Republican standard bearer. If his name came up as a complaint of what was wrong with the party establishment and why conservatives shouldn't have supported him, I always said, "McCain wasn't my first choice, he wasn't my second choice, but in the end, he was my only choice!" The crowd would usually applaud or visibly show their agreement with my assessment. Or it might be my proclamation that I was a "conservative before I'm a Republican." That one would almost always bring the house down, even at official Republican events.

So, imagine my surprise when, speaking before me at one meeting, Flores used one of my standard punch lines, along the lines of "I'm a conservative before I'm a Republican."

All of us in the room from my campaign, immediately looked at one another with eyes opening wide as if to say, *Did he just say that?* I was up on the stage and just looked at my wife and gave her the proverbial look of surprise and mouthed silently, "He just used my line!" and we shook our heads.

After the forum we all met and that was the first topic that came up with everyone asking, "Can you believe he's stealing your material?"

At the next meeting, to our stunned disbelief, he used another catch phrase of mine in a statement where he went first. We realized this was now going to be a standard practice at our subsequent live events. At least now we assumed it was purposeful. As I never scripted my speeches, it didn't throw off my performance, but it often kept me from using some of my *own* best material. After all, to someone listening for the first time, it's a great line, and they think Flores came up with it. If I were to repeat it when my turn came, people would think I was stealing *his* material!

While having to listen to Flores on stage using my talking points, I also had to fend off visual attacks from his personal entourage. I first experienced this at a forum in Waco during the runoff. As I spoke, my peripheral vision caught some extraordinary movement just below me, and I glanced down only to see his wife literally making faces at me! She would react--every time I would make a point--with an exaggerated, contorted expression of disapproval, then mouth different things like, "Oh, come on!" or "That's ridiculous!" throughout much of my talking. I was treated to my own little floor show of over-the-top gesticulations and animated dirty looks.

Positioned in the front row, this would often include turning to the audience sitting behind and sharing her reactions with them as well. Another close supporter also got into the act by pointing at me with his rolled-up program and mouthing, "You're crazy!" and such. I'm not sure what the actual purpose was, but it was mildly annoying and just seemed devoid of civil decorum. I have no idea what the audience thought, seeing it from their vantage point.

In the grand scheme of things, it was trivial and meant nothing really, but this type of activity became a staple at most runoff events and showed the personal nature this race was beginning to take.

One night, on our way back home to Waco from a donor meeting in Bryan/College station, one of my campaign chiefs and unofficial driver Scott said, "You know, there's the turnoff for Franklin." The small, rural town of Franklin was holding a Conservative Club meeting that night, and we had declined due to the conflict. But since we had finished earlier than expected, we decided to attend after all. Scott took the turnoff. Although late, we thought we could at least shake some hands. When we arrived a half hour later, a crowd of cars surrounded the meeting hall. This was a big meeting for this rural area that we would have missed.

As we entered, it just so happened that Flores was speaking. We walked in at the tail end of him making a declaration that "…the numbers showed that he couldn't even carry his own precinct. That's certainly not somebody who can beat Chet."

I felt my blood boil as I immediately realized he was referring to me. We busted him!

Obviously, he thought he had the venue to himself and was determined to go after me as I wasn't there. I was happy to think we blew up his plans by showing up late and unannounced. If he was going to say any more negative things about me, he was going to have to say it while I was sitting there listening. It was obvious that, once he realized I was in the room, he backed it down slightly from wherever he was going with that point. At the end of his talk, the audience gave him polite applause.

To Flores' disdain and my surprise, the host, seeing we had walked in, offered me the chance to speak as well. I bounded up to the podium and made the most of my unexpected opportunity. I felt like I was playing with house money and decided to let it rip. Knowing that I had interrupted Flores' attack on me, I decided to come as close as I'd ever come to attacking him *without* directly attacking him.

As usual, I vigorously expounded on the absolute necessity for conservatives to take this congressional seat. I don't know if I was pumped more than normal or the crowd was hearing what they wanted to hear, or maybe it was a combination of both, but they constantly interrupted me with applause and loud affirmations of my points. We were definitely connecting. Flores and his wife showed their displeasure at what was happening in the hall at this point.

It came to a head when I began my indirect Flores attack as to why I was the one who could defeat Chet, and I hoped they would give me the chance to finish the job we started. According to my wife and Scott, sitting nearby, Flores was getting physically agitated, and even verbally tried to refute my points.

"I've been fighting to get rid of Edwards for almost twenty years, and when we were battling tooth and nail last cycle, we got *no help* from anybody, and that includes people who showed up in this primary!"

"That's a lie," Flores said loud enough for anyone within ten feet to hear.

"I've lived and worked in this district all my adult life. This is my home and always has been. I didn't move into this district to run for Congress."

Flores and his wife were visibly animated.

"I'm not a Washington insider with connections to the power structure. I'm just a small business owner from Waco who represents the people of this area. Nobody recruited me to run once they saw that Chet was vulnerable. I ran because nobody else, including the party, was willing to do it."

"That's wrong," he grumped even louder to no one in particular.

"I'm the only one who's been vetted. There are no skeletons in my closet that Chet can bring up. I've been there. I'm the one who you'll know what you'll get."

"That's not true," came yet another retort from him.

"Yes, it'll take money to win this race but not *just* money. Chet outspent me by two million dollars, and I still almost beat him. I've proven I can stand toe-to-toe with him. Money's not the only answer, but we'll have enough to do what we need to finish the job."

"That's wrong. Not true."

If you based the success of the evening on pure optics, the enthusiastic applause I received at the end of my time spelled doom for Flores. It seemed the crowd was jazzed up by my passionate message. It was no contest, and he now appeared agitated. I assumed Flores was understandably angry because he saw his solo evening go up in smoke. After the meeting adjourned, I worked my way through well-wishers as an unorganized line soon formed of people wanting to shake my hand, pledge support, and talk to me.

Out of the corner of my eye, I saw Flores making his way to me while waving a sheet of paper in his hand. With people all around and a cacophony of loud conversations, he started excitedly shouting at me above the noise that I had "broken the pledge." I was trying to talk to the voters gathered all around me, but I realized that he was now standing just behind me waving the paper and loudly repeating that, "You broke the pledge!"

"What are you talking about?" I said as I turned, irritated at him interrupting my conversation.

"The pledge. You signed the pledge that said you wouldn't attack another Republican opponent! It's right here on the paper." He was now shaking it under my nose. "You signed it at that very first meeting, and tonight you attacked me," he accused aggressively.

"I didn't attack you," I sneered. "You're crazy."

A woman standing nearby in the now somewhat curious crowd snatched the paper from him and said, "Let me see that." After a moment reading, she shook her head and rolled her eyes, proclaiming, "This is ridiculous." She handed the paper back to Flores, then turned to me and said, "You just need to beat Edwards. We've got to get rid of him."

I turned back to her and said, "I agree, and that's why I want to finish the job."

I then continued on greeting well-wishers. I have no clue what Flores did at that point, and frankly I didn't care.

Sadly, it was indicative of where this whole thing was heading.

The Flores camp took an even more personal bent shortly thereafter. Supporters in the northern part of the district shared with us that Flores had bought a full-page newspaper ad in connection with a meet-and-greet in the northern district area, but the ad didn't just announce the meeting. The piece had the full page divided in half, with the heading: "The differences between Rob Curnock and Bill Flores." Below Flores' name was a long list of accomplishments, including all the professional, political, and social organizations he had ever been associated with and a list of his extensive business history. The other half of the page featured my name, and below it they graciously listed my background and all *my* accomplishments. Only there was just one entry: Former Sportscaster. The implication, of course, meant to show that I had no business running for Congress and was unqualified for the position. Although certainly not horrible and actually a standard political attack ad, this clearly signaled to us that the gloves were off, and they would be going after me personally.

The ad was dripping with utter disdain, but once I got over my initial impulse to respond angrily, I reluctantly had to admit it was actually pretty funny—in a mean, pathetic, and arrogant sort of way. I laughed it off to my supporters and began to make use of it in my talks at our own events, such as fundraisers. Rather than run from it, I would describe the ad to my supporters and tell them I took it as a huge compliment. In my mind, if you looked at it like it was a comparative scale, the ad was saying that, evidently, it took all of those organizations and accomplishments on Flores' side of the page to equal my lone sportscasting career. "Who knew?" My crowds would roar with laughter as I turned the disdain back on him.

In the meantime, it seemed Flores was sending out two to three full-color mailings to Republican primary voters per week in that final month. We couldn't begin to match his effective mailing effort, and had little resources, so we just soldiered on the best we could. From what we knew, Flores had already sunk more than $600,000 of his own personal money into this race, and the meter was still running. The stakes were getting higher and tensions were rising from his side of the campaign. Although our spirits were high, and we thought we were 'winning' the live events, we just didn't know what would happen as a result of the Flores postal bombardment.

I had never publicly called into question Flores' voting for Hillary Clinton in the Democratic primary in 2008, or his connection with George Soros, or his brief time living in the district. For various reasons, we just never publicly went there. I still didn't feel comfortable going the negative route. The next live forum would force my hand.

It was on Lynn Woolley's radio program on KTEM in Temple, the same radio program I had appeared on six years earlier. Both Flores and I agreed to appear on his program in spite of the fact that, at this point, I was fed up with Flores, and I'm sure he was with me as well. I didn't care anymore what the carefully-coached candidate Flores had to say. There was no real personal animosity; it was more of a Flores fatigue. After all, we'd spent a lot of time with each other over the last five months in an emotionally charged pressure cooker.

We began the show.

Woolley asked the standard conservative Republican questions and there was very little disagreement between the two of us. Thanks to his campaign staffer sitting next to him in the studio, Flores had become much more disciplined in formulating a conservative message and mantra than when he first began in this process. As the program wound down, the host suddenly looked over at me and said, "Okay, now I want each of you to ask the other a question. Rob, you go first."

I rolled my eyes and, with a complete lack of interest or passion, said, "Fine, Bill. Who'd you vote for in the last two general congressional elections?" unimaginatively repeating my question from weeks before. I didn't even look at him.

"Well, Rob, you asked me that question a while back in the Waco debate, and I was just kidding when I told you I voted for you—I didn't," he said, pleased with his new revelation.

Suddenly, I was yanked back to the moment. "You didn't vote for me?!" I asked as I whipped my head around to face him.

"No, I did *not*," he said with an air of defiance, like he was somehow making sure both I and the audience understood that he wasn't going to fall into *that* trap again. He continued on, "and two times ago I wasn't even in the district."

"But you didn't vote for me?" I asked again with a tone of puzzled disbelief.

"No, I did not," he exclaimed even more defiantly.

"Wow…"

At that moment it apparently dawned on him what he was actually implying. He quickly thrust his finger in the air and proclaimed, "but I didn't vote for Chet either."

Lynn basically ignored this last back and forth and moved onto something else and then ended the program. I was still focused on his curious answer to my question.

Driving back to Waco, I immediately got on my cell phone with our chief media director and said, "You're not going to believe this. Flores just admitted he lied on this live radio broadcast."

"You're kidding? I didn't hear it, what happened?"

"He said he was 'joking' back in that Waco forum when he said he voted for me. He can call it whatever he likes, but the bottom line is, he basically lied. He said he voted for me when he knew he didn't."

"But he clearly wasn't joking when he said that. That was obvious to everyone in the room."

"It doesn't matter. He just told a live radio audience that, in essence, he lied. And more pathetically, he's now asking for the Republican nomination, when he didn't even vote for the Republican nominee against Chet last time. Let's all figure out the best way to handle this, as soon as possible."

While still assessing our plan of action, a few days later my next one-on-one with Flores came in the northern part of the district. The forum was held in a local middle school gym and was filled with two-to-three hundred people crowding the bleachers of the large facility. The questioning produced few fireworks. Flores was now completely toeing what appeared to be his newly adopted conservative line and there was little major disagreement between us. As the event drew to a close, the moderator suddenly paused and said, "Okay, at this time we're going to let each of you ask a question of the other."

Here we go again.

This time Flores went first and attempted to show that I was nothing more than a former ignorant sportscaster by trying to trip me up with some query about the difference between financial and fiscal policies facing Congress. I quickly and correctly dispatched the question, but added that if I didn't know something, I was smart enough to find answers from those who did.

I stayed polite but decided to call him out.

"Bill, I've asked you twice now, and I've gotten two completely different answers. So, I'll try one more time. *Who* did you vote for in the last two congressional elections? And while you're at it, tell us who you voted for, for president, when you voted in the Democrat primary in 2008." I was going to force him to tell this partisan con-servative Republican crowd how he voted for Hillary Clinton.

I handed him the mic and listened intently.

"Like a lot of people, I knew that Barack Obama would be a horrible president, so in the primary I voted against Obama. Now, as to the other, I *misspoke* in Waco when I told you I voted for you.

And then I told you something else on the radio the other day. Let me tell you what really happened. I wanted John McCain to win in 2008, and I spent the entire Election Day in a phone bank making calls for McCain. By the time we finished, it was too late to vote. I never voted. I'm sorry, I just didn't get the chance." He then handed me back the mic for my rebuttal.

My mouth had fallen open, along with three hundred other mouths now silently looking down at us from the bleachers. You could hear a pin drop. It was the one answer I had never anticipated.

I recovered as quickly as possible. "First," I said, "I didn't ask you who you voted *against* in the Democrat primary, I asked you who you voted *for*." Pausing for effect, while I searched for exactly how I wanted to respond, I finally said, "But you didn't *even vote* for me in 2008?! How could you not vote in the most important election we've had in seventy years? I don't even know what to say."

The campaign had now taken a completely unexpected turn. With this latest admission on the part of Flores, I knew we now had to do something. This was so wrong; the voters had to know what was happening. Not only had he incriminated himself with the affirmation that he had blatantly misled everyone when answering what was in essence a silly, throwaway debate question, but he also clearly showed that he obviously didn't take the very foundation of democracy—his duty to vote—seriously.

And now he was running for Congress?!

My main criticism of my opponent had never been personal. I just thought that he had little understanding and desire for politics. I also thought he was simply a wealthy, connected opportunist who was taking advantage of an electoral situation that we had created through our hard work against Chet Edwards two years earlier. Aside from that, there had been no real personal animus and we generally kept things cordial.

But that had now dramatically changed in my mind. Never mind all the put-downs, campaigning tricks, and personal frictions; this was a new situation. To me, this was a question of character. When I had asked him that goofy little question, live on stage, he had no opportunity to consult with his campaign manager, speech coach, or anyone else on his paid campaign staff. He had to make a split-second decision to come up with a plausible answer.

At that moment, he had to choose. He could tell the truth and admit that he hadn't even *voted* in the last general election, and most assuredly his well-funded and heavily-backed campaign would be over. That's just something most primary voters would not easily overlook. Or…he could lie. He could say he voted for me and play along with the humor of the moment. He had to make a split-second decision with no ability to get advice. It was his first major political and character test in the campaign. In my mind, he failed miserably. I would no longer look at my runoff opponent in the same way.

The next day, we formulated a radio ad to let voters know about this new turn of events. They needed to be told of this seemingly insignificant incident which gave clear insight into the man wanting to push me aside so he could usurp the work we began two years before and face Chet in the fall. We thought this was an extremely serious flaw for a candidate. Most of my campaign leadership wanted to hit Flores, and hard, with no holds barred. The initial script specifically named Bill Flores and harshly called him out as a blatant liar who couldn't be trusted, now or later. After giving it some more thought, I decided we needed to back it down somewhat.

I personally reworked the script to soften it up significantly. The new version didn't reference Flores by name, but it did talk about "my opponent," first saying he voted for the Republican nominee, then saying he didn't, and then admitting he hadn't even voted at all.

"We need a conservative we can count on to get this congressional seat back. Vote for Rob Curnock for Congress."

That was it. There were no personal attacks, just a recitation of his own damning campaign words and past negligent electoral deeds. There was serious contention with my campaign staff who thought we were being way too benign.

We produced the spot quickly, letting a woman do the voicing. I guess, psychologically, I wanted to distance myself from it as much as possible, while still claiming it as an official Curnock for Congress campaign ad. Within a few days we had it on a couple of local talk radio stations in Waco and Bryan/College Station. I took a deep breath at the thought of my first not-positive primary spot, but at this point I was resigned to the fact that this was simply such a dumb and yet egregious act of callous disregard for the truth on so many levels, it just really couldn't be ignored.

CHAPTER 48

Last Blast from the Trib

Unexpectedly, Chet's attack dogs at the Waco *Trib* decided to get into the act with a request for me to meet with their editors. I was rather surprised that they wanted to talk, since this was a Republican runoff just for the opportunity to face Edwards. I couldn't remember them doing any kind of endorsements in Republican runoffs when there was a Democrat opponent waiting in the general election. After much internal debate, I finally decided I would go ahead and play their game. I figured that, even though we were on opposite sides of virtually every congressional issue, and they were there to protect Chet at all costs, perhaps I might get lucky, lightning could strike, and they would break with precedence and endorse me in a runoff. I've never felt the need to get the paper's endorsement for anything, but I thought it couldn't hurt if they did endorse me. So, I went.

It was a mistake from the get-go. The only lightning strike was on the top of my head.

The meeting consisted of the liberal editor, a reporter, the paper's new owner--a good man who had actually helped me some in the 2008 race before he bought the newspaper the following year--and me. The problem was, as part of the sale, the new owner kept two of the editors to help run the paper and provide continuity. To those of us who had initially cheered the ownership change, these were the most left-leaning partisan hacks he could have possibly kept on. It meant that very little had changed with the paper's content.

ROB CURNOCK

From the very beginning of our conversation, it was adversarial and antagonistic. We started off superficially polite, but as the questions began to take on a more ominous and attacking vein, I knew I was in for a battle. They clearly didn't like me, and I knew I didn't like them.

I doggedly stuck to my plan to keep my cool and not get angry, as that would not help me in the long run. But I also was determined to not absorb absurd charges and nasty comments without an answer. The editor began taking shots with antagonistic and pointed questions based on premises that I and any intelligent conservative would refuse to accede. One such example was where we got mired in a back-and-forth on whether or not Obama was actually a Liberal! Incredibly, he declared that everyone knew Obama was a centrist in the mainstream of American political thought. I was peppered with questions based on that very flawed premise.

I was having none of it and finally fired back: "You've got to be the only people on the planet who actually think Obama is a middle-of-the-road centrist. That's completely out of touch with reality."

A few times things got extremely heated, to the point where the new owner, who had been largely silent as he sat off to one side, finally felt compelled to speak up in an attempt to defuse the situation. But he was in a difficult position of trying to accommodate his editor and yet show me some modicum of respect. Only after his intervention would the editor head off in another direction of questioning.

One typical exchange came as a result of the sneering skepticism concerning the entire legitimacy of my candidacy, which was blatantly demeaning in and of itself. This pretty much summed up the entire hour-plus battle.

"What makes you qualified to be the congressman for District 17?"

I understood the intent of the query, and it could be considered a legitimate question, but the way it was asked left me shaking my head and smiling with my barely concealed contempt.

"The fact that I'm at least 25 years old and an American citizen," I said with an air of feigned disbelief and a tone of, *Duh, you dummies.*

And we were off.

"Yes, but you've never held any kind of elected office before, have you?"

"No, but that's not required to be a congressman."

"But shouldn't you have had some sort of elected experience? Anything? Shouldn't you have at least held a school board position, or any local elected office first?"

"No, that's the problem we have in America today. Our Founding Fathers never meant for the holding of a political office to be a career. The entire guiding principle of our system was that private citizens got involved in government, served their time in office, and then went back home to live under the laws that they had passed. We were never set up to have professional politicians. That's what's wrong with our country right now."

"So, are you trying to say that someone who serves on a school board is a professional politician?"

"No, *you're* saying that. I never said any such thing. I said we weren't meant to have a professional political ruling class. They intended for us to serve and get out, and that's the problem I have with people like Chet Edwards. He's been a professional politician his entire adult life and has lost touch with what it's like to live under laws he's passed."

The session lasted a little over an hour and, when we were done, I was mentally fatigued. It was definitely an unpleasant and stressful experience, even for someone like me who's never been afraid of a political argument. The problem I had of course was, what were they going to do with it? Would they actually break their own precedent and endorse in a primary runoff, or just remain silent and wait to protect Chet later in the general election?

I got my answer weeks later when, once again, it was people at my church who approached me thinking I knew all about the Waco *Trib* article they had read earlier that morning. They supportively gave me their opinions by recounting what they had unhappily read. I heard many comments like, "That was the most ridiculous thing I've ever seen the paper do; I'll bet you're furious."

"What are you talking about?"

"The *Trib*'s endorsement. What a hatchet job!"

That conversation was repeated over and over again all through my time at church that morning.

I never bought the paper and made the conscious decision to ignore it the whole day. But on Monday someone from our campaign staff brought in the editorial section from Sunday's paper.

Yes, it was a hatchet job alright. It was about as blatantly bad as it could be.

The editors headlined the page with their unprecedented decision to endorse Flores because he offered "nuanced, thoughtful views." They went on to admit that the paper didn't ordinarily make candidate recommendations in primary elections, but, because of "the strident tenor of the race," they were doing so this time. Okay, so at least my memory was good. I knew they hadn't ever done it before. But now, apparently, they would be doing it with a vengeance.

After definitively stating that they certainly didn't favor him over long-time incumbent Chet Edwards, they went on to explain that they liked his proposals which, "ironically, mirrors some of what President Obama proposed."

Hmmm.

Later on, they reiterated the importance that Flores "sides" with Obama on certain energy policies.

Hmmm.

However, in contrast, they decided that my "insight concerning a vast array of issues doesn't always withstand close examination."

Hmmm.

And they weren't happy with the fact that, although I displayed "more energy on the stump and in debates," they snarkily added that they wanted me to have more "credible experience in public service" other than my experience as "a sportscaster, video production entrepreneur, and perennial candidate."

Ouch!

That was the nicer portion. They dedicated a second, full page to their endorsement that would have even made the *Pravda* enthusiasts populating the national media blush.

This page was divided in half vertically. At the top of the left side was a crisp clear picture of Flores standing next to one of his yard signs. He was in focus, with a pleasant look on his face. Below this nice picture, suitable for framing of course, was a transcript of one portion of his question-and-answer dialogue with the editors.

It started with this hard-hitting, probing brainteaser: "Name some of the organizations that you've been associated with that will help you be an effective representative for the people of District 17?"

The softballs only got softer from there, eventually morphing into hard-hitting cotton balls. I was half expecting them to end with, "Please tell us how we here at the Waco *Trib* can help you defeat that ignorant, evil bas**rd Rob Curnock in this Republican primary runoff."

On the other side of the page there was I. The picture was out of focus, blurry, and representing a new standard of overall poor photographic quality. In the photo, I was seen reaching for something toward the camera and I had a look, on my contorted, disfigured face, like I was on the receiving end of a jalapeno-laced, super sour dill pickle and was not very happy about it. It was so bad, it was almost like an over-the-top parody of what campaigns do with an opposing candidate when it comes to placing their photos in ads.

Down below was the transcript of one of the more contentious running battles from the editorial board meeting. Again, dealing with my lack of elective experience. So, the takeaway from this perennial Waco *Trib* hit piece, courtesy of the highly-partisan Edwards-supporting sycophantic editors, was that the Republican voters of District 17 should definitely pick "oil and gas executive" Bill Flores to face Edwards in November. By their account, he wasn't a good campaigner, and he would be closer to Obama and some of his policies, but that would offer "greater credibility for Republicans in the fall."

Hmmm.

In our campaign, we were left marveling at how lucky Republican voters were, to get such good advice from the historically blatant Edwards supporters at the Waco newspaper.

All sarcasm aside, we took this as a back-handed compliment and a sign of their determination to keep me from getting a chance at any rematch with Edwards. Looking at it from a purely strategic standpoint, it was obvious that, for whatever reason, I was the candidate they feared for Edwards, so they did what they could to get me out.

From their Democrat standpoint, perhaps the editors believed that Flores was a rich oil executive with no elective experience himself; he was a very weak campaigner and hadn't really been vetted in his past business practices. In spite of the fact that he would have a lot of money, we had already proven in 2008 that this general race was not going to be determined with money alone. And besides, this time around, both Republican candidates would have all the money they needed. We believed that Flores was definitely the opponent they assumed Chet would have an easier time with. Their arguments against me were weak, and any thinking person should see right through them. But these editors clearly knew who they were trying to reach. Although generally fewer, overall, in the Republican Party, those coveted, low-information voters were being wooed by the paper's sirens of the Left.

This was not just a simple unprecedented endorsement. This was a page right out of the current Democrat handbook where you trivialize, marginalize, demonize, ridicule, and hopefully destroy your opponent.

The *Trib*'s editors weren't alone in this effort.

CHAPTER 49

Thirty Minutes Disposed

Meanwhile, Randall, far away in the Northeast, became more aggressive in his determination to either get money from us or destroy my candidacy. He decided, through his new Waco lawyer, to take it to court. He filed suit in McLennan County against the 2008 Curnock for Congress campaign with a motion to freeze all our campaign assets unless we paid him the money immediately. Curiously, was it just mere coincidence that he filed the suit in the only court with a Democrat judge left in McLennan County? All other courts had gone Republican over the last several election cycles. Again, it was clear that someone locally was steering him.

We, of course, were trying to win a congressional race. We knew his demands were without merit, so this seemed like nothing more than an attempt to divert our attention and resources to deal with him. I was unwilling to let him achieve his goal of disrupting my campaign any more than he already had, so I left the situation in the capable hands of my lawyer. I had no time, energy, or patience to deal with his nonsense.

Incredibly, Randall made the long trip to Waco for his hearing, which my lawyer later reported lasted about thirty minutes. I wouldn't have attended the hearing anyway, but it just so happened that we were in Burleson for a big forum that evening. Nonetheless, I was curious to know how it went and whether or not we would have all our assets frozen. My lawyer later gleefully gave me a play-by-play recounting of the entire court proceedings.

He said he had fun tying Randall into knots on the witness stand. With a Waco *Trib* reporter as the only other person in the courtroom, he had Randall admit that virtually everything he was claiming was not credible, was inaccurate, untrue, or just plain made no sense. Time and time again, when Randall was pressed to produce documents to bolster his claim or refute evidence contradicting his claim, he was left sputtering little more than, "That's not how I understand things." When it was all said and done, the Democrat judge never even looked up from the paperwork in front of him. In less than thirty seconds of deliberation, he denied all motions to take action on our campaign, while gaveling the proceeding closed.

Randall would have to skulk out of town with nothing more to show than some long plane rides.

Most assuredly, his lone consolation was that he would, indeed, get another hit piece in the Waco *Trib*. The *Trib* reporter dutifully wrote a story about Randall's hearing, without clearly stating that he was completely shot down in all his baseless demands. But the *Trib*, Randall, and our mystery Waco instigator probably got at least one thing they wanted: another "embarrassing" article reminding voters that the Curnock campaign still had a disgruntled former volunteer out there with a dubious claim that we had cheated him out of money we owed him.

Gratefully, I never had any dealings with Randall at any point in his extortion exercise. I honestly don't know what I would have done to him if I had.

CHAPTER 50

Escalation

A day later, after our first radio spots began playing, Flores and I were scheduled to debate on live television at the Waco NBC affiliate. That afternoon, while at the main headquarters in Waco, I got a call from a man identifying himself as the McLennan County Chief Appraiser. After introducing himself, he said he was calling to let me know that—as far as he was concerned—I had done nothing wrong in connection with my homestead tax exemption on my Cresthill property.

"What are you talking about?" I asked with complete confusion and total ignorance. I had purchased some incredible wooded land in town, with an old house on it, several years prior, with the plan of building a new house there some day.

"The Flores campaign is claiming that you've illegally home-steaded your Cresthill property and are saying that you're in legal trouble as a result. I think they're obviously trying to make something out of it. I only wanted to let you know that, as far as our office is concerned, you're not in any trouble."

Wondering what the heck was going on, I just decided to accept what he was saying at face value until I could figure out what he was talking about. "I appreciate you letting me know." And then chuckling a bit, I asked, "Can I quote you on that?"

"Sure, because that's what I just told the Waco *Trib* reporter who's doing a story about it."

Here we go again with the Trib. *Don't they ever let up?*

"Don't take this wrong," I added, "but are you an authority on this matter?"

I was relieved with the definitive response he gave me. "I'm the *final* authority."

I explained I wasn't aware of the problem. "What are they accusing me of?"

"They're saying you didn't live there when you established your homestead exemption on your Cresthill property for tax purposes."

In fact, I *had* lived in the house off and on when I first bought the property, I explained, with the intent to eventually tear down the old house and build a new one on the property. It was during this period when I became engaged and knew it would be ill advised to build a house without my future wife taking the lead on what would be *her* house. The run for Congress ensued shortly thereafter, and building that house fell far down the priority list. In Texas you generally homestead the place you want to legally protect. In case of lawsuits, bankruptcy, or whatever, the state's theory is that at the very least, no one can take away your home. Since it was my dream property, I wanted it protected. Minor tax savings never even entered into my equation.

He concurred. "From a legal standpoint, the law says you are allowed *one* homestead. According to our records, you have only one homestead, so there's no problem. That's all we care about."

I thanked him for taking the time to call me, jotted down his name, and assured him that I would be using his name if this went any further. The call left me to ponder at the desperate moves the Flores campaign and the Waco *Trib* were now making. I told everybody in the campaign office, including my wife, that, unbelievably, Flores was trying to make trouble over something about my homestead tax exemption, but it seemed so trivial, I still couldn't figure out what the heck they were getting at.

I got my answer a few hours later when we arrived for the debate at the KCEN TV station just south of Waco. I had already arrived and was mingling in the lobby with about a dozen or so supporters who had come to cheer me on. Flores rolled up in a black Suburban and walked in with a staff member in tow. He made a beeline to me through the crowd.

"Could I speak with you in private?" he asked tersely.

I said, "Sure," and we walked behind a door that led down an empty hall.

"I just wanted you to know that I'm fixin' to go negative and unload on you big-time-- starting tomorrow morning—if you don't pull that radio spot you're running," he said in a menacing, yet businesslike manner.

"And what kind of negative would that be?' I shot back, playing dumb, but wondering if he would actually tell me. I could feel the anger rising inside me.

"About the homestead."

That was it. Now I was ticked and came about as close as I'd ever come in any campaign to letting go and losing my temper with an opponent.

"My homestead? Well, you just go for it, big boy," I yelled at him while sticking my finger in his face. I'm not sure where the "big boy" reference came from, except that it was more polite than "as**ole."

He repeated his threat. "Okay, I'm warning you. Pull the ad or we start hitting you tomorrow morning."

I was angry and done talking. I flung open the door and made my way through the gathered crowd, which came to a hush as I walked through shouting, "Go for it, big boy. You do what you gotta do. You just go for it."

My wife and top volunteers quickly gathered around me just off of the lobby and wanted to know what happened. Still agitated, I said, "He's threatening to go negative on me over that stupid homestead deal he's concocted if I don't pull our radio ad."

"We're not going to, are we?" someone asked. "Obviously, it's hitting him where it hurts because he knows he screwed up and lied."

"Of course not. You heard me tell him what I thought he should do with this garbage. Frankly, I'm fed up with the guy."

I quickly regained my composure and went back to mixing with my supporters. I was truly grateful that all these good people would go out of their way to attend this thing and show their support for me. The debate wasn't set up for an audience, so they couldn't even go into the studio. They just wanted to demonstrate their solidarity with me. That meant a lot, and it showed the depth of support and loyalty we had from our volunteers in this endeavor.

Contrary to his stated threat, I didn't have to wait until morning for him to fire the first negative volley of his homestead salvo. The debate involved questions submitted by viewers live via the internet. Amazingly, right off the bat, someone communicated that they had heard that I had some tax discrepancies with my personal home and its homestead exemption. They wanted to know what I had done wrong.

Flores immediately launched into a contrived and obviously practiced diatribe about my illegally homesteading my Cresthill property. He claimed that I signed the paperwork while not actually living there and, therefore, was in violation of the law. He even just happened to have copies of my homestead paperwork in his notebook, which he brandished to the camera, the moderator, and anybody else that would listen or look. When he finished, the moderator asked for my comment.

I explained the back story as I did to the county appraiser earlier. "The law says that you can claim a homestead on one residence. That's what I have done. Drew Hahn, the county appraiser, called me today and assured me that I've done nothing wrong, even though Bill is trying to say I have. The accusation is ridiculous."

Flores interjected. "I have the paper here, and he signed it. Look, it's right here. Do you want to see it?" he pleaded with the moderator.

To his credit, the moderator looked at him with absolutely no affectation and said, "No, I think we've covered this topic. Let's move on."

Flores, still waving the paper, barked one last, "It's illegal!"

As a former TV guy, I could picture thousands of eyes rolling in front of TV sets all over Central Texas. Mercifully, we moved on and finished the debate with few fireworks.

Flores was a man of his word. The next day, his attack ad began running on the Dallas talk radio station WBAP, which covers much of the district, and it ran in the southern regions of the district, as reported by supporters there. Curiously, it did not run in Waco. I did not hear the spot, but it was described as being so over the top, the supporters couldn't imagine any Republican voter falling for it. It was described as being so bad that it was like a parody of a negative campaign spot, complete with scary music under an ominous announcer intoning the criminal and civil wrongdoings of that evil Rob Curnock. Evidently, the gist of it was that I had cheated on my taxes by illegally homesteading my second home, which was worth more than my old house, so I was cheating residents out of tax money for roads, schools, and other local needs. I was dishonest, had no integrity, and had no business running for Congress.

In conjunction with the radio spots, the Flores campaign also sent out a blast email to thousands of Republican voters, including me. I have to admit, this one bothered me. The email was a long, rambling screed which tried to make Flores' case that I had illegally made Cresthill my homestead in an effort to cheat on my taxes and rip off the residents of McLennan County. Not only did the attack email have pictures of both of our homes in question, but it also included the street addresses for each. This hit below the belt, and it was obvious to everyone in our campaign leadership that Flores and his campaign manager out of Washington were practicing a scorched-earth policy of campaigning. This was beyond the pale.

I hit the roof that evening when I got home and found Karen in tears.

Up to this point, she had been a trooper, cheerfully getting past all the difficult times we'd been through. She'd held up her end of the bargain with grace, dignity, good cheer, and a smile on her face. But now she was sincerely scared for our safety. This email went out to who knows whom, and any crazy person who hated me for any reason now had all the information they needed to "do something." The only thing missing was a map.

I always had a stoic attitude about running for Congress. Of course, it's not easy; if it was, everyone would do it. Only a fool would think that any candidate could make it through a heated congressional race unscathed. For me, it was always a matter of a higher calling and an ideological quest. I always figured, if I was obedient and supposed to be in politics, the Lord would take care of me. Before, it was always just me, but this was new territory. I sat and watched the woman I love, and wanted to protect at all costs, now truly in distress as a result of my being called into politics. This was one of the toughest moments in the entire affair. It was my fault that she was now in such pain and fear…and there was nothing I could do about it.

I hugged her and tried reassuring her that nobody would attack us in our home. It was definitely a hard sell for her to accept. Personally, I wasn't worried for myself, but her distress was tough to handle. As a Christian, I don't believe in violence to solve problems, but I'm thankful the good Lord didn't place Flores or his campaign manager in the room at that moment. Christian or not, I'm still a flawed human being, and it could have been a I John 1:9 moment.

As it was, I comforted Karen as much as possible and quietly thought, *I'm just glad this thing is drawing to a close. One way or the other, it's coming to an end.*

CHAPTER 51

The People's Choice

Our last joint appearance turned out to be a mini forum on the Mark Davis radio show. Davis was a periodic guest host for national conservative talk show host Rush Limbaugh. He had also enthusiastically supported and encouraged me in my effort to unseat Edwards in 2008. His radio show originated out of Dallas on WBAP, a powerful station that broadcasts over much of District 17. Davis was not willing to publicly choose sides in our runoff but wanted to give us some valuable air time to let District 17 voters have one last chance to hear us and make a decision.

Karen, Scott, and I headed up to the station and waited for our time to go into the studio with Davis. Flores showed up without his campaign manager but with another aide alongside. *Good. He'll be on his own and will have to speak for himself.* We all headed into the studio for a live, on-air discussion similar to the week before in Temple.

We were only going to have about twenty minutes, so right off the bat, Davis started digging aggressively to see where the two of us differed. He hit pay dirt on where we stood in the recent Texas gubernatorial primary. I was actually pleased with this line of questioning. Kay Bailey Hutchison challenged the incumbent Rick Perry for the nomination. As far as Texas Republican politics goes, Hutchison definitely represented the moderate wing of the party. Perry was more on the conservative side of things.

Davis exposed the fact that Flores had been a huge supporter of Hutchison, which included major financial donations. I supported Perry and was in fact reappointed by Perry to the small business advisory panel of the TCEQ. In my mind, this was very telling about on which side of the political divide we stood, and I was glad for primary voters to hear the distinction. To me, this was important because the Republican primary is dominated by voters who are definitely conservative.

After some other inconsequential back and forth, Davis caught me a little off guard by delving into what he had heard was the negativity that had arisen in this runoff. He mentioned the Flores ad that was now running on WBAP, confessing he hadn't heard it himself, but had been told it was pretty harsh. As I hadn't heard it either, I had nothing to say about it. Flores tried to deflect the accusation, then went on the attack with an attempt to ambush me.

"Mark, I gave Rob an opportunity to avoid all this. I told him to his face that I wouldn't run any negative ads if he would pull *his* negative ad, which he started running first. He refused, but I'll make the offer again, right here and right now. Rob," he said, now turning to me, "if you take your negative ad off the air, I'll pull mine, right now."

"Wow, maybe a breakthrough right here," Davis said, chuckling and amused with how this seemed to be playing out. "Well, Rob, how about it?"

I unloaded on Flores in a business-like manner. "First of all, I'm not running a negative ad. In our spot, we don't even mention your name. All we do is repeat what you've actually said in this campaign, and then at the end, we don't even make any judgments about what you've said. So, in my mind, we don't have a negative ad.

"Now, I personally haven't heard the ad you've been running, but those who have tell me it's pure garbage. So, the only one who's running a truly negative ad is you. No, I'm not pulling my ad."

"I can see I opened up a can of worms with this one," Mark laughed, and began to wrap up our segment. "We'll definitely be keeping our eye on this, but whatever happens, we know that either one of you should win and will be way better than Chet Edwards."

They went to commercial break, we said our goodbyes to Davis, and all headed down in the small elevator together. It was not a comfortable ride in that elevator with all that had happened in the last week or so. For the first few moments there was absolute silence, as Flores and I stood a few inches apart, flanked by Karen, Scott, and Flores' aide. Everybody's nerves were still raw following the live, on-air debate. I finally decided to break the uncomfortable silence and threw out an olive branch.

"Well, Bill, I agree with Davis. No matter which one of us wins, it will be better than Edwards, by far."

His mind was obviously still on the debate exchange, and Flores flashed eye contact and shot back, "You were the one that went negative first."

Just then the elevator arrived at the lobby floor. I was about to angrily respond about his campaign sinking to a new low with the personal attack when, unexpectedly, my wife behind me erupted.

Karen, bless her heart, had finally had enough. All her pent-up emotions, which had been building for the last several months, exploded out of her normally polite and smiling mouth. I was momentarily stunned as she unloaded on Flores at the top of her lungs.

"How dare you!" she screamed. "You're the one who lied about us and then put out pictures of our home!"

395

She moved toward Flores in a menacing way. Scott, standing behind her, grabbed her by the shoulders and held her back. Flores bolted out the opening elevator door. With no regard for my own safety, I instinctively stuck up my hand in front of her face as if to silently say, "Stand down; I've got this."

In hindsight…whew… I got away with it.

Flores made a beeline for the doors, and I took up Karen's mantle.

"You put pictures of our house on the internet, and you have the nerve to talk to me about going negative!" I shouted after him. "That's real classy…you jerk!"

He just walked off without turning around, putting up his hand to wave me off.

And that was it--our last personal contact before the election. I would have preferred something a little more congenial and sophisticated, but that was it.

Over the next several days, I heard a voice out of my past. My old "buddy" Phil Gramm began appearing on the District 17 airwaves. He was featured in a spot encouraging Republicans to vote for Flores. This was evidently part of the Washington establishment support that Flores was receiving. This was also the clearest indication of why it takes money to run an effective primary race. The Republican primary voters were being inundated with the negative Rob's-in-legal-trouble-for-tax-cheating ads in conjunction with the positive Gramm admonitions to support his "good friend Bill Flores."

That supplemented their postal game which was breathtaking in its scope. The typical Republican household, including our own, was receiving an average of two to three mailed pieces each week. Of course, it annoyed me when I saw some of my own campaign catch phrases that were "borrowed," appearing in writing, in these full-color, slick mailings. But there was nothing that could be done about it. We had to sit helplessly by and watch the onslaught unfold in slow motion. We could only hope that our domination of live events and overwhelming support from political activists and elected officials would somehow withstand the Flores financial juggernaut and translate into a grassroots victory.

Election Day came, and we once again made visits to a few polling places, but much of the time was spent on phones trying to get out the last-minute voters. Frankly, at this point, there was almost a numbness to the whole situation. The campaign had gone on for so long and had been so physically, intellectually, and emotionally draining for such an extended period of time, our mindset became "whatever will be, will be." We were just too tired on all levels to put up an aggressive mental fight to victory, especially when we had no financial means to answer back in any way. We absolutely wanted to win, but if the voters didn't want me to finish off Chet, I had nothing left in me to invest in an emotional fight. That turned out to be a healthy attitude when the votes came in that evening.

By the time the second round of results came in, it was all but over. There was no drama and no suspense. We were overwhelmed, and the percentages never changed all the way through. When it was all said and done, we lost two-to-one. It wasn't even close.

The runoff voters spoke clearly and definitively: they wanted Flores to finish the job I had started. I was crushed by that thought, and, ironically, although I was crushed emotionally, I was just too emotionally drained to even be devastated.

I had given all I had to give, in my quest to unseat Chet Edwards.

CHAPTER 52

Bittersweet

Flores' short-circuiting of the primary election season was indeed a wise move strategically. From my critical perspective as his opponent, I determined that his weak suit was clearly the basic elements of campaigning skills. Early on, he seemed uncomfortable pressing the flesh with average voters. He was not a good public speaker. He was never well-versed in the political issues of the day. He appeared unconcerned with local politics of any kind, and he was apparently unused to being criticized or questioned. Although he did improve over time, these shortcomings were fairly obvious to many engaged voters and political activists who showed up at the "live" events on the campaign trail.

But what he did have was an abundant supply of money, and money can either correct or cover over most flaws that a candidate might possess. For Flores, this turned out to be enough to get the job done. Since he seemed uncomfortable engaging with voters, he avoided them for the most part by jumping back in at the last minute. His money allowed him the luxury of blitzing *all* voters in the district with an incredible amount of political messaging, skillfully orchestrated by an experienced professional campaign manager and team. Even his initial lack of speaking talent was eventually transformed by a professional speech coach.

Money bought him the nomination, so in that sense, his opening declaration and proud assertion that "only *he* had the money to win it" at that first candidate meeting, turned out to be absolutely correct. Darn it!

Several weeks after the primary runoff election, I got a call from Flores. It was the first time we had spoken since election night when I conceded. Since we're both human, the conversation was strained and uncomfortable, to say the least, but I do give him credit for making an effort to reach out. After some awkward moments consisting of the common social formalities, he got right to the point.

"Rob, I'm going to need the list of your volunteers to move forward from here," he said with a matter-of-fact tone.

He was referring to the list of more than 1,600 people that had formally signed on to volunteer with our campaign. It was the one aspect of what we did that I was most proud of and grateful for. Ironically, virtually all of Flores' key people were paid staff. During the runoff, we joked internally that *all* of our people would and could be voting for me, whereas none of Flores' top people could even vote for him because they were all hired guns from out of town.

We may not have been able to raise a lot of money, but we had the grassroots activists enthusiastically dedicated to what we were doing. It was something that no other campaign in this primary could even come close to matching. We were also respectful of the amount of trust these people had put in us, and we were not going to do anything that might compromise that trust. That included our clearly-stated promise that we would not be passing along their personal information to anyone else.

I hesitated, because I didn't want to come off as being uncooperative, and I knew something like this was not unexpected. But in my mind, I had no choice.

"Bill, I'm sorry, but those people signed up with our campaign with the understanding that we would not be sharing their information with anyone. I'm really sorry, but I just can't give that list to you."

There was a slight pause while I assume he was pondering the meaning of what I was actually saying. Finally, he spoke up and, with all sincerity, asked, "Well then, will you sell it to me?"

Now it was my turn to try and ponder what was so difficult to understand. I said, "No, Bill, it's not for sale."

He paused for a moment, then went to his second order of business.

"We're going to hold a unity rally in a few weeks. Most of the other primary candidates have agreed to it and will be there. I think it's important for you especially to appear on stage with me to show that we're all unified and moving into the fall election to beat Chet Edwards. I'd like for you to be there."

While his request was certainly reasonable and common practice, as he was talking, all that kept running through my mind were the last weeks of the campaign, and his nasty personal attack ad. I thought to myself, *If you think I'm a tax cheat, a liar, would be going to jail, had no integrity, and had no business running for Congress, why on earth would you even* want *me to be on stage with you?!*

I kept my thoughts to myself and answered with a touch of sadness, "No, Bill, I think it's just too soon. Maybe somewhere down the road, but not now. It's too soon. But I appreciate the call; I really do. I'm sure we'll talk about it again sometime in the future."

"I understand; thanks for your time."

We never did talk again before the November election.

I would keep my word I had given to voters and assembled reporters on election night and *did* vote for the Republican nominee in the general election, but as for campaigning for Flores, I did have integrity. I knew it was expected of me to help out the winner of the primary and generally do whatever was asked of me. My problem was that I knew Flores politically better than anyone in the district, and I thought he had serious problems that precluded him from being the congressman he claimed he would be. I told my close friends and supporters that I knew Flores would vote "right" 90 percent of the time, and that was good, but it was that other 10 percent that would make a difference between him being a decent, yet standard establishment office holder and a truly conservative congressman fighting for real change in Washington.

Although I did get criticism from some Flores supporters for not getting out front during the general campaign, publicly I kept my thoughts to myself and my mouth shut. I was never asked to help Flores campaign against Chet, and I never volunteered. In a way, I was relieved, since I would not have to make that difficult choice. With the passing of time, much of the wounds and hard feelings had healed, and from a political standpoint, I definitely wanted a Republican victory, so it would've been hard for me to say no to any request for help. Ironically, the integrity I was accused of lacking, kept me from being a phony wannabe politician and enthusiastically stumping for someone I truly didn't believe in. But I knew he was exponentially better than Chet *politically*, and I would do no harm to jeopardize a Republican winning the seat.

I was only mildly surprised when, leading up to the general election, Edwards actually ran television ads in the fall exposing Flores' "truth" problem. He replayed the incident in that Waco primary forum relating to my innocuous question concerning voting habits. It was a fairly damning commercial, but in the end, it wasn't enough to make a difference. Edwards was so far gone politically from his Central Texas conservative district, that it had no real impact on the results. Edwards was defeated soundly and was finally halted from supposedly 'representing' a conservative Central Texas district.

After almost twenty years in office, Chet Edwards was no longer my congressman.

For me, the Flores victory was bittersweet. Although honestly not thrilled for Flores personally, I was very happy for the district and the country. We would finally get representation along the lines of what most of the district wanted and needed, and Nancy Pelosi had one less ally in Washington. In fact, the 2010 midterm election turned out to be quite good for Republicans all over the country, thanks to the absurdity of Obama's policies supported and promoted by the hard-left Democrats.

I could take satisfaction in the knowledge that my willingness to step out in 2008, when no one else would, in reality, set things in motion that would eventually result in the takedown of a prominent Democrat congressman. It really didn't matter which one of us got the nomination in 2010; Edwards was history. The incumbent Democrat congressman, along with his friends in the White House and Congress, was just too much out of step with most voters in Central Texas.

My political journey to lead Central Texas residents to the Promised Land of a conservative Republican representation lasted almost twenty years. Things weren't always done the way they should've been, and as a candidate, I surely made mistakes, but the journey continued forward, and, with the stunning results of the 2008 election, we saw the Promised Land but were never allowed to enter it. I knew conservatives would win this seat in the next cycle. However, for whatever reason, *I* was not chosen as the one to work in Congress for the good people of Central Texas. That honor and task was left to someone else. My five stones might have toppled Goliath, but it wasn't my hand that wielded the sword that beheaded the giant. That task would fall to Flores.

I am only grateful to have been used in a *small* way, for a monumental and seemingly impossible task, in the overall grand scheme.

Yes, I still felt the call, and it irked me that the congressional seat was being "wasted" on someone who wasn't willing to aggressively stand up and go toe-to-toe with the radical leftist Democrats working overtime to "transform" America. My personal sense of justice was also being sorely challenged by my feeling that, over a three-month span, someone with no real political background and no ideological compass had simply "bought" himself a seat by taking advantage of and walking through the door that we had opened up after a difficult twenty-year battle. Unfortunately, that's just a very common aspect of politics.

In spite of a fairly steady stream of requests for me to re-engage by well-meaning voters I would meet, I was in absolutely no financial position to run again. Karen and I had laid out a Biblical fleece, looking for a divine sign that if I was supposed to engage in *any* race, we needed to see a miraculous change in our financial situation. While the Lord could put me in Congress through the use of toothpicks if He wanted, like Gideon, we just wanted a sign that I was supposed go back into the fray. I was tired and wounded from fighting without the weapons that finances could provide.

CHAPTER 53

Unrealistic Expectations?

In spite of all my political knowledge and experience on numerous levels, the one aspect of running for a prestigious federal office that took me completely by surprise, was the connection that a successful candidate can make with his supporters. If your voters believe that you genuinely represent the things they sincerely believe in, there is indeed a real bond that develops. In many cases I found myself squarely between an honest disbelief that I meant that much to someone who only knew me from a political race, and an overwhelming sense of awe that I could engender such a genuine response in people.

For someone with less than pure motives or a cynical desire to control people, this can be a very easy way to lose sight of your own humanity and lead down a path that many career politicians seem to fall prey to: a callous willingness to further your own quest for personal power by taking advantage of the adulation and overall goodwill from your "base."

My first sense of the "godfather-like" power that some voters would assign to me came at a campaign stop in Temple during my first primary run. I was approached by a young man who was anxiously trying to get a job with the Texas penal system. It was clear he wasn't aware that this was a congressional race that had nothing to do with state government. However, he was touched by something I said in the meeting and evidently decided I was the one who he would support. Thus, he sought me out after the forum, patiently waiting in line with his resume and other paperwork. He asked very directly if there was anything I could do to help him.

I was caught off guard with his request but was struck with his sincere belief that I had the power to help him on any level. After all, this was just the primary and I was one of three novice candidates who were merely vying for the opportunity to face an incumbent congressman. And then, of course, I wondered why he sought me out of the three. For whatever reason, he decided I was the one who could help him, and I would be the one he was backing in this race.

I thanked him for his trust in me, and although, on a personal level, I truly wanted to help him, I had to politely explain that his job search was a state matter, and if I was successful, I would be involved in the federal system. I felt very helpless as I saw the disappointment come over his face. I didn't know if he would stick by me in the election, but I had no choice but to be honest. As a result, I left that meeting with the newfound realization that, rightly or wrongly, many voters were ascribing power to me that I certainly didn't have.

I got another lesson in humility, years later, in the general election when I was approached after a particularly successful meeting. I made it a habit of staying and talking to anyone and everyone who wanted to speak with me. My philosophy was that if a person was willing to take the time to talk with me, I'd give them as much of my time as prudently possible (especially if the line of people behind them was long). I figured it was a fair trade-off if I was hoping to get their vote. It was the least that I could do.

In fact, I actually enjoyed this part of campaigning and found myself connecting on many levels above and beyond politics. As such, my long-suffering wife and other campaign staffers had gotten used to the fact that I was almost always one of the last to leave the room at virtually any function, unless we were crunched for time and needed to leave sooner for some other commitment.

Early on in my political experience, I developed my own little style of interaction at most meetings where I was going to speak. Although I would "work the room" upon arriving, I always made it a point to keep conversations with voters before a speech to a bare minimum. Whenever possible I would say just enough to stay genuinely polite, but I was not interested in talking policy issues or cover topics that I would officially be discussing during my time at the podium. Quite honestly, it was simply a matter of not wanting to steal my own thunder. Maybe it was pride, but I wanted my speech to have the most impact on everyone that was in the room. The last thing I needed was for people to get bored thinking I was merely rehashing what I said to them before the meeting started.

This particular meeting was a small veterans function dealing with a lot of military matters. Normally this would be the perfect setting for Chet, but in keeping with his "Rob-is-persona-non-grata strategy," I had the forum all to myself.

I sensed it had gone well, and, in spite of his reputation as being a champion of all things veterans, I sensed that we had won some people over. I stressed our differences on the matter of Iraq. The Dems in Congress were always talking about how they supported the military, but in the case of the Iraq war, they certainly didn't support the mission and stated so boldly whenever the sympathetic media offered them a platform. I repeated my mantra that we could disagree with whether or not we should be there, but the bottom line is that as long we were there, we needed victory and could argue about being there after we had succeeded.

Afterwards, as I was finally heading for the door, I was approached by an older couple carrying an old, drab olive cold-weather military jacket from the Viet Nam war era (I recognized the style from seeing pictures of soldiers in Viet Nam.).

As I shook their hands, the husband began, "Rob we believe in what you stand for, and we know you'll stand up for the American military. Chet talks a good game, but he toes the line of Pelosi and the Democrats who don't support our men in Iraq."

"That's right," I affirmed.

"We believe you're going to win and you *are* going to be our next congressman."

"Well, thank you so much, I appreciate your confidence in me. I do think we're going to surprise a lot of people."

"We'd like to give you something that--once you get up to Washington--will help you remember why you're there. We'd be honored for you to have our son's coat which he wore in Viet Nam," he said very solemnly and with great emotion. "He died a number of years ago, and we want you to keep it." He held it out for me.

Truly touched, and rare for me, I was at a loss for words. Finally, I gathered my thoughts and responded as best I could, "I am unbelievably honored, but I can't take this. It belongs to you and your family."

"No, it would be more important for our next congressman to have it. It's a symbol of what we stand for."

I felt terrible about taking this precious item that meant so much to them, but it was clear that it meant even more to them that I take it. Choking down my own emotions, I acceded to their wishes and took the coat. It was clear that refusing it would have deeply hurt their feelings and would have been an insult.

So, as unworthy of this gift as I knew I was, I thanked them profusely and parted with yet another lesson in supporters' relations. It seemed like this was some variation on the Biblical widow's mite parable.

I never met these people before and most likely would never meet them again, but we had somehow made a connection on a level that is truly mystifying to me.

I honestly don't know if it was an aura of confidence that I was projecting on the campaign trail or if it was something else at work. Looking back on it, I have to assume it was something else at work, because anyone looking objectively at the race would've thought my confidence was perhaps a subtle sign of insanity...and that assessment probably includes many of my own close supporters.

Be that as it may, my own confidence was also shared by many--some, way beyond my own. There were a couple of instances where I was really left scratching my head in wonder.

I'd lost my second ill-conceived primary race and had absolutely no plans to ever run again. In spite of this very real fact-of-my-political-life, I ran into a couple of middle-aged men at a volunteer function for President Bush. They approached me and shared with me that they had supported me both times in the primary against Farley. They said they knew for sure that I was the one who could beat Chet, and they wanted me to get back in the fight. They also wanted to know what my immediate plans were politically.

I'd heard this kind of talk often from many well-meaning people, but I always just chalked it up to them being polite and wanting to encourage someone who had lost. I was in that frame of mind when one of the men suddenly blurted out, "...and quite honestly... we expect you to be running for President someday."

At that point, I literally did a spit take and burst out laughing. "What?!" Without realizing it or meaning to, I was coming very close to ridiculing them. "Yeah, right. You guys are funny."

They were not amused at my reaction.

I continued, "I appreciate your confidence in me, but that's just crazy. I'd be happy just to get a chance to represent us in Congress."

They doubled down and informed me that I had to get back into politics because it was clear to them, from seeing me campaign, that being in Congress was just the start for me.

"You're serious?!" I said stifling more laughter and executing a quick emotional pivot to seriousness. "Wow. That's never even remotely entered my thoughts, but, again, thanks for your confidence. I'm honored that you think so highly of me."

"We know what we see in you and we're telling you, you can't give up."

I honestly thought this kind of thinking was crazy. After all, I was a two-time primary loser who never even made it to the general election. Yet, incredibly, I actually heard that same exact expectation a few more times over the ensuing years, from very sincere and deadly serious supporters who evidently liked what I brought to the political table.

Again, it's that mystical bond with people who buy into what you stand for and what they hope you'll try to do once in office. It's an incredibly powerful force that is taken advantage of by too many professional politicians from both parties. If not carefully controlled, it leads to an arrogance and mindset that is the reason why so much of the power structure in Washington is completely out of touch with the average American voter.

For me, after completing a major campaign, I can look back and understand how important it is to be well grounded and squarely focused on what you're trying to accomplish in office as opposed to your own personal betterment. It's unbelievably easy to fall into a trap where you actually do start believing that you are special, even though, ironically, and I believe dangerously, you *are* special to many of your dedicated supporters.

Depending on how a person handles it, running for office can actually be the best thing that ever happened in your life...or the worst.

* * * * *

The Founding Fathers gave us this gift that we call the United States of America. Since the fragile beginnings of the Republic, many things have changed, and some not for the better. When assessed by the original documents, the United States government was never meant to be a corrupt, amoral, humanist system ruled by an entrenched political overclass exploiting a permanent underclass to amass power. I hope that most average, working-class, traditional Americans never give up on that original unique and fantastic idealism. I didn't, and I haven't.

And, as a result, in one congressional district in flyover country, a powerful incumbent was toppled against all odds. The world of politics does not have to be reserved for only the very wealthy or the very connected. Although, admittedly, it still definitely helps, as I discovered.

While rare, an average citizen or political neophyte can break through and reaffirm the idealism of the American political system. The nation saw this up close in the 2016 presidential election with Donald Trump. In many ways his success at breaking through with a shocking upset, while unique and unprecedented in the modern political era, in other ways reaffirmed some of the basic "rules" of today's American politics I experienced in my quest.

Although an outsider and political novice, he clearly demonstrated that personal wealth is extremely beneficial in a contested primary. Then in the general election, Trump clearly showed that plain-spoken ideology *can* overcome a vastly superior war chest, as he was able to negate the more-than-a-billion dollars Hillary Clinton brought to bear against him. As a result, he and his supporters secured the shocking upset victory.

Thank God this is still America where it can and does happen.

EPILOGUE

Following Flores' first re-election in 2012, I ran into a couple in a post office parking lot who, though previously unbeknownst to me, claimed to be loyal supporters. They implored me to consider finishing the job I had started. They wanted to move our country beyond "business-as-usual" in Washington and wanted me to challenge the man who had so abruptly and harshly ended my political journey to the halls of Congress. They graciously touched me with their sincerity and willingness to do whatever it would take to help me get back into the fight. They pledged to officially volunteer for my campaign—if I would just get out there again and lead them.

I sincerely thanked them for the kind words and incredible trust they placed in me. "I'm humbled and honored," I said, "but my financial situation has to be resolved. That being said, I guarantee you this, if I were to win the lottery, I promise I'd challenge Flores tomorrow!" I said with a laugh.

They nodded their heads and smiled with contented approval.

Suddenly, the man stopped and asked, "Have you bought a ticket lately?"

I laughed. "Nope, you got me there. I've never bought a lottery ticket in my life."

We all laughed, but the woman mockingly scolded me. "That makes it a little hard to do what you're supposed to do—if you won't even try."

The man reached for his wallet, pulled out a $20 bill, and shoved it into my hand. I protested. "I can't take that."

In spite of my objection, he became deadly serious and firmly declared, "I'm getting this race started today. I want you to go and buy twenty dollars' worth of lottery tickets. It starts right here, right now in this post office parking lot!" The woman nodded enthusiastically.

I've attended many fundraisers where many thousands of dollars changed hands for many different political office holders at many different levels. None of those will ever come close to the true amount of wealth that was pushed into my hand that day from just another average working-class citizen who was willing to take a stand and do anything that they thought would help save their country. That's the real challenge for those on the left who want to destroy traditional America. It may take a lot to get the average American riled up, but eventually leftists will face resistance from those otherwise powerless citizens who will not go down without a fight. The Trump election proved that.

I could have cried right then and there when this couple was willing to back up their words of support with their pocketbook.

That's just the kind of passion for America that could relight the fire in my belly…

Rob and Karen await 2008 election returns

CPSIA information can be obtained
at www.ICGtesting.com
Printed in the USA
BVHW082344210121
598397BV00006BA/31